# Register for Free Membership to

**s o l u t i o n s @ s y n g r e s**

Over the last few years, Syngress has published many best-selling and critically acclaimed books, including Tom Shinder's *Configuring ISA Server 2004*, Brian Caswell and Jay Beale's *Snort 2.1 Intrusion Detection*, and Angela Orebaugh and Gilbert Ramirez's *Ethereal Packet Sniffing*. One of the reasons for the success of these books has been our unique **solutions@syngress.com** program. Through this site, we've been able to provide readers a real time extension to the printed book.

As a registered owner of this book, you will qualify for free access to our members-only solutions@syngress.com program. Once you have registered, you will enjoy several benefits, including:

- Four downloadable e-booklets on topics related to the book. Each booklet is approximately 20-30 pages in Adobe PDF format. They have been selected by our editors from other best-selling Syngress books as providing topic coverage that is directly related to the coverage in this book.

- A comprehensive FAQ page that consolidates all of the key points of this book into an easy-to-search web page, providing you with the concise, easy-to-access data you need to perform your job.

- A "From the Author" Forum that allows the authors of this book to post timely updates and links to related sites, or additional topic coverage that may have been requested by readers.

Just visit us at **www.syngress.com/solutions** and follow the simple registration process. You will need to have this book with you when you register.

Thank you for giving us the opportunity to serve your needs. And be sure to let us know if there is anything else we can do to make your job easier.

SYNGRESS®

SYNGRESS®

# OS X for Hackers at Heart

## THE APPLE OF EVERY HACKER'S EYE


Ken Caruso
Chris Hurley
Johnny Long
Preston Norvell
Tom Owad


FOREWORD BY TOM OWAD
APPLEFRITTER.COM


Bruce Potter Technical Editor

| KEY | SERIAL NUMBER |
| --- | --- |
| 001 | HJIRTCV764 |
| 002 | PO9873D5FG |
| 003 | 829KM8NJH2 |
| 004 | GFR5J82S4D |
| 005 | CVPLQ6WQ23 |
| 006 | VBP965T5T5 |
| 007 | HJJJ863WD3E |
| 008 | 2987GVTWMK |
| 009 | 629MP5SDJT |
| 010 | IMWQ295T6T |

PUBLISHED BY
Syngress Publishing, Inc.
800 Hingham Street
Rockland, MA 02370

**OS X for Hackers at Heart**

Printed and bound by CPI Group (UK) Ltd, Croydon, CR0 4YY
Transferred to Digital Printing, 2013
ISBN: 1-59749-040-7

Publisher: Andrew Williams          Page Layout and Art: Patricia Lupien
Acquisitions Editor: Jaime Quigley  Copy Editor: Amy Thomson
Technical Editor: Bruce Potter      Indexer: J. Edmund Rush
Cover Designer: Michael Kavish

Distributed by O'Reilly Media, Inc. in the United States and Canada.
For information on rights, translations, and bulk sales, contact Matt Pedersen, Director of Sales and Rights, at Syngress Publishing; email matt@syngress.com or fax to 781-681-3585.

# Acknowledgments

Syngress would like to acknowledge the following people for their kindness and support in making this book possible.

Syngress books are now distributed in the United States and Canada by O'Reilly Media, Inc. The enthusiasm and work ethic at O'Reilly are incredible, and we would like to thank everyone there for their time and efforts to bring Syngress books to market: Tim O'Reilly, Laura Baldwin, Mark Brokering, Mike Leonard, Donna Selenko, Bonnie Sheehan, Cindy Davis, Grant Kikkert, Opol Matsutaro, Steve Hazelwood, Mark Wilson, Rick Brown, Tim Hinton, Kyle Hart, Sara Winge, Peter Pardo, Leslie Crandell, Regina Aggio Wilkinson, Pascal Honscher, Preston Paull, Susan Thompson, Bruce Stewart, Laura Schmier, Sue Willing, Mark Jacobsen, Betsy Waliszewski, Kathryn Barrett, John Chodacki, Rob Bullington, Kerry Beck, and Karen Montgomery.

The incredibly hardworking team at Elsevier Science, including Jonathan Bunkell, Ian Seager, Duncan Enright, David Burton, Rosanna Ramacciotti, Robert Fairbrother, Miguel Sanchez, Klaus Beran, Emma Wyatt, Chris Hossack, Krista Leppiko, Marcel Koppes, Judy Chappell, Radek Janousek, and Chris Reinders for making certain that our vision remains worldwide in scope.

David Buckland, Marie Chieng, Lucy Chong, Leslie Lim, Audrey Gan, Pang Ai Hua, Joseph Chan, and Siti Zuraidah Ahmad of STP Distributors for the enthusiasm with which they receive our books.

David Scott, Tricia Wilden, Marilla Burgess, Annette Scott, Andrew Swaffer, Stephen O'Donoghue, Bec Lowe, Mark Langley, and Anyo Geddes of Woodslane for distributing our books throughout Australia, New Zealand, Papua New Guinea, Fiji, Tonga, Solomon Islands, and the Cook Islands.

# Technical Editor and Contributing Author

**Bruce Potter** is a Senior Associate at Booz Allen Hamilton. Prior to working at Booz Allen Hamilton, Bruce served as a software security consultant for Cigital in Dulles, VA. Bruce is the founder of the Shmoo Group of security professionals. His areas of expertise include wireless security, large-scale network architectures, smartcards, and promotion of secure software engineering practices. Bruce coauthored the books *802.11 Security* and *Mac OS X Security*. He was trained in computer science at the University of Alaska, Fairbanks.

*First and foremost I would like to thank my family for putting up with me and my time constraints due to the many projects I am dealing with. I'd also like to thank The Shmoo Group for all the guidance and wisdom they have imparted on me over the years. Finally, a big thank-you goes to Syngress, for giving me the opportunity to work on an interesting enjoyable project.*

*Bruce wrote Chapter 7.*

# Contributing Authors

**Johnny Long** is a "clean-living" family guy who just so happens to like hacking stuff. Recently, Johnny has enjoyed writing stuff and presenting stuff at conferences, which has served as yet another diversion to a serious (and bill-paying) job as a professional hacker and security researcher for Computer Sciences Corporation. Johnny enjoys spending time with his family, pushing all the shiny buttons on them thar new-fangled Mac computers, and making much-too-serious security types either look at him funny or start laughing uncontrollably. Johnny has written or contributed to several books, including *Google Hacking for Penetration Tester"* from Syngress Publishing, which has secured rave reviews and has lots of pictures.

Johnny can be reached through his website, **http://johnny.ihackstuff.com**

*Thanks first to Christ without whom I am nothing. To Jen, Makenna, Trevor and Declan, my love always. Thanks to Bruce Potter for the opportunity to chime in on this one, and to my fellow co-authors. I hold you all in the highest regard. Thanks to Anthony K, Al E, Ryan C, Thane E, and Gilbert V for introducing me to the Mac. Thanks to Jaime Quigley, Andrew Williams and all of Syngress. I can't thank you enough. Thanks to Jason Arnold (Nexus!) for hosting me, and all the mods on JIHS for your help and support. Shouts to Nathan B, Sujay S, Stephen S, James Foster, Jenny Yang, SecurityTribe, the Shmoo Group, Sensepost, Blackhat, Defcon, Neal Stephenson (Baroque), Stephen King (On Writing), Ted Dekker (Thr3e), P.O.D., Pillar, Project86, Shadowvex, Yoshinori Sunahara. "I'm sealing the fate of my selfish existence / Pushing on with life from death, no questions left / I'm giving my life, no less"*
*from A Toast To My former Self by Project86*

*Johnny wrote Chapter 2 and Chapter 5. He also contributed to the technical editing of this book.*

**Ken Caruso** is a Senior Systems Engineer for Serials Solutions a Pro Quest company. Serials Solutions empowers librarians and enables their patrons by helping them get the most value out of their electronic serials. Ken plays a key role in the design and engineering of mission critical customer facing systems and networks. Previous to this Ken has worked at Alteon, a Boeing Company, Elevenwireless, and Digital Equipment Corporation. Ken's expertises include wireless networking, digital security, design and implementation of mission critical systems. Outside of the corporate sector Ken is co-founder of Seattlewireless.net one of the first community wireless networking projects in the U.S.

Ken studied Computer Science at Daniel Webster College and is a member of The Shmoo Group of Security Professionals. Ken has been invited to speak at many technology and security events including but not limited to Defcon, San Diego Telecom Council, Society of Broadcast Engineers, and CPSR: Shaping the Network Society.

Ken would like to acknowledge the great support he has always received from friends and family as well the unflagging patience of his editor at Syngress.

*Ken wrote Chapter 3.*

**Chris Hurley** (Roamer) is a Senior Penetration Tester working in the Washington, DC area. He is the founder of the WorldWide WarDrive, a four-year effort by INFOSEC professionals and hobbyists to generate awareness of the insecurities associated with wireless networks and is the lead organizer of the DEF CON WarDriving Contest.

Although he primarily focuses on penetration testing these days, Chris also has extensive experience performing vulnerability assessments, forensics, and incident response. Chris has spoken at several security conferences and published numerous whitepapers on a wide range of INFOSEC topics. Chris is the lead author of *WarDriving: Drive, Detect, Defend* (Syngress, ISBN: 1-931836-03-5), and a contributor to *Aggressive Network Self-Defense* (Syngress, ISBN: 1-931836-20-5) and *InfoSec Career Hacking* (Syngress, ISBN: 1-59749-011-3). Chris holds a bachelor's degree in computer science. He lives in Maryland with his wife Jennifer and their daughter Ashley.

*Chris wrote Chapter 4.*

**Tom Owad** is a Macintosh consultant in south-central PA and the D.C. area and vice president of Keystone MacCentral. He serves on the board of directors of the Apple I Owners Club, where he is also webmaster and archivist. Tom is owner and Webmaster of Applefritter, a Macintosh community of artists and engineers. Applefritter provides its members with discussion boards for the exchange of ideas and hosts countless member-contributed hardware hacks and other projects. Tom holds a BA in computer science and international affairs from Lafayette College, PA. Tom is the author of the Syngress title, *Apple I Replica Creation: Back to the Garage* (ISBN: *1-931836-40-X).*

*Tom wrote Chapter 7. He is also the foreword contributor.*

 **Preston Norvell** is a computer and networking geek. He has been fortunate to work as an administrator, engineer and consultant, and currently works as a network architect for a satellite communications company in the small town of Alaska, USA. He has pulled Ethernet cable through sewage melted by body heat, written the bill software for a utility, co-written a book on Mac OS X Security, designed and deployed systems and networks in places small and large, ported Open Source software to Mac OS X, and many other rather silly fun things.

In his off time he tinkers with computers and networks, thinks about collections databases for museums, purchases entirely too many DVD's, wastes too much time, cooks for friends when he can, enjoys a spot of tea now and again, and continues to add to the lived-in look of his dwelling at a reasonable pace. He also plans to take over the world with a vast army of mind-controlled, monkey-piloted robot minions.

*I would like to thank Bruce and the folks at Syngress for the opportunity to tag along on this project, as well as their patience and guidance. Apologies to my friends and co-workers for my absences and the late mornings with tired eyes and many thanks for their patience and support. Thanks also to Hershey for Good & Plenty's, Republic of Tea for Blackberry Sage and a little place in Chinatown for their white tea and lapsang souchong. And thanks much to the social insects all.*

*Preston wrote Chapter 1. He also contributed to the technical editing of this book.*

# Contents

# Foreword

"The computer for the rest of us" was never considered much of a hacker's platform. The original Mac didn't even have arrow keys (or a control key, for that matter), forcing the user to stop what he was doing, take his hands off the keyboard, and use the mouse. The Mac's case was sealed so tight, a special tool known as the "Mac cracker" was made to break it open. It was a closed machine, an information appliance. The expansionless design and sealed case of the Mac stood in stark contrast to the Apple II that came before it.

With its rich graphical interface and ease of use, the Mac became the standard for graphic artists and other creative types. Custom icons and desktop patterns soon abounded. The users that embraced the Macintosh for its simplicity began using ResEdit (Resource Editor) to modify system files and to personalize their machines. The Mac developed a fanatical following, and you could rest assured that each fanatic's system was unique, with the icons, menus, program launchers, windows, sounds, and keyboard shortcuts all scrutinized and perfected to meet his personal needs. My Color Classic even played Porky Pig's "That's all folks" each time it shut down (although the novelty wore off on that one pretty quick).

Mac OS X was met with some trepidation. It broke every program and system modification, it didn't have a proper Apple menu—and what on earth was this "dock"? Jef Raskin, who gave the Mac its name, wrote of Mac OS X, "Apple has ignored for years all that has been learned about developing UIs. It's unprofessional, incompetent, and it's hurting users." Bruce Tognazzini, founder of the Apple Human Interface Group, even penned an article titled "Top 10 Reasons the Apple Dock Sucks."

Mac OS X was an entirely different operating system. Most classic Mac OS applications were compatible, but only when operating inside a special run-time environment. All system extensions and user interface modifications were permanently lost. For many users, these changes are what made the computer "theirs" and they replied heavily upon their customizations to efficiently get work done. The loss was tremendous. And it was worth it.

Preemptive multitasking, symmetric multiprocessing, multithreading, and protected memory. Protected memory was the one I wanted most.

At a 1998 keynote, Steve Jobs showed off a mere dialog box, to great applause. The dialog read: "The application Bomb has unexpectedly quit. You do not need to restart your computer." I take it for granted on Mac OS X, but as I write this, I'm recalling occasions when Internet Explorer brought my entire system down multiple times in a single day.

Mac OS X promised to combine the power and stability of Unix with the ease of use of Macintosh. I was cautiously optimistic with early releases (I've been using Mac OS X since Developer Release 4).

Protected memory doesn't do much good when all your apps are running in the Classic Environment, and the user interface did indeed leave a lot to be desired. But with each revision, Mac OS X has improved dramatically. With Mac OS 10.4 Tiger, I no longer even have the Classic Environment installed, the user interface has improved to a degree that in many ways I far prefer it to that of Mac OS 9. Mac OS X has succeeded in combining the best of Unix with the best of the Macintosh.

The Macintosh has become "the computer for everybody." For novices, it remains the easiest computer there is. For enthusiasts, as in the old days, there is a vast array of third-party applications, utilities, and customizations, to tweak and improve the way the OS works. For hackers and programmers, there's the command line and the BSD Unix compatibility layer.

All the power, all the tools, and all the geekery of Linux is present in Mac OS X. Shell scripts, X11 apps, processes, kernel extensions… it's a unix platform. It's even possible to forgo Apple's GUI altogether and run KDE. Why you'd want to is another matter. While its unix core is what has made Mac OS X a viable platform for hackers and programmers, it's the user interface that has made it popular.

Apple's Terminal application is perpetually running on my PowerBook, but so is iTunes, iCal, and a slew of Dashboard Widgets.

If Apple hadn't moved to Mac OS X, I would have two computers. A classic Macintosh would be home to my "business" work—my email, calendar, word processor, etc. The other would be a Linux box, which I would probably connect to via an ssh connection from my Mac. Here would be the toys, the programming tools, the shell scripts, and everything I couldn't do within the confines of the old Mac. Thanks to the elegance and sophistication of Mac OS X, this isn't necessary. I've got every program I want to run and every tool I need to use on a single 4.6 lbs, 12" PowerBook.

*—Tom Owad*
*www.applefritter.com*

# Chapter 1

# A Network Admin's Guide to Using Mac OS X

## Solutions in this chapter:

- Running a Headless Mac
- Adding Interfaces to a Mac
- The Macintosh as a Router
- Mac OS X as a RADIUS Server

☑ Summary

☑ Solutions Fast Track

☑ Frequently Asked Questions

# Introduction

When looking at the state of networking on a Macintosh today, it is hard to fathom how much things have changed in the couple decades of its existence. New administrators and switchers will never know the worries and troubles of a network administrator trying to perform her job from a Macintosh, particularly those in heterogeneous networks. While Macintoshes have nearly always been able to network with each other with relative aplomb, performing random bits of networking was only for the very adventurous, or those willing to abandon the Mac OS for MkLinux (a Linux distribution that provided some of the foundations in early versions of Mac OS X and its still-born antecedent, Rhapsody). Beyond networking itself, managing networks was something of an issue for admins using Macs as their primary system as well.

But those were the old days, and a different generation, and in most senses, a completely different operating system. With this new operating system came the benefits of a well-known network stack (BSD, or Berkeley Software Distribution, sockets) and a host of standard UNIX tools at our disposal. Suddenly a whole range of networking tasks became easier and in many cases, free. Though the initial versions of Mac OS X had their shortcomings in a number of areas (whether it was performance, or bugs in various bits of code, or old versions of command line applications, or incorrect man pages), many of us immediately realized the available and impending power at our fingertips. Most of the issues were relatively minor and developers and hackers were able to work around any compiler or CLI (command line interface) issues they were faced with to bring many of the more popular open source projects to the operating system.

Each successive release of Mac OS X has extended its capabilities and utility in networking. With version 10.3 and more recently, 10.4, Mac OS X has truly begun to shake off its earlier neoteny and show an increasing maturity in the built-in toolset, as well as the tools available from third parties. Most of the top networking tools either work via the standard **./configure**, **make, make install** process, or are available via one of the popular ports systems. Most, if not all, of the man pages now reflect the versions of the command line tools that are included. The present is rosy indeed.

In this chapter we will play with some of these wonderful capabilities. We will first go about creating a functioning headless Mac complete with serial console access and printer logging suitable for use as a general purpose networking device. Since network admins often need more than one interface or IP (Internet Protocol) address for their work, we will take a look at adding interfaces, both logical and physical, to a Mac OS X system. Once we have more interfaces in the Mac, we will move on to providing routing services. Many networks require user authentication for access to various network devices for either VPN (virtual private network) access or administrative access to routers and switches, so we will see how to set up a Macintosh-based RADIUS (Remote Authentication Dial-In User Service) server utilizing an open source RADIUS server. Finally, throughout the chapter we will follow a number of tangents on smaller topics that affect the daily use of a Mac by network administrators. Since this is a chapter geared towards the network and systems administrator, we will be assuming some basic skills on the reader's part. As with all of the previous and remaining chapters of this book, a basic understanding of the Mac OS X UI (user interface) and CLI is required. Beyond this, readers will need at least a basic understanding of networking, from Layer 1 through Layer 7 (if you do not know what is meant by this, this chapter may not be for you, but just in case you need a refresher on it, see http://en.wikipedia.org/wiki/OSI_model). In addition some portions of this chapter will require installing or attaching interface adapters or other oddments of hardware to the Macintosh, so some ability to insert plug A into slot B or twist connector C in hole D may be required. Also, unless specified, the operating system in question will be the client version of Mac OS X v10.4 and since we will be compiling stuff here and there, the Developer Tools must be installed.

# Running a Headless Mac

The very idea of running a Macintosh sans display would seem to defy the very nature and intent of the platform. Most Mac users are attracted to the platform, at least in some small but significant way, by its lovingly crafted (if not occasionally schizophrenic) GUI (graphical user interface). To not connect a large, beautiful LCD display to one seems a painful waste in many ways. Due as much to the beauty of the interface as perhaps the historical desktop focus of the platform, many people probably cannot fathom the use of a Macintosh that has no directly attached output interface. But as Mac OS X has matured, the variety of applications and roles in which one might find a system has increased. Whether it is being deployed as a file server in an equipment rack (such as Apple's Xserve, a machine designed with the likelihood of being deployed headless), or as a machine in an Xgrid or a supercomputing cluster, Macs are showing themselves to be useful for far more than just the eye candy of their interfaces. In some sense this outside-the-box functionality is what this entire book is about, but for our current topic let us take a look at the variety of ways one can manage a headless Macintosh, with a particular focus on methods best used when making the Mac into something other than a desktop PC.

**NOTE**

Mac OS X Server itself comes with a wealth of utilities that provide an administrator with nearly all of the capabilities of the console itself. Between these applications and built-in VNC (Virtual Network Computing) support, a machine running Mac OS X Server is a rather capable machine when run headless and the fact that it was designed as such shows. Given this, much of this section will be geared towards the client edition of Mac OS X.

# Apple Remote Desktop

Apple Remote Desktop (ARD, www.apple.com/remotedesktop) is Apple's commercial remote management solution and can be used to manage any number of Macs, headless or not. Beyond just providing remote desktop control, ARD does quite a number of nifty things: software pushing, reverse sharing (so admins can show users how to perform tasks), remote process execution, system inventory, and much, much more (cue cheesy salesman). All said, it is a wonderful tool, but it is expensive (relatively… it is not free, as the rest of the remote management methods we will discuss are), and for a small number of clients, more powerful than most administrators need. This is especially true for those who have no need for a GUI at all and wish to use a

Macintosh as a server, or a more general-purpose network device. For those who really do want all that and a bag of chips, the following is a brief list of the features ARD provides:

- Automatic device discovery
- Automatic and manual remote software distribution
- Custom software packaging
- Hardware and software asset inventorying
- Scheduled and manual remote command execution
- Text chat with users
- Remote control

# VNC

VNC (www.realvnc.com) is an open source remote desktop management system. One of the beauties of VNC is its cross-platform nature; there is server software for every major platform and for many less popular operating systems. There are clients (used to control the remote desktops) for at least as many platforms, plus a couple platform-agnostic browser and java-based clients as well. Figure 1.1 illustrates a typical client and server relationship.

**Figure 1.1** VNC Client and Server

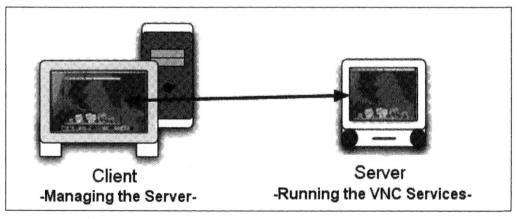

Client
-Managing the Server-

Server
-Running the VNC Services-

On Mac OS X there are two primary ways of providing VNC services. The easiest method is to use Apple's own Apple Remote Desktop services. As of version 2.0, the remote desktop control portion of these services is based on the VNC protocol, and as of v10.4, Apple bundles the server piece with every copy of Mac OS X. It can also be downloaded from Apple's site (www.apple.com/downloads/macosx/apple/appleremotedesktopupdate22.html) for Mac OS X versions 10.2.8, 10.3.x, and 10.4.x. The management application (the client) and the additional services it brings are what one pays for when one purchases ARD. To enable the server service, one only has to access **System Preferences**, choose the **Sharing** pane, and ensure that the **Apple Remote Desktop** item is checked. Upon first checking this item (or by clicking the **Access Privileges...** button), a sheet will slide down allowing an administrator to configure various bits for ARD. The only item of concern is the checkbox next to **VNC viewers may control screen with password:**. Check this box, enter a password, click **OK** and VNC is enabled and running on the system. Figure 1.2 shows the **Access Privileges** dialog box with this option selected.

**NOTE**

This terminology of *client* and *server* differs from Apple's terminology for ARD. For ARD the *clients* are workstations and servers running the ARD service. Clients are managed by an administrator with the management application. The term *server* does not directly apply in this context (though the client can be said to be running an ARD server).

**Figure 1.2** Enabling Apple Remote Desktop Client Services

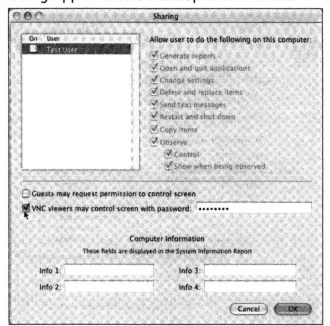

The other method of providing VNC services is to download OSXvnc (www.redstonesoftware.com/vnc.html) and configure it. OSXvnc is an open source implementation of the service implemented as an application that any user can execute. For those users who wish the service to start up at boot time, there is an option to do so (providing said users have administrative privileges on the system).

In general, OSXvnc is a faster and more configurable implementation, but the ARD implementation is more stable and has the added benefit of always being there (at least for Mac OS X v10.4, and later).

There are several free clients available for Mac OS X in various states of development, and the browser and java-based ones work in the predominant browsers on the platform. Table 1.1 presents some of the more common options:

**Table 1.1** Free Clients

| Name | Platform(s) | URL |
|---|---|---|
| Chicken of the VNC | Mac OS X | http://cotvnc.sf.net |
| RealVNC | Windows, *nix, Java | www.realvnc.com |
| TightVNC | Windows, *nix, Java | www.tightvnc.con |
| VNC for PocketPC | PocketPC 200x | www.cs.utah.edu/~midgley/wince/vnc.html |
| PalmVNC | PalmOS | http://palmvnc2.free.fr/ |

# SSH

The two previously discussed remote management options were both GUI-based and are more for those individuals who need access to the graphical tools. For those of us looking to use a Mac as more of a device for performing some network function, a graphical interface would seem to be an unnecessary overhead. This is one of the places that the venerable SSH (Secure SHell) steps up. Loosely described, SSH is a secure transport layer protocol that is used to provide a variety of services (commonly remote shells) to remote users.

Like any good *nix system these days, SSH services are built-in via the open source OpenSSH implementation, but are turned off by default. To enable them, access **System Preferences**, select the **Sharing** pane, and enable the **Remote Login** option. This will enable the service and cause it to start.

SSH is an immensely useful application that has far too many uses to enumerate (there are, in fact, whole books devoted to it), so we will not delve too deeply into this topic here, other than to say GUI or not, SSH can be very helpful to administrators of networks and systems alike. As an example, Figure 1.3 displays a user creating a SSH session to a remote host, then restarting the remote hosts RADIUS server.

**Figure 1.3** A Sample SSH Session by testuser to the Host test-users-mac-mini.local

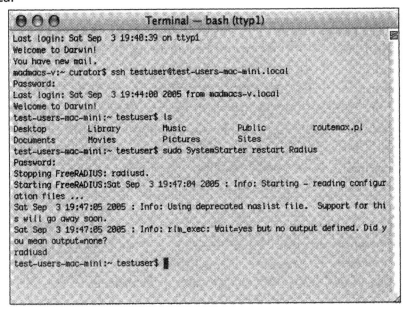

# Serial Console

So far, all of the methods of management we have discussed to this point require a network connection to be present for the system to be managed without a display. They also leave a GUI running (either because it is required or because it simply is not turned off); in the eyes of some this would mean that none of the above methods are truly headless. In the event of a network failure or misconfiguration, it very possible that a network administrator would lose network access to the headless Macintosh, thus requiring the administrator to run and grab a display and a mouse and keyboard to regain access to the system. Enabling the ability to log onto a Mac via a serial solves this issue. Besides, there is something inherently anachronistic and weird and cool in attaching a clunky old WYSE or C.Itoh vt100 terminal to a beautifully sculpted Macintosh. In certain circumstances (picture a 20-inch iMac or the fastest dual-processor G5 PowerMac), it is sure to cause screaming nightmares, or at least profound mental (but probably temporary) disturbance.

# Adding Serial Ports

The first task in getting access to a Mac via a serial connection is to physically get serial ports to connect to. The last time most Macs shipped with built-in serial ports was about 1998 when the last of the beige Macintoshes shipped. Since then the world has gradually migrated to a predominantly USB (universal serial bus) and Firewire world for peripherals (at least in the Apple world... many Wintel PCs still ship with serial and parallel ports, though it is no longer a given even there). Despite this change in peripheral interfaces, most network devices continue to use RS-232 for management ports. As luck and legacy would have it, a truly headless Mac is one such device.

**NOTE**

Apple's server systems, called Xserves, are the lone exception in being the only currently shipping Macintosh with serial ports (DB-9). In addition, these systems were designed specifically to be able to be run as headless systems with serial consoles as their primary console output.

Fortunately for us, a few manufacturers have created USB-to-serial adapters that solve this discrepancy in interfaces. Keyspan is one of the more popular brands and will be used here. While these USB dongles are typically meant to connect to a router, switch, or older model Palm device, they serve us well for our purpose. Making these devices function properly is generally as easy as plugging them into a free USB port and installing the appropriate drivers.

# Booting to the Console Instead of the GUI

Once the drivers are installed and the device connected, the next task is to configure the Mac to not boot to graphical environment. To do this we must find the new serial port's device path, enable the new serial point for tty use, and reroute the console to use it.

The first step in this task is to determine the device path of the new USB to serial adapter. This can be found by typing **ls /dev/tty\.\*** at the command line. This will generate a list of tty hardware devices on the system. The following is output from a typical modern system.

```
test-users-mac-mini:~ testuser$ ls -ls /dev/tty\.*
0 crw-rw-rw-  1 root  wheel    9,    4 Aug  6 21:46 /dev/tty.Bluetooth-Modem
0 crw-rw-rw-  1 root  wheel    9,    2 Aug  6 21:46 /dev/tty.Bluetooth-PDA-
Sync
0 crw-rw-rw-  1 root  wheel    9,    6 Aug  6 23:05 /dev/tty.USA19H1b1P1.1
0 crw-rw-rw-  1 root  wheel    9,    0 Aug  6 21:46 /dev/tty.modem
```

tty.modem, tty.Bluetooth-Modem, and tty.Bluetooth-PDA-Sync are typical of a modern system and in this case represent some built-in hardware in the test machine. The third item in the list is the Keyspan USB-to-serial adapter and it is the device we are interested in in this instance. The device label will vary depending on manufacturer, device model, and USB port. Copy the device path information (/dev/tty.USA19H1b1P1.1 in this case) to the clipboard, or to a scratch document, as you will need to enter it in the next step.

**NOTE**

If you are using a Mac with a built-in serial port, you may even see a tty.serial device, which can be used for this purpose as well, though you may still need some sort of adapter to convert from the old Mac-style mini DIN-8 connector to whatever kind of connector your management workstation has.

To complete the switch to a serial-based console access:
Modify the /etc/ttys file.

1.  Make a backup of the file, then using a text editor with administrative access open /etc/ttys.

2.  Locate a line near the top that begins with ""console "/System/Library/CoreServices…"" and comment it out by inserting a # symbol at the beginning of the line. This disables the GUI logon process.

```
#console
"/System/Library/CoreServices/loginwindow.app/Contents/MacOS/login-
window" vt100 on secure onoption="/usr/libexec/getty std.9600"
```

3. Next, insert the following text on a new line after the line we just commented out to redirect the console to the serial vty:

```
console          "/usr/libexec/getty serial.9600"  vt100    on secure
```

4. To enable serial port access via the USB adapter another line must also be added:

```
tty.USA19H1b1P1.1        "/usr/libexec/getty serial.9600" vt100 on
secure
```

The first field in this line denotes the device from the /dev directory as we determined above. The second field, between the quotation marks, is the command called when someone attaches to the interface. Most of the time this is *getty*, but can be almost anything (such as the line we commented out at the beginning of this modification, which uses *loginwindow* for console connections). The third field denotes the terminal type used by the connection, while the fourth and fifth fields determine whether terminal interface is enabled and whether root logons are permitted.

After this line has been added, save the file and reboot the system. The GUI logon should not appear and logons should be available via the attached serial interface.

## Connecting to the Headless Mac

To utilize their new capabilities, administrators need only connect their workstations to the Mac in question with some hardware such as a null modem cable and run their favorite terminal software with the appropriate configuration. Two of the more popular ways of connecting to a serial-based headless Mac (or any serial device for that matter) from a Mac are Zterm and minicom. Zterm is a freely downloadable (http://homepage.mac.com/dalverson/zterm/) GUI serial communications application. While perpetually in beta (the last update to the beta was released in 2002), Zterm is a program with a long history and a large feature set that makes it a useful tool for any network admin's toolkit. Minicom (actually a wrapper of sorts around kermit) is a venerable command line application that is open source (easily downloaded and installed via Fink or DarwinPorts) and free (as in beer). Though it is a command line application, it is menu-driven and rather easy to use.

In either case, administrators will need to set their communications application to 9600 bps, 8 data bits, no parity, and 1 stop bit with hardware flow control. For Zterm, this is accomplished by accessing **Settings | Connections** Figure 1.4). Administrators can change this setting in Minicom by pressing **Ctrl+A** and then **Z**, followed by **O** to bring up the configuration dialog box. Within this dialog box is a **Serial port setup** item that contains the necessary settings. Once all of the communications are in place, an administrator only needs another computer with a null modem cable or a terminal device to connect to the headless Mac and start using it.

**Figure 1.4** Zterm Connections Settings

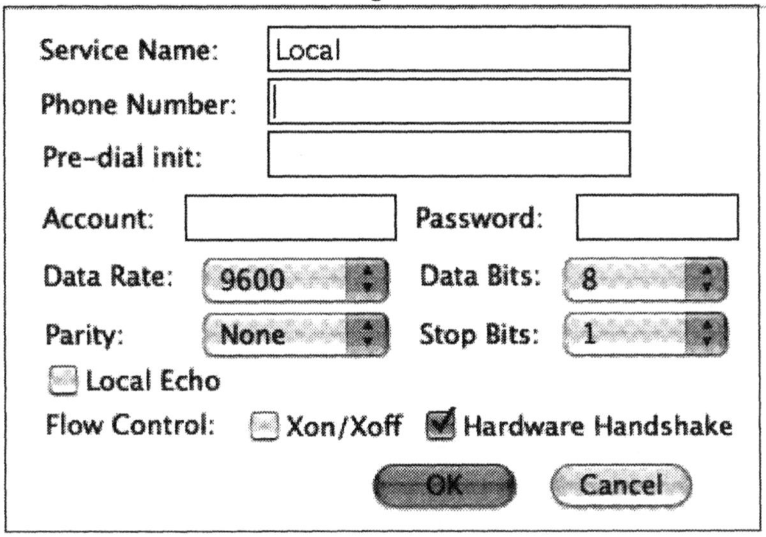

## Extra Credit: Serial over Bluetooth

For those looking for a more long distance approach to connecting to their Mac device serially, it is also possible to control one via Bluetooth, as shown in the following steps.

1. The first step in the process is to create a serial port device on the target device. Open the **Bluetooth** pane from **System Preferences**, and then select the **Sharing** tab.

2. Clicking the **Add Serial Port Service** will add a service named *SerialPort-1* in the column above (assuming no other serial ports already exist here).

3. To make this logical port accessible as a standard device and provide for some additional security, select the new port, then on the right-hand side, set the type to **RS-232** and check the box next to **Require pairing for security**". Figure 1.5 illustrates an example of this dialog.

**Figure 1.5** Adding a Bluetooth Serial Port

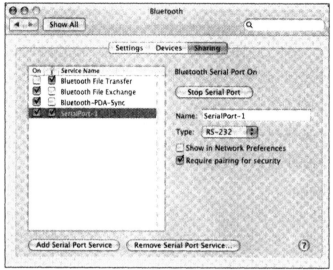

**NOTE**

Serial is, of course, not the only way to use Bluetooth to connect to a headless Mac. TCP/IP (Transmission Control Protocol / Internet Protocol) is also available, permitting one to use SSH or even VNC to control the Mac over Bluetooth.

4. The next step is to create a security pairing between the management device and the machine to be managed. From either device's GUI, select the **Devices** tab from **Bluetooth** pane, and then click the **Set up new device…** button. This will start an assistant that steps one through the setup.

5. Click the **Continue** button to advance past the welcome screen, and then choose a device type of **Any device** before clicking the **Continue** button again. The setup assistant will scan for nearby Bluetooth devices.

6. Select the appropriate one and click the **Passkey Options...** button. From the resulting dialog, ensure that the **Automatically generate a passkey** option is selected, and then click the **OK** button.

7. Clicking the **Continue** button should result in a page containing a six-digit number being displayed (as seen in Figure 1.6).

**Figure 1.6** Auto-Generated Passkey

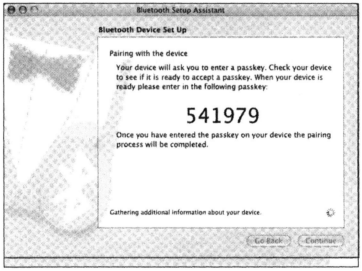

8. Shortly afterward there should be a dialog box on the other device (see Figure 1.7) in this pairing prompting for you to enter this six-digit number. Entering the correct number and clicking the **OK** button should result in a congratulations dialog on both machines.

**Figure 1.7** Pairing Request Dialog

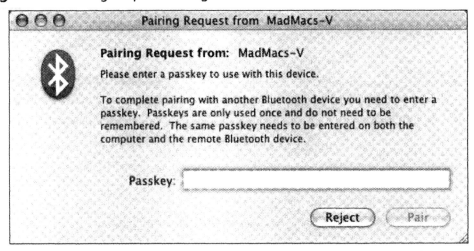

Just as when using a hardwired serial port (or serial adapter), the /etc/ttys file has to be modified to permit console access via the Bluetooth serial port. This is accomplished in the same way as any other serial device, with the device name being tty.SerialPort-1.

```
tty.SerialPort-1        "/usr/libexec/getty serial.9600" vt100 on secure
```

After making and saving the appropriate changes to /etc/ttys, the new configuration can activated with either a reboot or one of the following commands.

On Mac OS X 10.4 or later:

```
sudo launchctl reloadttys
```

On Mac OS X 10.3.x or earlier:

```
sudo kill -HUP 1
```

Once the two machines are paired and the modifications applied to the TTY system on the serving machine, it is necessary to go to the client side of the connection to further configure the serial connection:

1.  Open the Bluetooth preferences pane and select the **Devices** tab, then click the **Edit Serial Ports...** button. This will display a dialog that allows an administrator to create serial port devices based on the Bluetooth connection.

2. Click the plus (+) sign at the lower left of the box at the top. This will create a device and populate the lower portion of the dialog box, like that seen in Figure 1.8, with configurable settings.

**Figure 1.8** Adding a Client Device

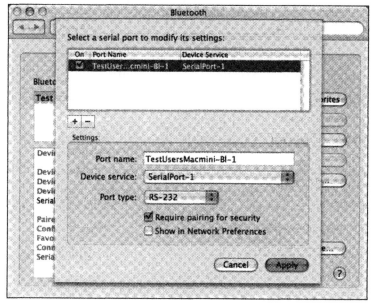

3. The **Port name** field can be left as is or set to something of the administrator's liking; this is the device name that the client machine's terminal application will use to connect to. The **Device service** drop-down menu contains the different kinds of serial ports being published by the serving machine; choose **SerialPort-1**. The **Port type** drop-down menu should be set to **RS-232** and the checkbox for **Require pairing for security** should be enabled.

4. Clicking **Apply** will save these settings. Terminal applications should now be able to connect to the device on the client side like it was any other device using the name given above.

## Notes From the Underground...

### Pretty (and Wireless)

A few vendors also make Bluetooth RS-232 (DB-9) dongles that can be affixed to the serial console port of a network device, allowing an administrator to manage it without being tethered by a cable.

## Extra Extra Credit: Logging to the Serial Port

While using the serial port as a terminal interface is certainly useful, a piece some administrators may find missing is the output of logging messages to the console (as many network devices do). This can be accomplished by modifying the /etc/syslog.conf file. To do this:

1. Create a backup of the file, and then modify the original with a text editor. Locate the following line:

   ```
   #*.err;kern.*;auth.notice;authpriv,remoteauth.none;mail.crit
           /dev/tty.serial
   ```

2. To enable the output of console messages, uncomment the line by removing the # symbol from its beginning, then modify /dev/tty.serial to indicate the particular serial device where the console output should go. Administrators may also wish to prefix *.notice; to the beginning of this line to have common notifications output to the serial line. For those administrators familiar with syslog, it is possible to customize the output to the serial console to suit the situation. Figure 1.9 shows sample output from a system with serial logging enabled.

**Figure 1.9** Sample Output of Logs on the Serial Port via Bluetooth as Seen in Zterm

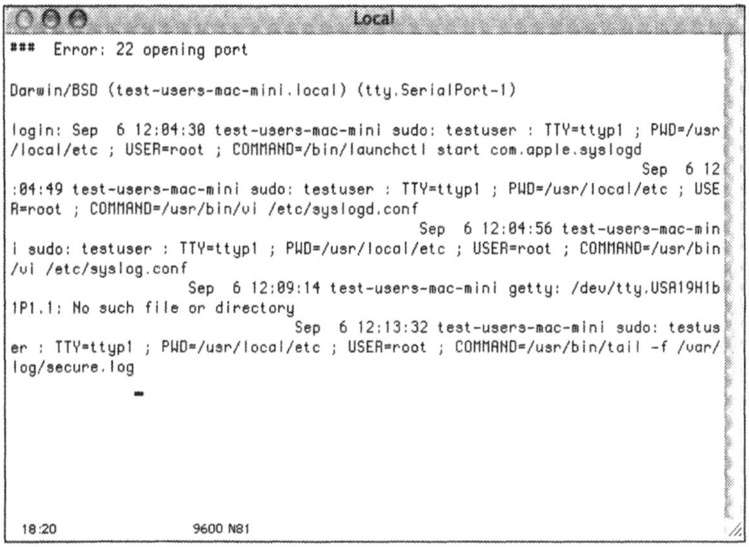

```
000                           Local
### Error: 22 opening port

Darwin/BSD (test-users-mac-mini.local) (tty.SerialPort-1)

login: Sep  6 12:04:30 test-users-mac-mini sudo: testuser : TTY=ttyp1 ; PWD=/usr
/local/etc ; USER=root ; COMMAND=/bin/launchctl start com.apple.syslogd
                                                              Sep  6 12
:04:49 test-users-mac-mini sudo: testuser : TTY=ttyp1 ; PWD=/usr/local/etc ; USE
R=root ; COMMAND=/usr/bin/vi /etc/syslogd.conf
                                    Sep  6 12:04:56 test-users-mac-min
i sudo: testuser : TTY=ttyp1 ; PWD=/usr/local/etc ; USER=root ; COMMAND=/usr/bin
/vi /etc/syslog.conf
                           Sep  6 12:09:14 test-users-mac-mini getty: /dev/tty.USA19H1b
1P1.1: No such file or directory
                                    Sep  6 12:13:32 test-users-mac-mini sudo: testus
er : TTY=ttyp1 ; PWD=/usr/local/etc ; USER=root ; COMMAND=/usr/bin/tail -f /var/
log/secure.log
             ▄

18:20            9600 N81
```

### Notes from the Underground…

#### The Next Logical Step

It is even possible to connect a printer to the serial port and have logs printed out it in real time. "Why?" one might ask (though such questions are somewhat irrelevant in a book ostensibly about hacking). I know of a company that had its Linux server's security log output to an old dot matrix printer filled with green bar paper. Since the server room was in the inhabited space in the office, logons and other security events were instantly and audibly announced to everyone nearby. It was a rather low-tech, but highly effective alarming system since the server was rarely ever logged into directly.

# Adding Interfaces to the Mac

Serial interfaces are not the only things that can be added to a Macintosh. Network administrators who want to do interesting things with Macs and networking often need to add additional interfaces to their systems. The reasons to add network interfaces to a Macintosh are numerous: creating a multi-interface firewall or router, simulating a switch, adding 802.3ad interface aggregation, or just providing another media type (such as fiber).

# Physical Interfaces

Out of the box, Mac OS X supports more than a dozen families of network interfaces:

- Airport
- Airport Extreme
- DEC 21x4
- Broadcom 440x, 5701, 52x1, 54x1
- National Semiconductor MacPhyter II (DP83816)
- Intel 8254x, 8255x
- Realtek 8139
- 3Com 3c90x
- Apple built-ins (Firewire, Ethernet, and Bluetooth)

For all of these devices, installation and configuration is relatively easy; it is as simple as purchasing a supported piece of hardware installing it into the appropriate PCI or Airport slot. The next time an administrator opens the **Network** pane in **System Preferences**, she will be alerted to the arrival of a new interface and it will be added to the list of configurable interfaces. It will also appear in the standard suite of command line tools (Ethernet interfaces appear as en$N$, FireWire interfaces as fw$N$). Third party manufacturers such as Asante or Small Tree are nearly as simple, with the added step of installing drivers.

For administrators who see the Mac Mini as an attractive and powerful little network device, its lack of expandability in the interface realm would seem to be an issue. To a certain extent, this can be true; no PCI slots means no really easy way to upgrade. But PCI is not the only place that new network interfaces can be installed; as with serial ports, the USB2 interface can come to the rescue. Most of the usual suspects that manufacture consumer-grade networking equipment (Linksys, D-Link, etcetera) make USB-based

10/100 Ethernet adapters. While not a perfect solution (particularly on older, USB1.x systems where the 12Mbps theoretical maximum throughput of the specification is a severe bottleneck), it is a very serviceable solution and can turn an already nifty, inexpensive system into something much more useful for a network administrator. Unfortunately, none of the major adapter manufacturers ship drivers for Mac OS X (though most of them do for their WiFi adapters). But lucky for us, there is a thriving open source community that provides functional drivers to fill in the gaps. Drivers for the most popular USB NICs (network interface cards) can be downloaded for free from Sustainable Softworks (www.sustworks.com/site/news_usb_ethernet.html). Installation is as easy as downloading the disk image and running the appropriate installer. Once installed, configuring the interface is the same as any other interface on the Mac.

# Interface Aliases

Sometimes an administrator needs to add additional IP addresses to a particular interface; perhaps for virtual hosting, or to assist in troubleshooting networks, connecting to local hosts with addresses on foreign subnets, or migrating a system from one subnet to another. This process can be achieved either via the GUI or the command line, though the GUI is certainly the easier of the two options.

## GUI Configuration

To add an interface alias via the GUI:

1. Open the **Network** pane of **System Preferences**, then select **Network Port Configurations** from the **Show:** drop-down list.

2. Select the interface you wish to alias and click the **Duplicate** button to the right of the list. This will open a dialog sheet that prompts for the interface to named; accepting the default or typing in a new name and clicking the **OK** button will add the alias interface to the list below (usually at the bottom of the list).

3. Once added, the alias interface can be configured like any other interface (interfaces that require authentication, like Airport and modems, do not require that passphrases or account information be re-entered).

4. Clicking the **Apply Now** button saves the configuration, maintaining the changes through any reboot.

# Command Line Configuration

In the event that an administrator is running a headless Mac, it is still possible to add aliases via the command line. Making the changes through the command line is a little more cumbersome, though relatively straightforward. To add an alias interface via the command line type the following:

```
sudo ifconfig <INTERFACE UNIT> alias <IP_ADDRESS> <NETMASK>
```

**NOTE**

The *interface unit*, also known as the *BSD name* for an interface, is a short string usually consisting of two or three letters followed by a number that is a unique identifier for a particular interface on a particular system. These interface units are typically used by command line or BSD subsystem components to reference the:

- en*N* – Wired and wireless Ethernet
- fw*N* – Firewire
- lo*N* – loopback
- gif*N* – gif tunnel
- stf*N* – IPv4-to-IPv6 tunnel

… and many more.

For example, to add the IP address 172.31.13.254 with a 24-bit mask to the built-in Ethernet port on a Macintosh, an administrator would type the following at the command line:

```
sudo ifconfig en0 alias 172.31.13.254 255.255.255.0
```

Making these changes stick between reboots is a little more difficult though, and requires a little shell scripting to make it work. This is most quickly accomplished with a *StartupItem*. How this is done depends on whether an administrator is dealing with Mac OS X Server or the client edition. On Mac OS X Server, Apple has already included a StartupItem called *IPAliases* that handles creating aliases via a configuration file.

1. To add aliases on startup, use administrative privileges create a text file at /etc/IPAliases.conf:

```
sudo pico /etc/IPAliases.conf
```

2. Next, any number of alias addresses can be added, one per line, to this file in the form of "<INTERFACE UNIT>:<IP_ADDRESS>:<NETMASK>". The following is the equivalent to the above ifconfig command:

```
en0:172.31.13.254:255.255.255.0
```

Any number of interface aliases can be created in this file in this way.

3. The next step in adding aliases is to modify the /etc/hostconfig file and append the following to enable the StartupItem.

```
IPALIASES=-YES-
```

4. Once this change has been made and the file saved, a simple reboot or **sudo SystemStarter start IPAliases** at the command line will enable the new interface aliases.

Bringing this functionality to the client edition of Mac OS X is a bit more cumbersome, given that Apple has not included the same startup item for desktop users. One way to make this easier is to simply copy over the StartupItem from a Mac OS X server to the appropriate location on the machine running the client. The other way is to create a similar script by hand:

1. The first step in doing this is to create a StartupItem directory:

```
sudo mkdir -p /Library/StartupItems/IPAliases
```

2. Next, create a file named StartupParameters.plist in the new directory and open it for editing. Insert the following text into this file:

```
{
        Description           =         "Add IP aliases to interfaces";
        Provides              =         ("IPAliases");
        Requires              =         ("Network");
        Messages              =
            {
                    start  =      "Adding IP aliases";
                    stop   =      "Removing IP aliases";
            };
}
```

3. Save this file, then set the appropriate permissions by entering **chmod 444 /Library/StartupItems/IPAliases/ StartupParameters.plist**. Then, create a file named IPAliases in the same directory, and open it for editing. Insert the following text into this file:

```
#!/bin/sh

. /etc/rc.common

StartService ()
{
if [ "${IPALIASES:=-NO-}" = "-YES-" ]; then

ConsoleMessage "Adding IP aliases…"

# add lines as necessary, one per to add aliases
# mirror these lines in the StopService function
# with a '-alias' to remove aliases upon command

/sbin/ifconfig en0 alias 172.31.13.254 255.255.255.0

fi
}

StopService ()
{
ConsoleMessage "Removing IP aliases…"
```

```
# add lines as necessary, one per to remove aliases
# mirror these lines in the StartService function
# with a 'alias' to remove aliases upon command

/sbin/ifconfig en0 -alias 172.31.13.254 255.255.255.0
}


RestartService  ()
{
        ConsoleMessage "Removing and re-adding aliases for fun"
        StopService; StartService;
}


RunService "$1"
```

Once the file has been saved:

1.  Its permissions must be set appropriately by typing **chmod 555 /Library/StartupItems/IPAliases/IPAliases** at the command line.

2.  The /etc/hostconfig file must then be modified as it was with Mac OS X Server by appending **IPALIASES=-YES-** to it. Here too, executing **sudo SystemStarter restart IPAliases** or rebooting will cause the new StartupItem to take effect. Aliases can be added or subtracted as needed through this StartupItem.

# The Macintosh as a Router

With multiple interfaces comes the ability to do more interesting things with a Mac. Chief among these, at least from a networking standpoint, is routing. A small, low power device such as a Mac Mini or an iBook expanded with USB-based Ethernet ports can serve as a quick and effective device for pushing packets between networks. While not an exhaustive view of routing on Mac OS X, this section will serve to show how to perform some basic routing tasks with a Macintosh, including installing a third-party open source routing engine called Zebra.

# Basic Host Routing

Like most modern operating systems, Mac OS X sports the ability to perform basic routing. Routes can be added to the host statically to allow it to connect to remote subnets as needed. It also ships with the ancient (venerable maybe even, it has been around since 4.2BSD, circa 1983) *routed*, which provides a general RIP (Routing Information Protocol)-capable routing daemon.

The current host routing table can be viewed with the **netstat -rn** command at the command line, or the GUI **Network Utility** (choose the **Netstat** tab, and select **Display routing table information**). The GUI output is shown in Figure 1.10.

**Figure 1.10** View netstat –r Results in a GUI

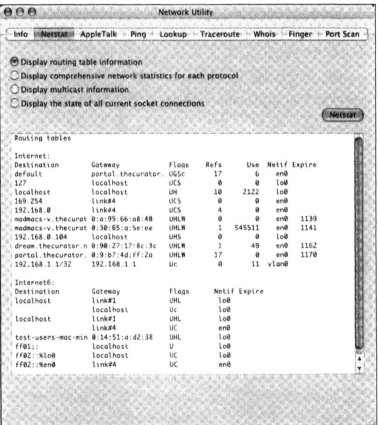

As with many UNIX-based operating systems, a Mac OS X system's routing table can be modified using the **route** command line utility.

1. To add a route, type **sudo route add &lt;NETWORK_ADDRESS&gt;/&lt;BITS&gt; &lt;GATEWAY&gt;** at the command line. For example, to send packets destined for the 172.16.16.0 Class C network to the gateway at 192.168.24.1:

   ```
   sudo route add 172.16.16.0/25 192.168.24.1
   ```

2. Deleting a route is very much the same, except it is done using the **delete** keyword:

   ```
   sudo route delete 172.16.16.0/25 192.168.24.1
   ```

3. To make these routes stick beyond a reboot, it is best to create a StartupItem to do so. To do this, first create a directory for the StartupItem by typing the following at the command line:

   ```
   sudo mkdir -p /Library/StartupItems/Addroutes
   ```

4. After the directory is created, create a text file named StartupParameters.plist in the new directory. Insert the following text into the file and save it:

   ```
   {
           Description         =       "Add additional IP routes";
           Provides            =       ("AddRoutes");
           Requires            =       ("Network");
           Messages            =
               {
                   start   =       "Adding additional IP routes";
                   stop    =       "Removing additional IP routes";
               };
   }
   ```

5.  Then create a text file named Addroutes and insert the following text (saving it when complete):

```
#!/bin/sh

. /etc/rc.common

StartService ()
{
if [ "${ADDROUTES:=-NO-}" = "-YES-" ]; then

ConsoleMessage "Adding additional IP routes…"

# add lines as necessary, one per route
# mirror these lines in the StopService function
# with a 'delete' to remove routes upon command

/sbin/route add 172.16.16.0/25 192.168.24.1

fi
}

StopService ()
{
ConsoleMessage "Removing additional IP routes…"

# add lines as necessary, one per route
# mirror these lines in the StartService function
# with a 'add' to remove routes upon command

/sbin/route delete 172.16.16.0/25 192.168.24.1
}

RestartService  ()
{
        ConsoleMessage "Removing and re-adding aliases for fun"
        StopService; StartService;
}

RunService "$1"
```

6. Finally, set the appropriate permissions on these two files:

```
sudo chmod 0444
/Library/StartupItems/Addroutes/StartupParameters.plist
sudo chmod 0555 /Library/StartupItems/Addroutes/Addroutes
```

Upon reboot or activation with SystemStarter, the new startup items will take effect.

**NOTE**

There are other aspects of the **route** command not covered here; the man pages contain information on the more esoteric possibilities such as metrics and Link Layer routes.

# Basic Static Routing

The above route commands modify the host's routing table and route packets for the host itself, but do no forwarding of packets for any other hosts attempting to use this system as a router. To do this we need to enable packet forwarding on the Mac, which is done by modifying some system variable with the **sysctl** command. The following command enables routing from the command line (there is no currently no GUI equivalent):

```
sysctl  -w net.inet.ip.forwarding=1
```

For IPv6-enabled systems, this command is slightly different:

```
sysctl -w net.inet6.ip6.forwarding=1
```

To make this setting survive reboots, administrators can create a file in /etc named sysctl.conf. This file can contain any number of lines, each with a sysctl setting. To enable IP forwarding at boot, insert the following into this file:

```
net.inet.ip.forwarding=1
net.inet6.ip6.forwarding=1
```

# Basic Dynamic Network Routing

Basic static routing only enables forwarding for static routes. If an administrator wants to make a Mac into a more capable router and use dynamic routing protocols, a routing engine must also be used. Mac OS X includes one such engine, called *routed*. This daemon understands three basic dynamic routing protocols: RIPv1, RIPv2, and IRDP (ICMP Router Discovery Protocol). To enable routed to operate as the system's routing process at boot time, a StartupItem is created; unless an administrator wants to get tricky with their configuration, there is no need for a configuration file; all local interface subnets will be broadcast. However, if there are interfaces that RIP updates should not be accepted or sent on, or networks that should not be added to the route tables, a file can be created at /etc/gateways with additional settings in it. The following lines in the file would individually turn off all routing updates from an interface, set a RIPv2 passphrase, and set a subnet that will not be sent in updates:

```
if=en0, passive
passwd=Killr0y
net 10.100.10.0/24 gateway 192.168.0.1 passive
```

Once the configuration, if any, is complete, the next step is to create a StartupItem to start routed at boot time.

1. Just like the previous discussions, we make a directory first:

   ```
   mkdir  -p /Library/StartupItems/routed
   ```

2. Next we create a text file within this directory named StartupParameters.plist and populate it with the following text:

   ```
   {
           Description         =       "Add additional IP routes";
           Provides            =       ("AddRoutes");
           Requires            =       ("Network");
           Messages            =
               {
                   start   =       "Adding additional IP routes";
                   stop    =       "Removing additional IP routes";
               };
   }
   ```

3. Third, we create a file in the directory, name it *routed*, and insert the following script:

```
#!/bin/sh

. /etc/rc.common

StartService ()
{
if [ "${ROUTED:=-NO-}" = "-YES-" ]; then

ConsoleMessage "Starting route daemon…"

/sbin/routed

fi
}

StopService ()
{
ConsoleMessage "Stopping route daemon…"

          /usr/bin/killall routed
}

RestartService ()
{
          ConsoleMessage "Restarting route daemon…"
          StopService; StartService;
}

RunService "$1"
```

4. Finally, we set the permissions on the files:

```
sudo chmod 0444 /Library/StartupItems/routed/StartupParameters.plist
sudo chmod 0555 /Library/StartupItems/routed/routed
```

---

**NOTE**

By now readers have probably noticed that we are making a lot of StartupItems for various items in this chapter. More information is available at the following URLs:

- www.macdevcenter.com/pub/a/mac/2003/10/21/startup.html
- http://developer.apple.com/documentation/MacOSX/ Conceptual/ BPSystemStartup/Articles/StartupItems.html

There are many different facets to creating these scripts, and Tiger added an additional wrinkle to startup scripts with **launchd**. Information on creating launchd style scripts can be found at the following URLs:

- www.macgeekery.com/tips/all_about_launchd_items_and_ how_to_make_one_yourself
- http://developer.apple.com/documentation/MacOSX Conceptual/ BPSystemStartup/Articles/ DesigningDaemons.html
- http://developer.apple.com/documentation/MacOSX /Conceptual/ BPSystemStartup/Articles /LaunchOnDemandDaemons.html

---

# "Real" Routing with Zebra

While routed is generally solid and has been around for a while, it does not support more modern routing protocols and it is not as adaptable or configurable or as easy to use as one would hope. Fortunately for administrators wanting more features in their Mac routers, there is an open source project named Zebra. Zebra consists of a primary routing process called *zebra* (go figure) and five other processes that manage specific routing protocols. The main zebra daemon is responsible for kernel routing tables, interface addressing, and passing routing updates between the other daemons. The other five daemons are named after the protocols they support and are touched on as we continue.

# Downloading and Installing Zebra

One can download Zebra from the project's website (www.zebra.org/download.html). There is no binary installer for Zebra, so you must download the tarball and compile it manually. We will walk you through it:

**WARNING**

We will be assuming here that Xcode version 2.1 (the latest as of this writing) is installed.

1. Make a destination directory for downloading the source:

   ```
   sudo mkdir -p /usr/local/src
   sudo chgrp admin /usr/local/src
   sudo chmod g+w /usr/local/src
   cd /usr/local/src
   ```

2. Download the latest source from ftp://ftp.zebra.org/pub/zebra:

   ```
   curl -O ftp://ftp.zebra.org/pub/zebra/zebra-0.95.tar.gz
   ```

3. Set the gcc version back to 3.3 for compatibility reasons:

   ```
   sudo gcc_select 3.3
   ```

4. Compile and install the software:

   ```
   cd zebra-0.95
   ./configure
   make
   sudo make install
   ```

5. Return the gcc version back to the default version:

   ```
   sudo gcc_select 4.0
   ```

6. As with most system daemons we need a way to start them at boot time, which we will do with a StartupItem. First we make the directory:

   ```
   sudo mkdir  -p /Library/StartupItems/zebra
   ```

7. Next we need to create a text file within this directory named StartupParameters.plist with the following text:

```
{
        Description          =          "Zebra Routing Engine";
        Provides             =          ("zebra");
        Requires             =          ("Network");
        Messages             =
            {
                    start  =          "Starting Zebra services…";
                    stop   =          "Stopping Zebra services…";
            };
}
```

8. Next, create a file named *zebra* in the directory and include the following text:

```
#!/bin/sh

. /etc/rc.common

StartService ()
{
if [ "${ZEBRA:=-NO-}" = "-YES-" ]; then

ConsoleMessage "Starting Zebra services…"

            # Start the routing manager, handles general
configuration
            #    and static routes.
/usr/local/sbin/zebra -d

# Start routing protocol engines
#    -- Only start those actually being used

# BGP
# /usr/local/sbin/bgpd -d
# OSPF for IPv6
# /usr/local/sbin/ospf6d -d
# OSPF for IPv4
```

```
# /usr/local/sbin/ospfd -d
# RIPv1, RIPv2
# /usr/local/sbin/ripd -d
# RIP for IPv6
# /usr/local/sbin/ripngd -d


fi
}


StopService ()
{
ConsoleMessage "Stopping Zebra services…"

        # Stop the routing manager
        if pid=$(GetPID zebra); then
               kill -TERM "${pid}"
        fi


        # Stop routing protocol engines
        if pid=$(GetPID bgpd); then
               kill -TERM "${pid}"
        fi


        if pid=$(GetPID ospf6d); then
               kill -TERM "${pid}"
        fi


        if pid=$(GetPID ospf); then
               kill -TERM "${pid}"
        fi


        if pid=$(GetPID ripd); then
               kill -TERM "${pid}"
        fi


        if pid=$(GetPID ripngd); then
               kill -TERM "${pid}"
        fi
```

```
        }


RestartService   ()
{
                ConsoleMessage "Restarting Zebra services…"
                StopService; StartService;
}


RunService "$1"
```

Before the services can be started at least minimal configuration files must created for the routing manager and the protocol engines that are intended to be used. We will look at this next.

## Configuring Zebra for Routing

The default location for Zebra's configuration files is /usr/local/etc. The installer creates a sample file for each of the daemons as daemon_name.conf.sample (zebra.conf.sample for the routing manager, for instance). To create a basic configuration for each daemon, simply create copies of the appropriate files (minimally, for Zebra itself) in /usr/local/etc without the .sample suffix. The included files contain enough information for the services to start and to permit access via Telnet.

Once the configuration files are in place, the daemons can be started with SystemStarter as normal (**sudo SystemStarter start zebra**). The first steps upon starting the daemons should be basic configuration. This includes providing hostnames, passwords, IP addresses, and any needed static routes to the system.

**NOTE**

It is also possible to fully configure the daemons before starting them via the configuration files. In either case (Telnet or direct file modification) the individual commands are the same, as long as location within the file is properly maintained. The intent here is to demonstrate basic configuration the way it would be completed on a production device, and it is easier to write the configuration from the vty session.

Connect to the vty interface of the main routing manager by connecting with Telnet to port 2601. When prompted for a password, use the default of **zebra**. This should set the session to a Router> prompt. This initial mode is read-only with very limited access. To enter privileged mode, type **enable** at the prompt and enter the default password, **zebra**. This mode is largely read-only, with the exception of the ability to the system configuration and some session parameters, so we need to enter configuration mode to make further modifications. This is done by typing **config term** at the Router# prompt.

**NOTE**

Astute and experienced users will note that the commands and configuration files used by Zebra are very similar to Cisco's own IOS. This is very true, but only to a point. Zebra resembles something like an IOS that was forked at about IOS version 10. While it shares a number of basic syntactical features, the Zebra syntax is also very different from what Cisco administrators would see today (and in many ways, happily less complicated, but also less feature-rich). Zebra for instance, does not use wildcard masks like IOS, but tends to use CIDR (Classless Inter-Domain Routing) notation instead. It also has a different method of dealing with named access lists; they are created with the **access-list ...** command rather than IOS's **ip access-list extended...** command, and are the more limited standard access lists rather than the extended variety. Rather than as in IOS (in most cases anyway), whose configuration is monolithic with all available functionality being available in one place, Zebra splits the dynamic protocols off into additional processes with their own configuration files. Though the differences are many, most administrators familiar with IOS will be able to find their way around Zebra with ease.

This mode (evidenced by the prompt changing to Router(config)#) is read/write and changes are instantaneous, though not automatically saved. To set the hostname for the routing engine (informational only, but useful when multiple devices are under one's domain), type **hostname Zeblah** (where Zeblah is a name that can be replaced with something more appropriate to the situation, but probably less silly).

It is a good idea to set the logon and enable mode passwords away from the default as well. This is done with two commands:

```
password somep@Sw0rdthatsrea77yl0ngandg00d
enable password some()therp@Zwerdthatsalsoreall EElo|\|gandg00d!
```

It is also a good idea to encrypt passwords in the configuration, so if a configuration is leaked it will still be difficult for someone to obtain administrative access:

```
service password-encryption
```

If an administrator wishes to add additional IP addresses to interfaces beyond those set at the OS level (via the **ifconfig** command, or GUI, as shown earlier) it is possible to do this within Zebra as well.

**TIP**

It is probably better to add the extra addresses through the zebra process if the reason for the additional addresses and interfaces is for routing. It is cleaner and easier to manage in the long run.

To add IP addresses to an interface, enter configuration mode (if not already there), then enter interface configuration mode for the interface you wish to configure. The general command for this is **interface <INTER-FACE_NAME>**. The prompt will change accordingly and allow you to enter subcommands for the interface (of which IP addressing is just one). The following example enters interface configuration mode, then adds an IP address of 10.10.10.10 (with a subnet mask of 255.255.255.0) to interface en0:

```
Router(config)#
Router(config)# interface en0
Router(config-if)#  ip address 10.10.10.10/24
```

Notice that the prompt changes accordingly. Additional addresses can easily be added with additional instances of the **ip address** subcommand. Once added, these IP addresses show up in ifconfig output as seen in the following snippet:

```
en0: flags=8863<UP,BROADCAST,SMART,RUNNING,SIMPLEX,MULTICAST> mtu 1500
        inet6 fe80::214:51ff:fe0a:d238%en0 prefixlen 64 scopeid 0x4
        inet 192.168.0.104 netmask 0xffffff00 broadcast 192.168.0.255
        inet 10.10.10.10 netmask 0xffffff00 broadcast 10.10.10.255
ether 00:14:51:0a:d2:38
        media: autoselect (10baseT/UTP <half-duplex>) status: active
        supported media: none autoselect 10baseT/UTP <half-duplex>
10baseT/UTP <full-duplex> 10baseT/UTP <full-duplex,hw-loopback> 100baseTX
<half-duplex> 100baseTX <full-duplex> 100baseTX <full-duplex,hw-loopback>
```

The other major piece of functionality the Zebra routing manager provides is static routing, the configuration of which is performed in general configuration mode (to exit interface configuration mode, type **exit** at the prompt). The general form of a route statement is **ip route** followed on the same line by a destination network in one of two forms:

- **A.B.C.D/M** The network address in CIDR notation
- **A.B.C.D W.X.Y.Z** The network address and subnet mask in dotted-quad notation

This is continued with a next hop location in one of three forms:

- **M.N.O.P** The IP address of the next hop
- **INTERFACE** (en0, or en1, or ppp0, for example) The interface out of which packets should be pushed, usually used for point-to-point links
- **Null0** A special interface of sorts that makes packets go poof, into a black hole rather than being processed further

For example, the following would add the network 172.16.16.0/25 with a next hop of 10.10.10.254 and route packets destined for 10.100.100.0/24 into the floor:

```
ip route 172.16.16.0/25 10.10.10.254
ip route 10.100.100.0 255.255.255.0 null0
```

While all of the above changes take effect immediately, if the machine is rebooted (or gods forbid, the daemon crashes), any configuration will be lost. To save the configuration, exit configuration mode (using the aptly named

**exit** command) and enter **write memory**. This will write the configuration out to the configuration file.

---

**NOTE**

Like the Cisco IOS, Zebra has the concept of a difference between a startup configuration and a running configuration. Changes to the configuration of a running process are effective immediately, but will not survive a restart of the process. Only by writing the running configuration out to the startup configuration will the changes survive a reboot.

---

The other daemons included with Zebra take the next step and provide dynamic routing services. Each of these processes is configured separately with separate configuration files (as discussed earlier in this section) and separate vty servers. Table 1 2 describes the default ports for each of the zebra services and a basic description of its functionality.

**Table 1.2** Zebra Processes, Ports, and Functions

| Process | Port | Function |
| --- | --- | --- |
| zebra | tcp 2601 | Zebra primary process |
| ripd | tcp 2602 | RIPv1/v2 server |
| ripngd | tcp 2603 | RIP IPv6 server |
| ospfd | tcp 2604 | OSPF server |
| bgpd | tcp 2605 | BGP server |
| ospf6d | tcp 2606 | OSPF IPv6 server |

Each routing protocol's daemon's configuration is similar to that of the zebra process. For each protocol in use, it is still proper to set the hostname and the two passwords. The process is exactly as seen above, except that you Telnet to a different port and the default enable password for the other daemons is blank. Each daemon also has to be configured with the networks it will be announcing via the protocol it governs, which is enabled with the **network** command. The following are examples of how each protocol uses this command to announce 10.10.10.0/24 to neighbors:

- RIP (ripd.conf)

```
! enable RIP (defaults to version 1 unless specifically set
! with the 'version' command
router rip
      network 10.10.10.0/24
```

- RIPng (ripngd.conf)

```
! enable RIPng
router ripng
      network 10.10.10.0/24
```

- OSPF (ospfd.conf)

```
! enable OSPF
router ospf
! announce the network (here we will assume it is area zero)
      network 10.10.10.0/24 area 0
```

- OSPF6 (ospf6d.conf)

```
! enable OSPF6
router ospf6
! announce the network (here we will assume it is area zero
! and there is no "network" command for v3 (IPv6) so we will use
! interface en0 as the interface for area 0
      interface en0 area 0.0.0.0
```

- BGP (bgpd.conf)

```
! enable BGP (here we will assume it is ASN 1)
router BGP 1
      network 10.10.10.0/24
```

---

**WARNING**

Since each process's password is blank by default, it is a very necessary part of configuration to set it to something more secure. And no, *zebra* is not good. Nor is *good* good.

---

Beyond the basics, the daemons typically need additional, protocol-specific configurations. These parameters depend quite a bit on which protocol is being used and how it has to be implemented to suit a particular network. In fact, the number of different ways an administrator can deploy these protocols is rather large (even when counting the subset of "correct" ways), so we will only touch on some basics here. The man pages and online documentation can assist greatly in tailoring the configuration to suite the needs of the network and its administrator(s).

# Mac OS X as a RADIUS server

In addition to providing routing services as a network device, Macintoshes also have the capability of providing services to other network devices. One such common service is RADIUS, a standard AAA (authentication, authorization, and accounting) protocol used by many administrators to provide logon and monitoring services to their network devices for security or change management. Figure 1.11 illustrates a simplified view of the process of a user attempting to access a router that uses RADIUS to authenticate its administrative users. After a client requests access, the device, typically referred to as the NAS, sends the requestor a request for credentials. The NAS bundles up this request and fires it off to the RADIUS server. Both NAS and RADIUS server are pre-configured with each other's host addresses and a pre-shared key that is used to authenticate each other and provide a basis for encryption of the user-supplied credentials. Upon receipt of credentials from the NAS, the RADIUS makes a determination of whether the credentials are valid. This lookup may be done in a local user database, UNIX password store, WindowsNT user database, an LDAP (Lightweight Directory Access Protocol) instance, SQL database, or all of the above, and can be compared against various filter rules defined on the RADIUS server. Once the determination of success or failure has been made, it is sent to the NAS, which then responds appropriately to the requestor (usually by either granting access, or re-prompting for authentication).

**NOTE**

Some readers may note the references to *NAS*, which stands for Network Access Server, and wonder why we keep using that term for the device when what we are talking about is a router. The reason is in one word, legacy. A company named Livingston Enterprises developed RADIUS, and they made... you guessed it, network access servers. RADIUS, in fact, stands for Remote Authentication Dial In User Service, and as such is used by ISP's far and wide for modem and PPPoE (Point to Point Protocol over Ethernet) access. For this reason a great many RADIUS implementations call a client application or device a NAS.

**Figure 1.11** Basic RADIUS Process

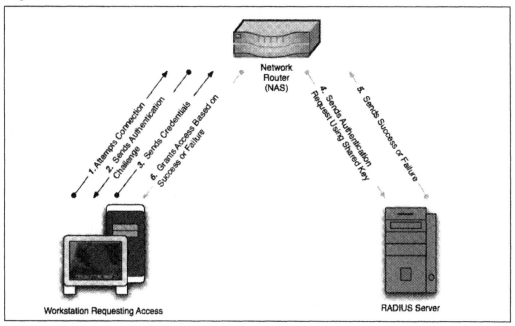

In this section we will discuss configuring a popular open source RADIUS server for providing authentication services to Cisco routers, and then we will move on to making a Mac OS X server the backend user store.

# FreeRADIUS

FreeRADIUS is one of the more popular and capable open source RADIUS servers (OpenRADIUS, YardRadius, ICRADIUS, and Gnu-RADIUS are others). It supports a number of datastores, has 50+ vendor dictionaries (used to tailor the RADIUS protocol to a specific vendor's needs), supports a variety of protocol sub-types, and has other nifty, enterprise features like load balancing. For those familiar with Livingston Enterprises' configuration format FreeRADIUS provides a similar syntax. FreeRADIUS is a fully featured and complex product that manages a complex and multi-faceted protocol, so what we show here is just the tip of its iceberg of functionality.

Since FreeRADIUS does not yet compile happily on Mac OS X, FreeRADIUS is easiest installed from an installer package available from the Internet (http://home.sw.rr.com/jguidroz/radius.html). On this site there is a disk image containing an installer for the server and a separate one for the necessary StartupItem. The installer installs the bulk of the FreeRADIUS install in /usr/local/freeradius. While the installer does all the copying of files and such, it is currently necessary to manually create the log file:

1. Type the following on the command line:

```
sudo mkdir -p /usr/local/freeradius/var/log/radius
sudo touch /usr/local/freeradius/var/log/radius/radius.log
```

2. The current installer also needs a little help with permissions on the StartupItem:

```
sudo chown -R root:wheel /Library/StartupItems/FreeRadius
```

3. To cause the service to start at boot time, append the following line to /etc/hostconfig:

```
RADIUSSERVER=-YES-
```

4. The next thing to do is to start the service and test the installation:

```
sudo SystemStarter start Radius
sudo radtest bob hello localhost 1812 testing123
```

This should return something similar this:

```
   Sending Access-Request of id 240 to 127.0.0.1:1812
        User-Name = "bob"
        User-Password = "hello"
        NAS-IP-Address = test-users-mac-mini.local
        NAS-Port = 1812
   Reply-Message = "Hello %u"
```

If the response is different, there must be an issue with the install that must be troubleshot before moving on (an exercise left to the reader). Once the service is installed and tested for basic functionality, it is time to create NAS definitions so that the RADIUS server has something to do by adding at least one NAS definition to the /usr/local/freeradius/etc/clients.conf file. It is a good idea to set the default example to the side for use as a template or reference in creating a new one. The following content would create a definition for a Cisco router at an address of 192.168.0.250 and with a shared secret of *FractAlgorithm*.

```
client  192.168.0.250   {
        secret        =        FractAlgorithm
        shortname     =        portal
}
```

Now that the RADIUS has something to do, it is time to give it something to do it with by adding users to the /usr/local/freeradius/etc/raddb/users file. As with the clients.conf file, it is best to make a backup of the default, then start from scratch using the examples in the default to create entries in the new file. The following definition creates a user named *ciscoadmin* with a password of *BantyVervet*.

```
ciscoadmin      Auth-Type := Local, User-Password == "BantyVervet"
```

The final component of authenticating administrative users on Cisco devices with FreeRADIUS is configuring the Cisco device. To add this ability, an administrator must enter config mode and enter the following commands (we will assume a bare configuration, not previously configured for AAA authentication and that the RADIUS server is located at 192.168.0.104):

```
! enable modern AAA services
aaa new-model
! create a local backup user account, in case of RADIUS failure
username localadmin secret JerseyHowler
```

```
! setup aaa login for RADIUS with fall back to local authentication
aaa authentication login USERAUTHEN group radius local
aaa authorization network GROUPAUTHOR local
radius-sever host 192.168.0.104 auth-port 1812 acct-port 1813 key
BantyVervet
! set the vty's to use USERAUTHEN login configuration
line vty 0 4
login authentication USERAUTHEN
! set the console to use USERAUTHEN login configuration
line con 0
login authentication USERAUTHEN
! exit line config mode
exit
! exit config mode
exit
```

Though these changes will take effect immediately, one must, of course, save the running configuration to make the changes permanent. As soon as the changes have been made and the RADIUS daemon is started on the Mac, administrators should be able to use a username and password pair as described in the users file to log on to their routers.

## Mac OS X Server Integration

Administrators lucky enough to manage Mac OS X Server systems can install FreeRADIUS on a server and use Open Directory to authenticate users. This provides an added benefit of providing a more centralized user database, making it easier to control access to systems. This process is only a little more complicated than setting FreeRADIUS up to use its local database. First, Open Directory must be configured to permit the queries against its database, and then LDAP authentication must be added to the RADIUS configuration:

> **NOTE**
>
> It is possible to run the RADIUS server on a box other than the Mac OS X Server machine, but then you should use TLS encryption, which is not covered here.

1. The first step is to ensure that the Mac OS X Server installation is up to the task. From a basic functionality standpoint, we will assume that Open Directory is properly installed and functional. On top of this, the directory must permit directory binds. This is permitted using the Server Admin.app application.

2. Open the application, select the **Computers and Services | Open Directory | Policy | Binding**. Enable the **Enable directory binding** and **Require clients to bind to directory** options in the **Directory Binding** section (Figure 1.12).

3. Click **Save**.

**Figure 1.12** Directory Binding Settings

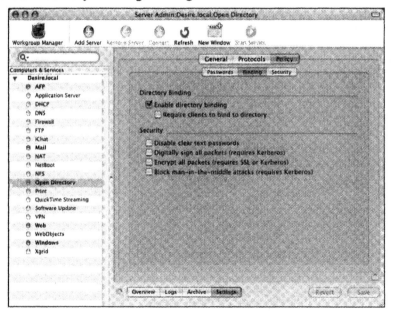

4. Assuming that Open Directory is happily up and running, the next step in the configuration is to configure the LDAP section of /usr/local/freeradius/etc/radiusd.conf. Locate the line beginning "ldap {"; this begins the LDAP module definition, which is ended by a "}". Modify the line beginning "server =" to replace "ldap.your.domain" with the DNS name or IP address of the Open Directory server (if the FreeRADIUS install is on the same box, "localhost" will do).

5. The line that begins with "basedn =" should also be modified and the sample string replaced with the basedn of the Mac OS X Server. For systems that use NetInfo as their primary information store, this can be located by using **niutil** from the command line, where SERVER is the hostname of the server:

```
niutil -readprop -t SERVER/network /machines/SERVER suffix
```

On systems that do not use NetInfo databases as their primary store, such as Open Directory Masters, this can be found in Server Admin.app, by selecting **Open Directory | Settings | Protocols**. The basedn can be specified as the information in Search base: field (Figure 1.13).

**Figure 1.13** Finding the BaseDN

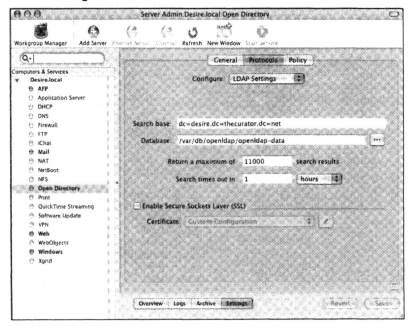

6. After the basedn information is included, identity and password fields should also be inserted into the configuration file. The identity field is a fully qualified distinguished name (FQDN) for a valid user on the system to be used during username/password searches. The password entry is self-explanatory and is the password that goes with the identity for use when binding to the directory to perform searches.

The rest of the entries in the ldap{} section can be left as is. The following is an example ldap{} section for the radiusd.conf file:

```
ldap {
        server = "localhost"
        identity = " uid=testuser,cn=users,dc=test,dc=example,dc=com"
        password = supergreatpassword
        basedn = "dc=test,dc=example,dc=com"
        filter = "(uid=%{Stripped-User-Name:-%{User-Name}})"
        start_tls = no
dictionary_mapping = ${raddbdir}/ldap.attrmap
ldap_connections_number = 5
        timeout = 4
                timelimit = 3
                net_timeout = 1
}
```

7.  Once the ldap{} section has been properly modified, locate the authorize{} section, which begins with "authorize {". In this section, locate a line that reads "#   ldap" and remove the comment character (#) from the beginning of the line. Next, locate the authenticate{} section (starting with, you guessed it... "authenticate {"). About halfway through the section there is the following:

```
#Auth-Type LDAP {
#       ldap
#}
```

8.  Remove the # characters from beginning of each line and save the file.

9.  The next step is to modify the users file and insert the following line, which will enable LDAP lookups for user requests:

```
DEFAULT Auth-Type := LDAP
```

**WARNING**

Users defined in the users file take precedence over this *DEFAULT* setting. The LDAP server will only be queried if the user account attempting to authenticate is not defined.

10. Saving this file and restarting the radiusd process (**sudo SystemStarter restart Radius**) will enable the new authentication source. Users should now be able to authenticate to the requested resources with their Directory Services password.

**NOTE**

RADIUS has a great number of uses and potential variations in configuration that we cannot begin to cover here. As previously noted, there are a variety of backend user databases, a couple different ways of performing, and a variety of client side users such as the recently popular 802.1x protocol for wireless and wired port security. For those wanting more, we suggest reading RADIUS, by Jonathan Hassell (2002).

# Summary

Mac OS X has a lot of networking capabilities that get lost in the background of million-color interfaces and candy-like buttons. Here we have looked at but a few. There are many more awaiting enterprising administrators with the will and the need to push the limits of their machines.

# Solutions Fast Track

## Running a Headless Mac

☑ A variety of solutions are available, both graphical and non-graphical.

☑ Serial ports already exist or are easy to add to most Macs and can be used as an out-of-band connection method.

☑ Bluetooth is another alternative physical interface, providing a wireless serial connection.

# Adding Interfaces to the Mac

☑ Physical interfaces can be added via expansion slot or by USB device.

☑ Physical interfaces can be extended with virtual interfaces (aliases) via GUI or CLI.

# The Macintosh as a Router

☑ Basic static and RIP-based dynamic routing is built-in.

☑ Advanced routing protocols and easier configuration can be added with Zebra.

☑ Zebra supports RIP, OSPF and BGP in IPv4 and IPv6 versions.

# Mac OS X as a RADIUS server

☑ RADIUS is used to provide authentication, authorization, accounting services to a variety of network devices and services.

☑ There are a variety of open source RADIUS servers available; FreeRADIUS is one of the more developed and popular options.

☑ Basic file-based backend for FreeRADIUS is relatively easy, and it can also be backended in an LDAP server such as Mac OS X Server's Open Directory.

# Frequently Asked Questions

**Q:** I do not see a Bluetooth preferences pane in System Preferences.app. What gives?

**A:** The most likely answer is that you do not have a Bluetooth adapter installed in your system; only recently has this become the norm rather than the exception. Fortunately for you, every major manufacturer of networking peripherals seems to make USB Bluetooth tokens and they are even compatible with Mac OS X. These devices retail for about $30 and are available at most any computer parts store.

**Q:** Now that I have all of these network interfaces attached to my Mac, I cannot seem to access the Internet, or get to other networks outside those defined on my interfaces, how come?

**A:** Your default gateway probably no longer points where it should. If you have multiple interfaces (physical or logical) where the router address is defined, Mac OS X sets the default gateway to the interface that is highest in the list under Network Port Configurations (in the Network preferences pane). Simply dragging the entry for the appropriate interface to the top of the list should put everything back to working order.

**Q:** Why would anyone want to use a non-GUI method of remotely managing a Mac?

**A:** There are a number of reasons to eschew the GUI for the command line in remotely managing a Mac. Perhaps an administrator does not wish to disturb the user operating at the console, or the connection between client and server is too slow or choppy to use a GUI like VNC, or the managed machine is a dedicated server that simply lacks the need for direct console access and could use the spare CPU cycles elsewhere. Or maybe the admin just does not have a monitor around and really, really needs to do something important with the system.

**Q:** You speak of connecting a Mac to a Mac over a serial cable, what about Windows or Linux?

**A:** This is easily achieved through any of the standard applications typically included in either operating system, and any other third-party serial terminal application that supports the vt100 terminal type. On Windows this would be the venerable HyperTerminal, and on Linux it is usually minicom.

# Chapter 2

# Automation

## Solutions in this chapter:

- **Using Automator**
- **Understanding AppleScript**
- **Bash Scripting**

☑ **Summary**

☑ **Solutions Fast Track**

☑ **Frequently Asked Questions**

# Introduction

Apple's Mac OS X operating system is extremely intuitive and user-friendly; there is a powerful depth to the system, which we have been exploring throughout this book. We have discussed ways that OS X can be used to perform all sorts of tasks, but even the most intuitive tasks can become repetitive. Thankfully, Apple has provided some mechanisms that can help before the repetitive stress disorder sets in. In this section, we'll discuss several ways tasks can be automated. Some of these methods are more difficult to learn than others, so we've organized this chapter in order of relative complexity.

We start by looking at "Automator," a drag-and-drop automation system initially released with OS X 10.4 (Tiger). This system is easy for beginners to grasp, but the functionality is somewhat limited because applications must be written with automation hooks before they can be called from Automator. AppleScript expands on Automator's capabilities, allowing for complete control of the OS X system, including automation of Graphical User Interface (GUI) events such as mouse clicks and movements. AppleScript is a very human-friendly language, and well written. AppleScript reads just like English commands when read aloud. Because of its similarity to English, AppleScript is much more intuitive than *bash scripting*, which relies on the commands and syntax that UNIX gurus have used for decades. Bash scripting is not entirely intuitive (it was created for techies by techies), and as such wins the prize for least user-friendly of the automation solutions we will discuss. Bash scripting is extremely powerful, however, and places the ability to hold your system firmly in the palm of your sweaty hand. Fumbling the *rm* command or deleting a file instead of appending to it can cause all sorts of problems and are relatively easy mistakes to make. Regardless, no discussion of OS X automation would be complete without a visit to the Berkeley Software Distribution (BSD) subsystem, home of the *bash shell*.

This section provides a mixture of reference information, instructional demonstrations, and basic overviews that will have you automating your Mac in no time.

# Using Automator

There are many different options when it comes to automating tasks on Apple's Mac OS X operating system. Apple's Automator is an automation assistant application, which does not require any programming knowledge and makes even fairly complex automation tasks as easy as "point and click." Automator uses simple steps known as *actions* that can be easily assembled into a process known as a *workflow*. Actions and workflows are assembled within the Automator application (see Figure 2.2), which is installed in the *Applications* folder of Mac OS X 10.4 and later. Automator can be launched from the */Applications* folder or from a context menu like the one shown in Figure 2.1. A context menu is activated with either a right-click or a CTRL-click

**Figure 2.1** Creating a Workflow From the Context Menu

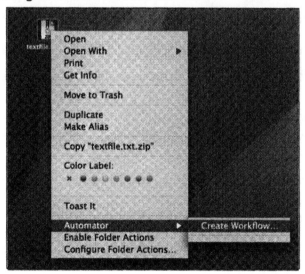

When Automator is launched this way, a new workflow is created and a "Get Specified Finder Items" action is placed in the first position of that workflow, as shown in Figure 2.2.

**Figure 2.2** The Automator Application

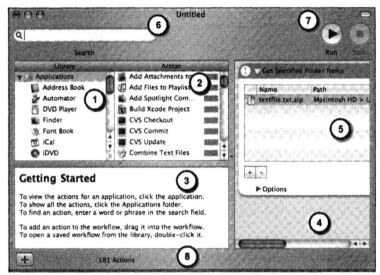

The Automator display is divided into several distinct sections (or panels):

1.  The *Library* panel lists all of the available libraries (or groups) of actions and creates workflows. A library can be added at any time by clicking the **+** sign at the bottom-left of the Automator window. When you click on a library, the actions contained in that library are displayed in the Action panel.

2.  The *Action* panel lists all of the available actions contained in the currently selected library. This panel changes based on which library is selected in the Library panel.

3.  This panel displays information about the action currently selected in the Action panel. When no action is selected, the "Getting Started" screen is displayed.

4.  The workflow panel lists the actions contained in the current workflow. The workflow shows the list of actions that will be executed when this automation is run. The actions are interpreted from the top down. When Automator is launched from the Applications folder, this panel is initially blank. Building a workflow is as simple as dragging actions into this panel.

5. An action may have several options, each of which can be specified here. Each action has its own "box" within this panel, and each action is numbered and executed in order. Changing the order of actions is as simple as dragging them above or below other actions. The *Action* panel is described in more detail below.

6. This field allows you to search for text within Automator. This is most often used to search for a specific action. When a search is complete, the results are displayed in the Actions panel, with relevance bars showing next to each search item. The "search" field is often the quickest way to locate a specific action.

7. Once a workflow is created, it can be run (or stopped) with these buttons.

8. The status bar displays various types of information during the creation and execution of a workflow. This text updates throughout the phases of your workflow creation and testing.

The action display (see Figure 2.3) consists of several sections as well:

**Figure 2.3** The Action Display

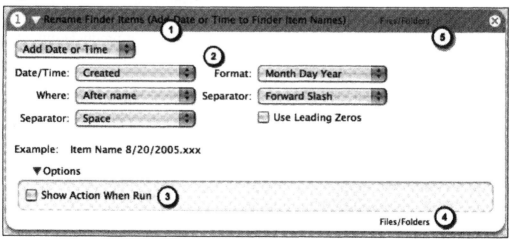

1. The title bar of an Action displays several items. First, at the far left is a number that displays the order of this action. Since actions are executed in order, the action marked with a "1" is the first to be executed in a workflow. The arrow next to the number allows you to expand or contract the display of the action. Contracting the display

allows you to see many more actions on the screen at once. A description of the action is displayed next, followed by an "X" on the right-hand side of the title bar, which allows you to delete the action. This removes it from the workflow and renumbers the actions below it, effectively bridging the gap created by the missing action (assuming the inputs and outputs align).

2. Each action has a distinct set of options that can be set in this area. This area will change based on the type of action, because some actions have more options than others.

3. In some cases, you may want to set the action's options *while the workflow is running*. Selecting "Show Action When Run" will allow you to modify these options as the workflow is running.

4. This area shows the output from this action. In this case, a list of files or folders is output from this action. This indicates that the next action must accept files and folders as input to the action.

5. This area of the title bar shows what should be input into this action. In this case, this action expects a list of files or folders to be passed into it. Red text color indicates an error. Since the "Rename Finder Items" action requires input, it cannot be the first action in a work-flow. To correct this, you must insert an action that produces output of the type *Files/Folders*. Put another way, Automator cannot rename files or folders unless it is first told which files or folders are to be renamed. The handling of inputs and outputs is one of the primary difficulties when creating workflows.

# Creating a One-shot Automation

If you have ever had to rename a group of files, you probably know what a laborious task it can be. Automator makes it simple. Let's create a simple workflow to help automate this task. Start by launching Automator from "Applications | Utilities." If a workflow is already loaded, you can create a new workflow by pressing **Command-N**. Select a group of files within Finder and drag them into the workflow panel. This will create a "Get Specified Finder Items" action, populating it with the list of files you selected (see Figure 2.4).

**Figure 2.4** The "Get Specified Finder Items" Action

| Name | Path |
|------|------|
| DSCN2626.JPG | Macintosh HD > Users > johnnylong > Pictures > iPhoto Lib |
| DSCN2646.JPG | Macintosh HD > Users > johnnylong > Pictures > iPhoto Lib |
| DSCN2654.JPG | Macintosh HD > Users > johnnylong > Pictures > iPhoto Lib |
| DSCN2657.JPG | Macintosh HD > Users > johnnylong > Pictures > iPhoto Lib |
| DSCN2644.JPG | Macintosh HD > Users > johnnylong > Pictures > iPhoto Lib |
| DSCN2659.JPG | Macintosh HD > Users > johnnylong > Pictures > iPhoto Lib |

(1) ▼ Get Specified Finder Items    Files/Folders ▼

▶ Options    Files/Folders

Next, click on the Finder library within the Applications folder of the Library panel, and select the **Rename Finder Items** action (see Figure 2.5). Drag this action to the workflow window, dropping it in the second position, or simply double-click the action to insert it at the end of the workflow.

**Figure 2.5** Selecting An Action From a Library

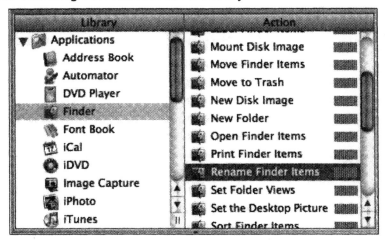

Automator is extremely user-friendly (see Figure 2.6). It presents a warning message indicating that the inserted action may alter your files. Clicking the **Add** button adds a copy action into the workflow, while clicking **Don't Add** would simply insert the rename action. Since our goal is to rename files, we will click **Don't Add**.

**Figure 2.6** Insertion Action May Alter Files

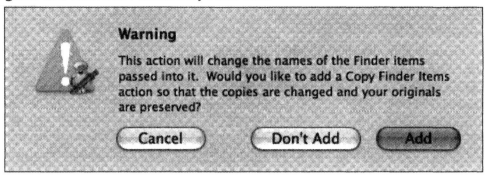

The rename action (see Figure 2.7) has many different options, but for the purposes of this example, we will opt to add the text "Vacation" followed by a space, to the beginning of each file name. This is done by first selecting the "Add Text" option from the drop-down box, and setting the "before name" value to the word "Vacation" followed by a space.

**Figure 2.7** Rename Action

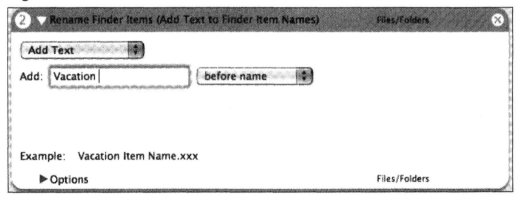

After filling in the options for this action, clicking the **Run** button executes the action and the files are all renamed.

This simple process highlights Automator's ease of use, and reveals how workflows are built. However, this is a simple automation that is only effective for renaming a specific group of files. We've created a one-shot. Let's make this automation more useful, giving it the capability to rename files on the fly.

# Creating a More Versatile Automation

To create a more versatile renaming workflow, we begin by highlighting the first action in the workflow and pressing the **delete** key (or clicking the **x** in the upper right-hand corner of that action) to delete it. Since this action listed the files that were to be renamed, we will replace it with an action that will prompt the user to select a list of files to rename.

From the Library panel, select the "Finder" folder in the "Applications" directory. After clicking the Finder application, select the "Ask for Finder Items action," and drag it to the first action position in the workflow. Within this action, select the file type, choose a starting location and a prompt, and check the "Allow Multiple Selection box" (see completed action and workflow should look like the one shown in Figure 2.8).

**Figure 2.8** A Versatile File Renaming Workflow

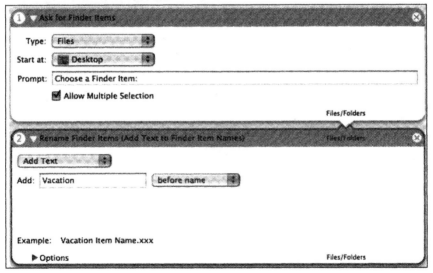

When this workflow is run, a dialog box is presented, and after selecting a list of files and clicking the **Choose** button, the list of files are fed into the second action, which renames the files just as before. This is an extremely simple Automator workflow, but is much more versatile than the first example. As you develop more automations, you'll want to save your work, so that the automations can be run or changed as you see fit. Let's take a look at various options for saving our work.

# Saving Automations as Applications and Workflows

An automation can be saved as either a workflow or an application via the "File | Save or File | Save As…" menu items (see Figure 2.9).

**Figure 2.9** Automator's Standard Save Options

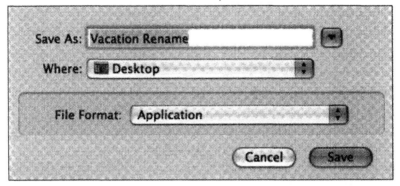

When saved as an application, an automation becomes *executable*. Double-clicking the application's icon (see Figure 2.10) runs the automation.

**Figure 2.10** Automator Application Icon

The application file format is portable, meaning it can be sent to other Mac users and executed, but this format is rather large (e.g., our simple *Vacation Rename* automation grows to over 800K when saved as an application). This is because Mac applications contain not only an executable program (our automation in this case), but other files including preference files (*.plist* files) and foreign language support files. The Automator application also contains a copy of the actual workflow file. These files can be viewed by clicking **Show Package Contents** from the "Vacation Rename" application's context menu (see Figure 2.11).

**Figure 2.11** The "Vacation Rename" Application's Contents

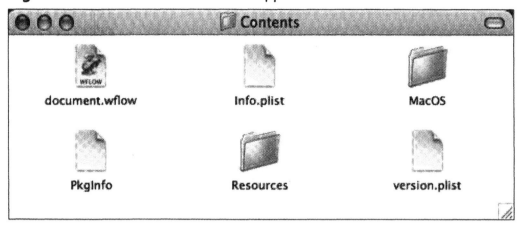

### Notes From the Underground...

## Drag-and-Drop Goodness

Automator applications can be copied to the dock or run from any location you choose, just like any other application. You can also drag a pile of files onto an Automator application's icon, executing actions on those files even if the application is sitting in the dock. To do this, however, your automation must have a compatible first action to grab those incoming files. A great finder action for this purpose is the "Get Selected Finder Items" action. Replacing the "Ask For Finder Items" action in the "Vacation Rename" script with the "Get Selected Finder Items" action will make it drag-and-drop ready.

An automation can also be saved as a workflow, a basic single-file format with a *workflow* file extension. When launched, this type of file opens in Automator, allowing you to view the actions within or make changes (see Figure 2.12). Both workflows and applications can be modified later by opening them from within Automator.

**Figure 2.12** Workflow Icon

# Saving Automations as Plug-ins

A plug-in is an application extension. Saving an automation as a plug-in via the "File | Save As Plug-In Automator" menu item saves your automation as a workflow file, but the workflow file itself is placed in a subdirectory under "/Library/Workflows/Applications."

There are many different types of plug-ins, and the list continues to grow as developers create plug-in hooks for various applications. Do not be surprised if the list of available plug-in types grows over time. Let's take a look at the default plug-in types that are currently shipped with Mac OS X.

## Finder Plug-ins

Saving an automation as a Finder plug-in creates a context menu entry for your automation. For example, saving the "Vacation Rename" automation as a Finder plug-in will create the context menu item shown in Figure 2.13. The items selected in Finder will automatically be fed into the first action in the workflow, so make sure that action is expecting Finder items as input.

**Figure 2.13** Automations Saved as Finder Plug-ins

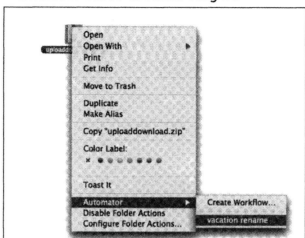

# iCal Alarms

The Mac OS X calendar application, iCal, can be used to launch automations at a specific time and date. Automator performs two steps when an automation is saved as an iCal alarm: an entry is created for the current time and date, and the automation is made available as an alarm for other dates. As shown in Figure 2.14, the automation can be used as an alarm by creating an iCal entry, setting the *alarm* to *Open file*, and selecting the name of the automation to be executed. The automation can be set to execute before, during, or after a specific time.

**Figure 2.14** Automation Triggered By Time or Date

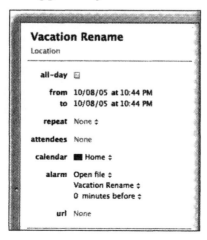

# Image Capture

Not only can an automation take a picture from a digital camera (thanks to the "Take Picture" action), it can also be set to execute after images have been captured from the camera by saving the automation as an "image capture" plug-in. This is especially handy for the "Vacation Rename" script, which prepends the word "Vacation" to selected files. By saving this automation as an image capture plug-in, it can be run directly from the image capture dialog.

# Print Workflow

If an automation is saved as a *print workflow* plug-in, it can be run from any print dialog box. This type of plug-in requires a *.pdf* file as input to the first action. As shown in Figure 2.15, several print workflow automations are installed automatically with OS X. These can be found in the */Library/PDF Services* folder, and are all very simple workflows which accept PDF files as input.

**Figure 2.15** Print Workflow Automations Automatically Installed with OS X

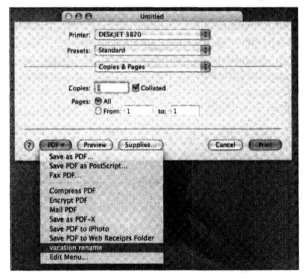

# Folder Actions

The AppleScript Utility (located in */Applications/AppleScript*) allows you to enable and configure two very interesting features: *folder actions* and the *Script Menu*. Folder actions are disabled by default; however, enabling them (through the "Folder Actions Setup" screen of the AppleScript Utility) allows you to run either AppleScript or Automator actions when the contents of a folder are modified or accessed. Folder actions can also be enabled or modified from the "Context" menu by right-clicking (or CTRL-clicking) a folder in Finder (see Figure 2.16).

**Figure 2.16** The "Folder Actions" Screen

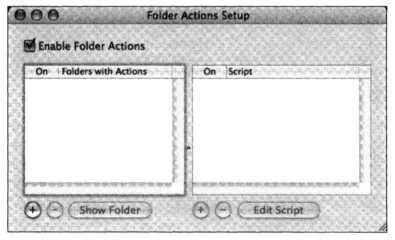

After clicking the **Enable Folder Actions** box, the Folders and Scripts sections become available, letting you select which folders will trigger which actions. The **+** button in the folders section adds a folder, and the **+** button under the scripts section adds an action. Selecting a folder and a script in this screen will cause the action to be launched whenever the contents of the folder are modified.

You can save Automator workflows as folder actions via the "File | Save as Plug-In" menu, or by saving the workflow to a folder and enabling it as a folder action through that folder's Context menu. There are several folder actions installed along with OS X. To set a folder action on your home desktop folder (e.g., right-click the **Desktop** folder in finder, select "Attach Folder Action," and select the *add – new item alert.scpt* action. Whenever an item is added to the desktop, this action will fire, displaying an alert dialog (see Figure 2.17).

**Figure 2.17** Basic Folder Action At Work

## Script Menu

The Script menu, when activated via the AppleScript Utility (found in */Applications/AppleScript*), places a script icon on the menu bar found at the top of the OS X screen. This menu provides quick and easy access to various scripts. Workflows can be added to the Script menu by saving them as "Script Menu" plug-ins or by saving them directly to the */Library/Scripts* folder. Figure 2.18 shows the *Vacation Rename* workflow, as it would appear in the script menu.

**Figure 2.18** The "Workflow Saved to the Script" Menu

As shown in Figure 2.19, there are many different scripts supplied with OS X. We look at some of these scripts in the next section, as we begin to explore AppleScript.

**Figure 2.19** The Script Menu Provides Instant Access to Local Scripts

Notes From the Underground…

## Multipurpose Menu

The Script menu can be used for just about any purpose. Try dragging a folder or even a URL into your */Library/Scripts* folder. Whatever you drag into that folder becomes accessible through the Script menu. AppleScript programs can also be saved here.

# Hacker-friendly Automator Actions

There are many different actions to choose from, but some actions are more interesting for true hackers at heart. This section takes a look at some of the more interesting actions and how they can be used.

# Automator | Run AppleScript

We cover AppleScript in a bit more detail in the next section, but if Automator just isn't powerful enough for you, get "under the hood" and use raw AppleScript within a workflow. As shown in Figure 2.20, the AppleScript can be typed (or pasted) right into the action's field. Notice that the input and output types are listed as *anything*. This passes the power onto you, the developer, and you'll have to process what comes in and what goes out. Beware the old adage: "Garbage in, garbage out."

**Figure 2.20** The "Run AppleScript" Action

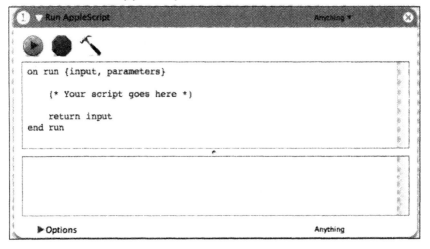

```
on run {input, parameters}

    (* Your script goes here *)

    return input
end run
```

# Automator | Run Shell Script

The *Run Shell Script* action allows you to run scripts within a workflow. As shown in Figure 2.21, shell, PERL, or Python code can be executed within this action. The script can be entered in the provided text box, and input can be passed into this script as either standard input (*stdin*) or as individual arguments, depending on how your shell script is designed to accept them. We'll see this action again in this chapter's final section.

**Figure 2.21** The "Run Shell Script" Action

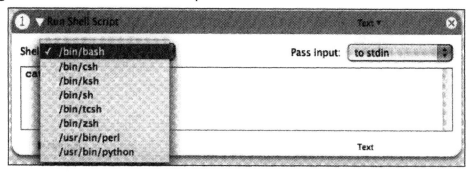

# Automator | Run Web Service

The *Run Web Service* action allows you to execute an eXtensible Markup
Language (XML)/Remote Procedure Call (RPC) protocol/Simple Object
Access Protocol (SOAP) program with various parameters. The default Run
Web Service action provided with OS X queries the California Highway
traffic system to determine if there are any reported accidents. This example is
limited, however, in that you must enter a highway name into the action. This
is extremely impractical; however, it was discovered that the parameter field of
this action accepts AppleScript commands. By modifying the workflow with
an updated parameter field and a front-end AppleScript dialog (see Figure
2.22), this workflow will accept user-supplied highway parameters and pass
them into the Run Web Service action. This can be used with other XML-
RPC SOAP interfaces to allow easier user interaction.

**Figure 2.22** The "Run Web Service" Action

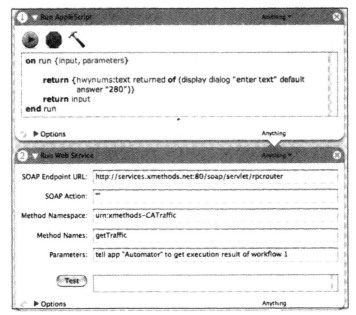

While Automator has limitations, these types of "hacks" keep popping up, making Automator more powerful and flexible.

# Automator | View Results

The *View Results* action is simple and necessary for workflow debugging. When used in a workflow, this action displays the results of whatever action preceded it. If you insert a shell script or an AppleScript action before this action, this action will display the return value of that script. If you want to pass a value *through* an action, you must take care to purposefully pass that value through with a *return* statement. For example, the AppleScript action used in Figure 2.23 (the last figure in the *Automator | Run Shell Script* section above) did not include a *return input* command. Because of this, the script sent the return value from the *display dialog* command. In that case, the value of the shell script was lost to the rest of the workflow.

**Figure 2.23** The "View Results" Action

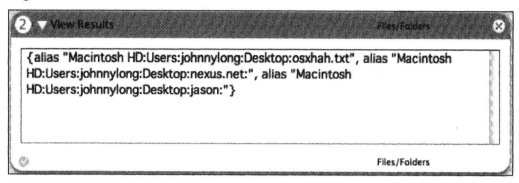

# Finder | Set the Desktop Picture

Although this action seems simplistic, it highlights the flexibility and ease of use of Automator. By creating a simple workflow and saving it as an application, you can set the desktop picture by dragging an image onto this application's icon (see Figure 2.24). The icon can be placed in the dock or in many other places. Also, this workflow can be saved as a finder plug-in, allowing you to set the desktop picture by right-clicking on an image and selecting the action from the "Automator menu."

**Figure 2.24** One Action, Drag-and-drop Wallpaper Update!

# Image Capture | Take Picture

This action takes a picture (Figure 2.25) from a locally connected camera and saves the image to the "Pictures" folder. This action requires no input; Although it's easy to imagine this type of action being used for practical jokes, there are (admittedly few) *legitimate* uses for this action as well. Remember though, "What goes around comes around!"

**Figure 2.25** Snapping Photos With Automator

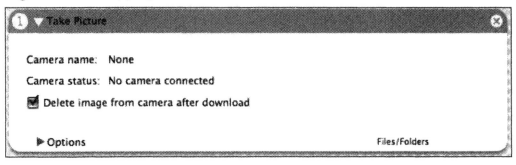

Want to create a surveillance camera with your Mac? The workflow shown in Figure 2.26 does just that.

**Figure 2.26** Automator in "Surveillance Cam" Mode

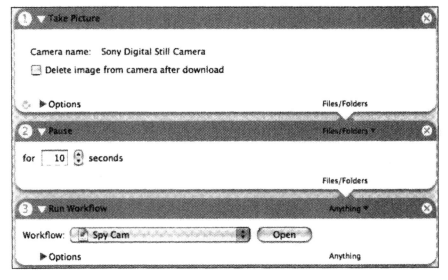

This workflow (named "Spy Cam") begins by snapping a picture, which is saved to the camera and the "Pictures folder." The second action (Automator | Pause) pauses for ten seconds, and the third action (Automator | Run | Workflow) runs the workflow in a continuous loop, snapping pictures every ten seconds. This workflow can be modified in a number of ways, and can send pictures to a remote location via File Transfer Protocol (FTP) or Secure Shell (SSH).

# Mail | Add Attachments

There are quite a few actions than trigger various Mail events, including *New Mail Message*, which launches Mail with optional pre-filled text (see Figure 2.27). However, the "Add Attachments To Front Message" action is quite handy, allowing you to not only create and send a message, but add a file as an attachment as well. This action provides a handy way to fire off all sorts of e-mails, including notifications from Automator-embedded AppleScript and *bash shell* commands. We will look at this type of embedding in this chapter's final section.

**Figure 2.27** "New Mail Message" Action

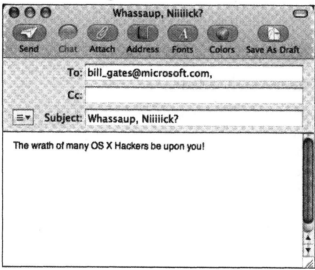

# PDF | Encrypt PDF Document

This action allows you to encrypt the contents of a PDF document, and is included with OS X 10.4 as a print plug-in, which is accessible from the standard print dialog. As shown in Figure 2.28, this action requires a password (and verification), and accepts PDF files as input.

**Figure 2.28** Encrypt PDF Document Action

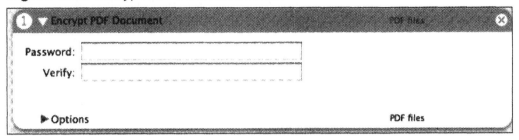

# PDF | Watermark PDF

This action allows you to add a watermark to a PDF document. It is quite robust, allowing you to set all sorts of options including whether the watermark should be placed under or over the text, where it should be placed, the angle is should be skewed to, and the transparency of the image. This lets you personalize any PDF document, and once it is set up, it is easy to use. When using this action, consider checking the "Show Action When Run" option, which allows you to make changes to the watermark's configuration on-the-fly (see Figure 2.29).

**Figure 2.29** Watermark PDF Action

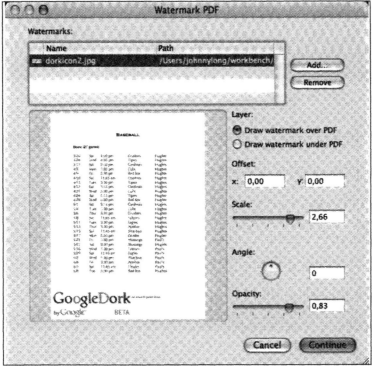

## Safari | Download URLs

This action saves URLs as local files (see Figure 2.30). URLs can be pumped into this action from a variety of places including bash scripts, AppleScripts, or the "Safari | Get Specified URLs" action.

**Figure 2.30** Download URLs Action

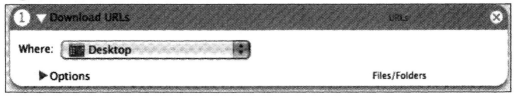

## Safari | Get Link URLs

This action outputs a list of links found at the URL location supplied as input. This action, along with other Safari actions, allows you to create a simple Web page crawler with relative ease. The list of returned links can be filtered with the "Safari | Filter URLs" action (see Figure 2.31).

**Figure 2.31** The "Get Link URLs from Webpages" Action

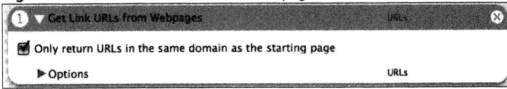

## Safari | Filter URLs

The *Filter URLs* action allows you to display URLs that match a particular search criteria. As shown in Figure 2.32, this action can be configured to search within various parts of a URL, and the searches can be "stacked" enabling fairly complex binary (AND, OR, NOT) search operations.

**Figure 2.32** The "Filter URLs" Action

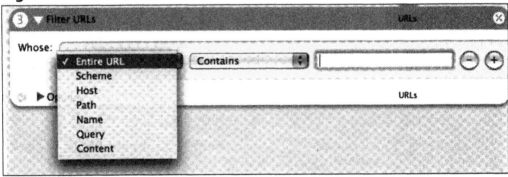

This action can be used in conjunction with other actions to create interesting workflows (see Figure 2.33).

**Figure 2.33** A Version Tracker Auto-download Workflow

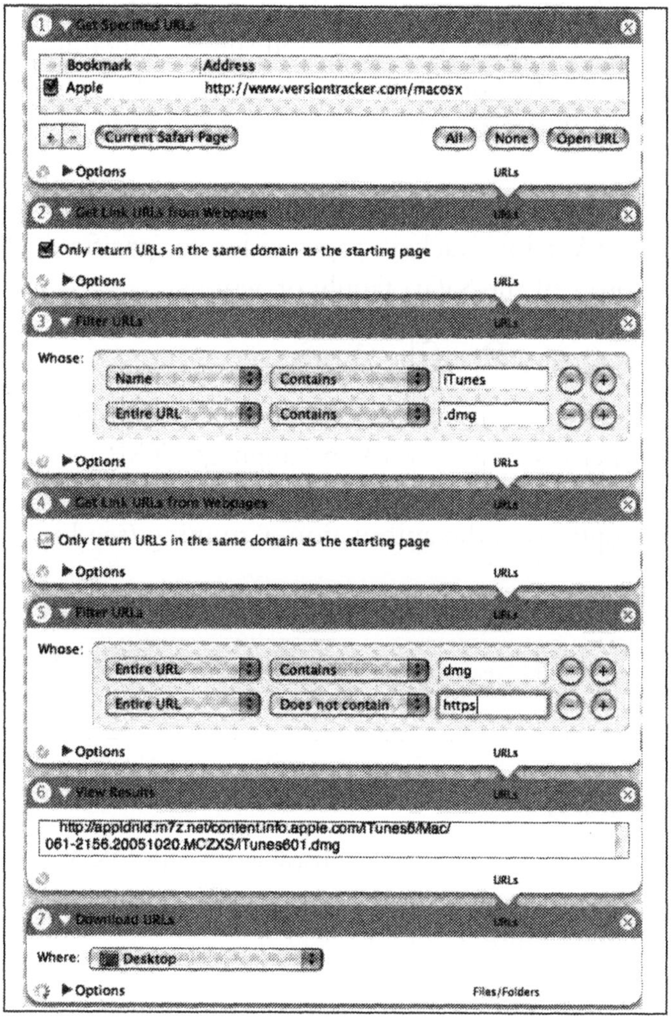

This workflow connects to the Version Tracker Mac OS X front page (action one) and gathers all the *versiontracker.com* links found on that page (action two). The third action locates all iTunes-related disk images (*.dmg* files) by searching the URLs for *iTunes* and *.dmg*, respectively, and action four downloads the pages pointed to by those URLs. This step effectively downloads Version Tracker's description page for each piece of software that contains a link to the software itself. The fifth action then searches those description pages for the links that point to the *.dmg* files. Since these links will point outside of *versiontracker.com*, the "same domain" checkbox is unchecked. This action also searches for links that do not point to Hyper Text Transfer Protocol Secure sockets (HTTPS) sites, since these links point back to *versiontracker.com*. The View Results action shows, which links survived the selection process, and the last action downloads these links to the desktop. By changing the word *iTunes* in action three, additional software can be located and downloaded.

Although this may seem like a lengthy action, it makes short work out of bouncing between Version Tracker's pages to locate specific downloads, and highlights the power of the Safari family of actions.

## System | System Profile Action

This action allows you to capture any number of system information and diagnostics as either eXtensible Markup Language (XML) or text. When setting the "Show Action When Run" option, it presents a dialog box allowing you to set these options as the automation is running (see Figure 2.34).

**Figure 2.34** The "System | System Profile" Action

## XCode Actions

After installing the XCode developer's tools from the OS X installer disc (as described in the Pen Testing chapter), several actions become available in the XCode Library (see Figure 2.35).

**Figure 2.35** The "System | System Profile" Action

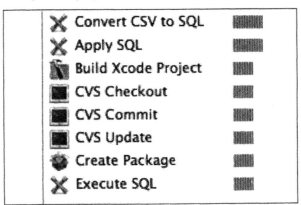

Although most of these functions only apply to die-hard programmers, they might come in handy as you travel farther down the long, dangerous road of the OS X hacker. Keep an eye out for more actions as developers begin including them with their software.

# Understanding AppleScript

AppleScript is an English-like language that is used to develop script files. These script files can be used to automate the actions of many different applications on the Mac, including those with graphical interfaces. Beyond simple automation, AppleScript can be used to write full-blown programs, and with the help of AppleScript Studio (included in "/Applications/AppleScript" with a standard OS X install) AppleScript programs can be built with powerful, flexible graphical interfaces.

AppleScript is billed as being user-friendly, but do not be mistaken, it is a powerful programming language and as such is not intended for non-techies. We will only cover the basics here, as true mastery of AppleScript will require more than a quick glance at a portion of a chapter. What we will try to do, however, is get you up and running fairly quickly. We will take the hacker's approach to this problem, showing the basics first, and then diving headlong into some Apple-provided scripts.

## Introducing the Script Editor

An AppleScript file, in its most basic form, is a single file with a *.scpt* extension. Although you can use a hardcore editor like *vi* to sling code in a terminal session, the Script Editor holds several distinct advantages, including a "record" mode, syntax highlighting, in-line auto-complete, and script control icons. Of course nothing's stopping you from using *vi*, but unless you're just trying to show off, the Script Editor really is more efficient. Files saved from the Script Editor become binary files; therefore, you cannot edit them from *vi*. However, a *.scpt* file created from *vi* (or any editor) can be opened from the Script Editor without incident. The Script Editor is installed in the */Applications/AppleScript* directory. Its deceivingly simplistic interface is shown in Figure 2.36.

**Figure 2.36** The Script Editor

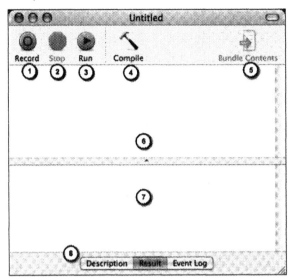

Although the interface is rather simplistic, a great deal of functionality is packed into this small space.

1.  This button places the Script Editor into "record" mode, allowing it to capture events from recordable applications, like many of those included with the OS X operating system.

2.  This button stops the recording process.

3.  This button runs a script. If the stop, run and record buttons are confusing, you may be a bit shocked when it comes time to use AppleScript, but let your burning desire to be an OS X hacker spur you on none the less. If anyone asks about your button confusion, just mumble something about *being used to vi*, and most average techies will nod knowingly and eventually leave you alone!

4.  This button compiles a script, checking it for errors and reporting the context of any error. Compiling a script also applies a color-coding that helps keep the script visually organized.

5.  A *bundle* is a collection of programs and support files contained in a folder, which appear to be a single application. AppleScripts can be saved as scripts or application bundles. If the script is saved as a

bundle, this icon will become available to allow you to view and modify the contents of the bundle.

6. This is where the AppleScript goes.

7. This is the data panel. Its contents change based on whether the "Description," "Result," or "Event" logs contain data.

8. These tabs activate the Description, Result and Event logs, respectively.

# Hello, World!

What's a quick and dirty guide to any programming language without a "Hello, World!" script? Figure 2.37 applies this time-honored programmer's tradition to the AppleScript language.

**Figure 2.37** Hello, World!

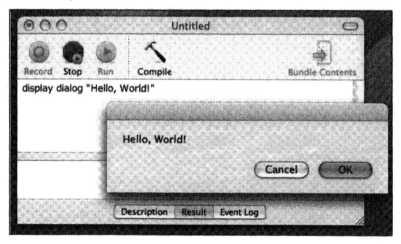

As you type text into the script pane, the Script Editor will display your text in a purple color to indicate that this is *uncompiled*, or untested code as outlined in the *Formatting* section of the Script Editor's *Preferences* settings. After entering the text, you can simply click the *Run* button to compile and run the script, or press the *Compile* button followed by the *Run* button to compile and run the script in separate steps. Either way, Script Editor will test the script for errors (displaying any error text in a pop-up dialog box) color-code the script again based on the *Formatting* preferences.

In the case of this simple program, the *display dialog* text will be colored blue to indicate that these are application keywords, and the "Hello, World!" text will be colored black to indicate that this is a value, or a string. The color-coding helps get a quick-look picture of your program's various components. Assuming no errors were made in the creation of the script, a dialog will be displayed, and the program will track and display which of the two buttons you clicked, displaying the results in the data panel, under the "Results" tab.

# Recording Actions

If you're anxious to get your hands on the AppleScript programmer's cheat code, the *record* button may be exactly what you're looking for. This little button will seriously jump-start your AppleScript Kung Fu. Bear in mind that this is cheating, and you'll be missing out on some of the real power and flexibility of the language if this becomes your sole source of education, but regardless it's a great place to start. The recording features of the Script Editor make automation fairly easy, and are roughly equivalent to the process of creating an Automator workflow, but AppleScript ultimately allows for greater flexibility and more control over applications than Automator's actions.

The simplest way to test out the recording features of Script Editor is to test it on an application like Finder. First, begin a new script in Script Editor by pressing *Command-N*, or by selecting *File | New* from the menu. Click the *Record* button to begin recording, and launch Finder from the dock. Launching Finder will cause the following lines to appear in the script window:

```
tell application "Finder"
    activate
    select Finder window 1
```

In technical terms, these lines are called *statements*. One of the primary purposes of an *AppleScript* statement is to send *Apple events*, or actions, to applications. In the statements listed above, "activate" and "Select Finder window *1*" are both Apple events. Applications execute these actions, and return events back to the script, through what's known as the AppleScript *extension*, the translator between *script* statements and actual events. These return events can then be analyzed and used to have an effect on the flow of the script. There's a basic flow of events back and forth between the script and the applications, which creates a basic *input* and *output* of Apple events. This is the primary reason that the Automator shows inputs and outputs for each action in a workflow. Automator is essentially a graphical, easy-to-use interface to AppleScript.

Back to the Script Editor, further playing with the Finder window while still in record mode creates more statements in the script window, which may look something like this:

```
select Finder window 1
set position of Finder window 1 to {317, 168}
set toolbar visible of Finder window 1 to true
select Finder window 1
set target of Finder window 1 to folder "Desktop" of folder
"johnnylong" of folder "Users" of startup disk
select Finder window 1
```

Click the **Stop** button to finish the recording process; the script window will "close out" the recorded script with a line like this:

```
end tell
```

As you can see from the generated script, the AppleScript syntax is very easy to read, and can be read out loud as a list of simple instructions describing the actions performed with the Finder application. To test the generated script, click the **Run** button in the Script Editor. You should see your Finder window's actions repeated at a very fast rate of speed.

One of the problems you are bound to run into by "programming" in this way is that your operating environment is constantly changing. A statement such as *select Finder window 1* is dangerous, especially if there are no Finder windows. Closing out all of your Finder windows and re-running the above script will demonstrate this point. As shown in Figure 2.38, AppleScript complains that there *is no* "Finder window 1." A "real" programmer would check for the existence of a "Finder window 1" and you should too if you intend to create anything other than frustrating scripts.

**Figure 2.38** AppleScript Cheat Codes Fall Short

# AppleScript Save Options

Like Automator workflows, AppleScripts can be saved in a variety of formats via Script Editor's *File | Save As...* menu item. Let's take a look at the more common save formats.

## Script

This option saves the script as a single file with a *scpt* extension. When launched, this type of file opens in Script Editor, allowing you to modify, execute, or save the file as another type. Scripts can also be opened from Script Editor with the **File | Open** command.

## Application (Applet)

This option saves the script as an executable file with an *.app* extension. When launched, this type of file executes the script. By default, applications can also be opened from Script Editor with the *File | Open* command, although checking "Run Only" will prevent this type of file from being edited.

## Bundles

*Bundles* are folders that appear as a single file to Mac OS X, even though they contain various support files. Most large applications on OS X are packaged as bundles, the contents of which can be viewed by selecting "Show Package Contents" from the bundle's context menu. When launched, a script bundle opens in Script Editor, just like a standard script file. By contrast, an *application bundle* runs the script when launched. Both of theses types of bundles can be opened from Script Editor through the *File | Open* command, unless the

"Run Only" option is checked when the file is saved. Bundles are a preferred option if your script uses files that may not be available on all systems (e.g., if your script plays a movie file or calls a script that you created, these files can be included in the bundle so that they are available to the user when the bundle is opened). Bundling resources is beyond the scope of this chapter, as we will include most resources (like shell scripts) within the AppleScript or workflow document itself.

# Script Assistant

If you're adventuresome enough, you could dive right in and start manipulating this code, but without a few hints you just might find yourself poking around in the dark. Consider enabling the *Script Assistant,* which provides language "hints" based on what you type into the script window. To enable the Script Assistant, check the "use Script Assistant" box in the **Preferences | Edit** panel, and restart Script Editor. After the restart, you can press the **esc** key to engage the Assistant. To test Script Assistant's auto-complete feature, type the first letter or letters of a function (e.g., the letters "s" and "e," the beginning of the **set** command. At this point you can either press the **esc** key to see a list of terms beginning with the letters "s" and "e," or submit to the Assistant's best guess by pressing **Option-ESC**. You can also press **F5** (or **Function-F5** on a PowerBook) for a list of suggested words (see Figure 2.39).

**Figure 2.39** Script Assistant's Power of Suggestion

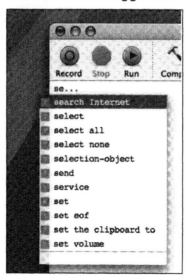

By using the arrow keys or the mouse pointer, you can complete a selection, and with a press of the **Enter** key or a click of the mouse the completed phrase can be inserted into the script (e.g., the current system volume can be adjusted by selecting the "set volume" action). However, this does not make a complete command, and if you try to run a script that consists of little more than set volume, Script Editor says you need to supply a value for the command. In this case, it is pretty easy to guess that the command is looking for a number from one to ten, with ten being the full-on setting.

# AppleScript Dictionary

Since applications accept commands of different types, the logical question to ask might be, "What applications allow which commands?" Fortunately there is a quick and easy way to answer this question thanks to the AppleScript dictionary. When launched from "Script Editor's File | Open Dictionary" , the dictionary first asks for the name of a specific application (see Figure 2.40).

**Figure 2.40** AppleScript Dictionary Applications

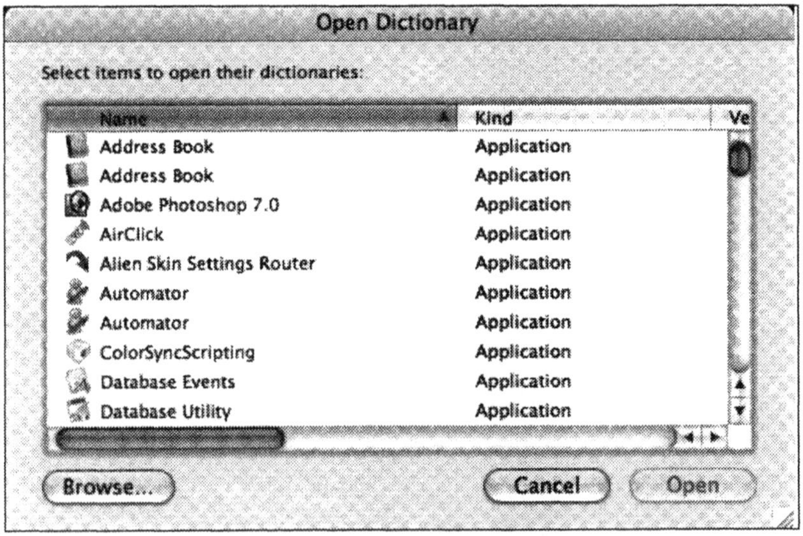

After selecting an application, the dictionary displays a screen similar to the Safari application's dictionary (see Figure 2.41).

**Figure 2.41** A Typical AppleScript Dictionary Page

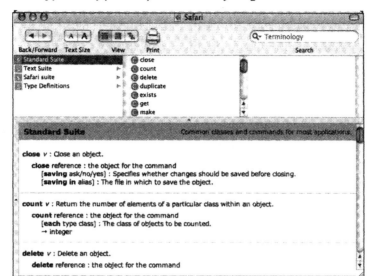

Although it is easy for an amateur to get in too deep, the dictionary provides a basic outline of what can be done within each application. The most common commands are listed as soon as an application's dictionary is opened, and can help lead the way through automating that application's actions. If you notice that Script Editor's record mode doesn't change while in record mode, there's a good chance the application has no scriptable actions. When combined with the Record" feature and the Script Assistant, it is possible to plod through just about any automation in very little time.

AppleScript is powerful, however, and poking around in the dark in this fashion will only take you so far. The next section looks at basic AppleScript syntax, describing (at a very high level) some of the most common elements of the language.

# Not Quite An AppleScript Language Guide

There is a lot to AppleScript, and there are tons of books and Web sites dedicated to the topic. This section looks at some of the basics to help you get started. One of the best guides to the language is free from Apple, and is aptly named the *AppleScript Language Guide*. It is available in PDF or Hypertext Markup Language (HTML) format, and is available from Apple's developer documentation page at *http://developer.apple.com/documentation*. If you've already memorized the entire language guide, feel free to skip ahead, saving this section for when the Ginkgo Biloba wears off.

# Comments

*Comments* are most often used to document a program, and as such they are essentially ignored in AppleScript. AppleScript supports two types of comments: the *compound* comment, which begins with the characters " `(*` " and ends with the characters `*)` and the end-of-line comment, which begins with the characters `--`."Everything within a compound comment is ignored, and everything after an end-of line comment is ignored. For example, the following lines are all considered comments:

```
(* I'm not
quite
dead yet *)
--Nothing to see here, carry on
```

# Statements

Our little recording exercise produced a pretty decent script, most of which revolved around tweaking Finder. As such, the entire script encompassed a single (albeit lengthy) statement, beginning with a "tell" and ending with an "end tell":

```
tell application "Finder"
[...]
end tell
```

This is a *compound* statement, meaning it occupies more than one line. By contrast, a *simple statement* is written on one line:

```
tell application "Finder" to select Finder window 1
```

Notice that this command includes the word *to*. This is an indicator that an action is included in this statement. If the word *to* is not followed by an action an error will be generated. In summary, *compound* statements relay multiple actions, while *simple* statements relay a single action.

# Line Breaks (The ¬ character)

Simple single-line *AppleScript* statements can be broken into separate lines for readability. This is accomplished with the "¬" character, which can be generated using either *Option-L* or *Option-Return*. Some of the scripts listed in this section take advantage of this. For example, this is interpreted as a single line:

```
tell application "Finder" to ¬
select Finder window 1
```

# Capitalization

AppleScript is not case sensitive. You can use all lowercase characters, all uppercase characters, or any combination of the two, including the infamous *pSYKO fONT* and *cAmElBaCk* notations. You can even code in *h@x0r* speak with some limited success, but keep in mind that the backslash ("\") and double quote (") characters have special meaning when used within strings. These characters (and others) can be escaped with a backslash character (e.g., use "\\" to represent a backslash and "\" to represent a literal double quote). When you run or compile code in the Script Editor, capital letters are used in some places to improve clarity although this is not required by the language.

# The "the"

The word "the" is a courtesy word in AppleScript. It can be used to clarify statements for readability. A statement such as:

```
tell application "Finder" to select Finder window 1
```

can be written:

```
tell the application "Finder" to select the Finder window 1
```

without changing the effect of the code. It is possible to go overboard, especially if you use commands like:

```
set the toolbar visible of the Finder window 1 to the true
```

If you must code like this, try mumbling about "steganography" or "philosophy of code obfuscation" and watch as the hardcore techies nod and grunt knowingly.

# Variables and Basic Mathematical Operations

Variables are objects in a program that may take on different values. For example, to set the variable *CatName* to *FluffyButt*, use the following statement:

```
set CatName to "FluffyButt"
```

Notice that the word *FluffyButt* is in quotes. This is because the word FluffyButt is a string, or collection of characters treated as a single unit. An undefined word such as FluffyButt used without quotes is treated as a variable, and variables must be defined. Therefore, the command:

```
set CatName to FluffyButt
```

would fail unless the variable FluffyButt had been defined earlier in the program. Variables can also be set to numeric values:

```
set WIS to 1
```

This statement would set the variable *WIS* to "1". This (and any) variable can be modified, but numeric variables can be modified *mathematically*. For example, the *WIS* variable can be incremented with a statement such as:

```
set WIS to WIS + 1
```

Variables can also be compared using specific comparison operators. For example, the following expressions check to see if WIS is equal to, greater than, or less than one, respectively:

```
WIS = 1
WIS > 1
WIS < 1
```

These operators could be represented "verbally" as well:

```
WIS is equal to 1
WIS is greater than 1
WIS is less than 1
```

These expressions check whether WIS is not equal, is greater than or equal to, or is less than or equal to one, respectively:

```
WIS ≠ 1
WIS ? 1
WIS ≤ 1
```

Since the characters used to represent these comparisons are shorthand, special character combinations must be used within Script Editor to represent them, or they could be expressed "verbally":

```
WIS is not equal to 1
WIS is greater than or equal to 1
WIS is less than or equal to 1
```

Table 2.1 shows the representations, equivalents, and Script Editor shorthand of the most common comparison operators.

**Table 2.1** Common Comparison Operators

| Operation | Shorthand | Keystroke(s) | Equivalents |
|---|---|---|---|
| Equal to | = | = | Is<br>equals<br>is equal to |
| Not equal to | ≠ | Option-equal | Is not<br>Is not<br>equal<br>Is not equal to |
| Greater than | > | > | Is greater than<br>Comes after |
| Greater than or equal | ≥ | >= | Is greater than or<br>equal to |
| Less than | < | < | Is less than<br>Comes before |
| Less than or equal | ≤ | <= | Is less than or<br>equal to |

Other mathematical operations can also be performed. For a complete list, search the AppleScript Language Guide for "AppleScript operators."

# Looping (Repeat)

Without loops, programming becomes a bleak landscape of one-shot actions. AppleScript offers a lot of flexibility when it comes to loops. Apple calls these *repeat statements*, and as such, the basic loop is performed with the *Repeat* command. A *repeat* statement begins with the word "repeat." The end of the statement is marked with "end" or "end repeat."

The most basic use of this command will continually repeat a command. This script adds flair to the Finder recording we made earlier:

```
repeat
        tell application "Finder"
                set position of Finder window 1 to ¬
                {random number from 1 to 100, random number from 1 to 100 }
        end tell
end repeat
```

Running this script will set your first Finder window and dancing like a hyper-caffeinated Linux hacker at a Defcon rave.  will continue until either the script is stopped with the Script Editor's **Stop** button, or the Finder window is closed with something such as **Command-W**. Variations of the *repeat* command allow for more fine-grained control (see Table 2.2).

**Table 2.2** Repeat Loop Variations

|  | Description | Example |
|---|---|---|
| Repeat | Repeat indefinitely. This loop can be terminated with the exit command. | ```Repeat    Display dialog    "Forever" End Repeat``` |
| Repeat (number) Times | Repeat a fixed number of times. | ```Repeat 1 Times    Display dialog "Once" End Repeat``` |
| Repeat While (boolean) | Repeat while *boolean* is true. If *boolean* evaluates as false, the loop will not execute. | ```set WIS to 10 Repeat while WIS > 1    set WIS to WIS - 1    Display dialog WIS End repeat``` |
| Repeat Until (boolean) | Repeat until boolean is true. If boolean evaluates as true, the loop will not execute. | ```Set WIS to 0 Repeat until WIS ≥ 10    Set WIS to WIS + 1    Display dialog WIS End repeat``` |
| Repeat With (loopVariable) From (startValue) To (stopValue) | Repeat, incrementing *loopVariable* from *startValue* to *stopValue*. Loop terminates when *loopValue* equals *stopValue*. | ```Repeat with WIS from    0 to 10    Display dialog WIS End repeat``` |
| Repeat With (loopVariable) In (list) | Repeat, setting *loopValue* to each value in (list). Loop terminates when list is exhausted. | ```Repeat with WIS in ¬    {1, 2,    "FluffyButt"}    Display dialog WIS End repeat``` |

# Learning By Example: Interactive Dialogs

Since we cannot plumb the depths of the AppleScript language in these short pages, we instead take a look at some of the pre-written scripts installed with OS X in the */Library/Scripts* directory, and modify them for our own purposes. Along the way we will get a good feel for practical AppleScripting, and set the stage for integrating Automator, AppleScript, and shell scripting in this chapter's final section.

## A Simple Mac Help Script

The */Library/Scripts/Basics/AppleScript Help* script (see Figure 2.42) launches the "Help Viewer" application and displays the AppleScript "Help" topic.

**Figure 2.42** A Basic Non-interactive Help Viewer

Although this script is only moderately helpful, it can be made better by searching for "Help" on a "user-supplied" topic, and adding the ability to search Apple manual (*man*) pages as well as Apple Help. To do this, we will need to figure out how to prompt for user input. This is accomplished through an expanded *display dialog* statement.

## Interactive Dialog Boxes

The basic *display dialog* statement displays a simple message and two buttons (**OK** and **Cancel**), as shown in the "Hello World!" example. This basic dialog can be expanded to accept user input with the addition of a *default answer to the display dialog* statement:

```
display dialog ¬
        "What would you like help on?" default answer "AppleScript"
```

This command produces a dialog with a text input field (see Figure 2.43).

**Figure 2.43** Dialog With Text Input

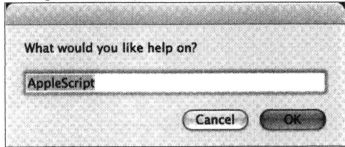

This dialog is useless unless we write some code to handle that user input. The result variable holds the result of the last command executed. When a script finishes running, the "Results" panel of the Script Editor window shows the last value of the script's results variable (see Figure 2.44).

**Figure 2.44** Tracking the *results* Variable with Script Editor

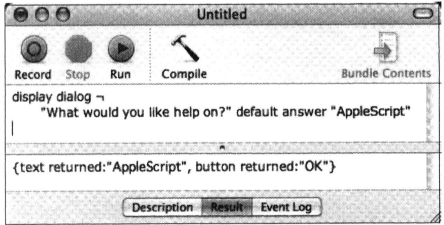

In this case, the text field contained AppleScript and the **OK** button was clicked. These values were stored in the "text returned and button returned"

values of the return variable, respectively. An *if* statement can be used to test the text entered into the input box:

```
display dialog ¬
    "What would you like help on?" default answer "AppleScript"
if text returned of result is "AppleScript" then
    display dialog "You entered AppleScript"
else
    display dialog "You didn't enter AppleScript"
end if
```

Notice that we are checking the value of *text returned of result,* and not simply *text returned.* We must properly reference these values as belonging to *result.* We could also use an *if* statement to check which button is pressed, although pressing the **Cancel** button will cause the script to terminate:

```
display dialog ¬
    "What would you like help on?" default answer "AppleScript"
if button returned of result is "OK" then
    display dialog "You pressed OK!"
else
    --this line will never be reached if Cancel is pressed!
end if
```

However, checking the value of both the text returned and button returned values this way will not work as expected. This is because the return variable is dynamic, meaning it is constantly updated whenever a statement is executed. This includes *if* statements. Once the *if* statement runs, there is a whole new return value, and the return value of display dialog is overwritten. Because of this, the *return* value must be grabbed immediately after the *display dialog* statement. The */Library/Scripts/Finder/Add to File* script does this in a very elegant fashion- with a single *copy* statement:

```
copy the result as list to {the prefix_or_suffix, the button_pressed}
```

This *copy* command takes the text returned and button returned values in the return variable and assigns them to *prefix_or_suffix* and *button_pressed,* respectively. We could use this to improve our *Apple Help* script, by introducing similar code:

```
display dialog ¬
    "What would you like help on?" default answer "AppleScript"
copy the result as list to {help_topic, button_pressed }
```

```
if button_pressed is "OK" then
      display dialog "You pressed OK, and entered " & help_topic & "!"
else
      --this line will never be reached if Cancel is pressed!
end if
```

Now that *help_topic* and *button_pressed* contain the text entered and the button clicked, respectively, we can use these values throughout the script as needed without fear of return being overwritten. The first *display dialog* command in our *if* statement reveals the value of *button_pressed* (OK) as well as the value of *help_topic* using the *&* character, which effectively "glues" strings together into a *unified output* statement.

Testing the button returned of a simple two-button dialog (with **OK** and **Cancel** buttons) is rather pointless, since clicking **OK** will continue the script and clicking **Cancel** will terminate the script. The ultimate goal of this exercise is to create a script that will display either *man* pages or *Apple Help* pages, which calls for an overhaul of our dialog's buttons. Adding additional buttons to a dialog is rather easy:

```
display dialog ¬
      "What would you like help on?" default answer ¬
      "AppleScript" buttons {"Man", "Apple Help", "Cancel"}
```

**Figure 2.45** An Updated Three-button Help Dialog

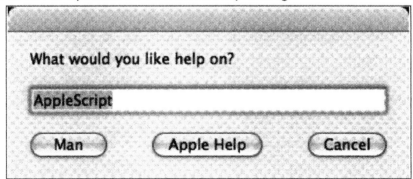

This code results in the dialog box shown in Figure 2.45. Determining which buttons the user clicked is as easy as updating our *if* statements to reflect the new buttons. Our updated script, along with three buttons, a *copy* statement to catch the dialog's return values, an updated *if* statement, and the code from */Library/Scripts/Finder/Add to File* to launch *Apple Help* is shown below:

```
display dialog ¬
    "What would you like help on?" default answer ¬
    "AppleScript" buttons {"Man", "Apple Help", "Cancel"}

copy the result as list to {help_topic, button_pressed}

if button_pressed is "Man" then
    display dialog "You pressed the \"Man\" button!"

else if button_pressed is "Apple Help" then
    tell application "Help Viewer"
        activate
        search looking for help_topic
    end tell


end if
```

The **Cancel** button works just as it did before, terminating the script. Clicking the **Apple Help** button launches the Apple Help application and automatically performs a search for *help_topic*, the text entered in the dialog box. The *man* (manual) lookup section of the script is unfinished, and displays a dialog box, but *man* is a *Terminal* command (specifically a shell command, which we'll cover in the next section), but a visit to the Script Editor's dictionary for Terminal reveals the *do shell* command. This command (wager a guess?) *runs* a *shell command* within Terminal. To view a manual page for a specific topic, we would normally run *man* followed by the name of the topic. In terms of our *Apple Help* script, we would run a *shell* command of *man* followed by the *help_topic* variable, using the "*&*" (ampersand) to "glue" the command together:

```
if button_pressed is "Man" then
    tell application "Terminal"
        do script "man " & help_topic
    end tell
```

By plugging this into the *if* statement, we arrive at our finished script, which accepts user input and will look up topics in wither *man* or *Apple Help*, depending on which button is clicked:

```
display dialog ¬
        "What would you like help on?" default answer ¬
        "AppleScript" buttons {"Man", "Apple Help", "Cancel"}

copy the result as list to {help_topic, button_pressed}

if button_pressed is "Man" then
        tell application "Terminal"
                do script "man " & help_topic
        end tell

else if button_pressed is "Apple Help" then
        tell application "Help Viewer"
                activate
                search looking for help_topic
        end tell

end if
```

This may seem like a long explanation for a fairly simple script, but user interaction via AppleScript comes in very handy, especially if you plan to integrate Automator workflows, AppleScript, and shell scripting—a very powerful combination. The next section discusses bash scripting, and the final section of this chapter integrates Automator, AppleScript, and bash into a powerful and flexible application.

# Bash Scripting

With OS X sitting on a full-blown BSD UNIX foundation, power users can take advantage of *UNIX shell scripting*. While not as sexy as Automator workflows or AppleScripting, UNIX scripts are insanely powerful, granting access to do pretty much anything with (or *to*) your system. Running UNIX shell scripts as the root user can be extremely dangerous, especially if you make a syntax error. Consider this fair warning. You are entering the realm of the *die-*

*hard* OS X hacker, where system failure and eternal Unix bliss are separated by mere keystrokes!

Most of the magic of UNIX shell scripting occurs from the command-line interface (CLI), brought to Mac OS X as the Terminal application. (The "testing" chapter of this book discusses the Terminal application in more detail. If you have not read that section, you may want to familiarize yourself with it before diving into scripting. When you launch Terminal, you are presented with a shell prompt. By typing in commands at this prompt, you are requesting that the shell perform some action. If you were to collect these commands and place them in a file, executing this file from the shell would in turn execute each command within that file. A file that contains a list of *shell* commands is referred to as a *shell script*. There is little or no difference between running commands from the shell and running commands from a shell prompt. Either way, the shell executes the commands. These commands most often reference other programs that exist on the system, but each shell has its own set of built-in commands that control program flow, perform variable comparison, interact with the user, and so on.

Since *shell* commands are text-based, any text-based editor can be used to create a shell script. However, command-line editors such as *vi* or *nano* are a much better option for creating and testing shell scripts than the more cumbersome graphical OS X equivalents, because the latter require that you leave the Terminal window. The back-and-forth process of testing and editing your scripts can be cumbersome, and most advanced shell scripters find it easier to edit and test scripts from within a single Terminal window, especially because individual *shell* commands can be tested from the shell prompt before being committed to a file.

# Foundations of Shell Scripting

In this section, we will first lay out some of the foundations of bash scripting. We will talk about syntax and common conventions (which admittedly are a bit dry, but necessary), and then we will discuss some programs commonly called by shell scripts, including *grep*, *awk*, and *sed*. We will wrap up this section by examining how these commands and conventions can be wielded as a powerful combination that complements your expanding OS X Hacking toolkit.

# Selecting a Shell

OS X ships with many different UNIX shells installed, including *bash*, *tcsh*, and *zsh*. There really is no *best* shell, but we focus on the extremely popular *bash* shell. The bash shell can be run by simply running bash from the Terminal prompt, or bash can be set as the default shell through "Terminal's Preferences" window.

# Permissions and Paths

Shell scripts are essentially text-based programs that must be executed. To execute a shell script, you must first set the file permissions of the script so that OS X recognizes it as an executable program. Although this can be done through the graphical *Get Info* menu, it is much easier (since you are using the Terminal anyhow) to set the file permissions from the command line with the change mode *(chmod)* command. We won't go into a full discourse on UNIX file permissions (run *man chmod* through the Terminal or your handy *Apple Help* script) but sSimply running *chmod +x filename* will marks *filename* as an executable program.

In addition, OS X relies on a *PATH* variable to keep informed about of where executable files are located. The current path can be displayed by running *echo $PATH* from the terminal prompt. OS X will looks in these directories for executable programs, which meaning means you must either place your scripts in one of these directories, add your script directory to the path by exporting a new *PATH* variable (with bash's *export* command), or tell OS X where to find your script each time you run it. We discussed this in more detail in the pen testing chapter, but for now, we'll settle with *telling* OS X where to find our script each time we run it. This is accomplished by providing the full path to the script at the Terminal prompt. For example, if our the script is called *nappyscript* and it is in the */tmp/scripts* directory, we can run */tmp/scripts/nappyscript* at the Terminal prompt. As an alternative, if we are inside the */tmp/scripts* directory, we can run *./nappyscript*, as the period (.) and the forward slash (/ [often termed the "dot slash"]) indicates that the script is in our the current directory. Either way, remember to set the proper file permissions and remember to tell OS X where your script is located.

## Notes From the Underground…

### Look, Ma! No File!

Although we are making a lot of references to shell scripts, *shell* commands can be run directly from the shell prompt, without first placing them in a file. In fact, testing a script right from the shell prompt is a great way to test pieces of the script. Shells like bash are amazingly good at figuring out what you are trying to do, and well-formed multi-line commands present no problem when run directly from the prompt.

## Common Conventions

Shell scripts often start with a single line that indicates which shell (or inter-preter) is to be used to execute the script, and where that shell is located. This line begins with a pound sign (#) followed by an exclamation point (!). Theses symbols are often referred to as a "shabang." For example, the first line of an OS X bash script should read:

```
#!/bin/bash
```

While this first line is optional, it is recommended that you include it, since different shells have slightly different syntax. Executing a bash script from a *tcsh* prompt will feed *bash* commands and syntaxes into *tcsh*, producing unexpected results.

Although shell scripting is extremely powerful, it is also odd in many respects. Here is a breakdown of some of the things to keep in mind:

- **Capitalization matters.** Most shells are case sensitive, because UNIX is case sensitive. Variable names and command names must use proper capitalization. From a UNIX perspective, "Bash," "bash," and "BASH" describe three different things.

- **Spaces can be tricky**. Most shells are finicky about spaces. The reason for this is simple: the space is the universal "dividing character" that separates commands from arguments. When sending a command to a shell, for example the *ls -la* command, the first "word" is the name of the command (*ls*) and the following "words" are arguments to the *ls* command (*-la*). Do not recklessly add or delete spaces from the example scripts in this section.

■ **Shells rely on external commands.** One thing that makes shell scripting so powerful is that it ties together the best features of many external programs. As a shell programmer, you need to be keenly aware of the syntax of the external commands you are asking the shell to execute. Knowing shell syntax is useless if you are fumbling your way through the *grep*, *sed* and *awk* commands that you are relying on.

■ **Pipes can break.** The output from one program can easily be fed into another program, and that output can be fed into another program, and so on- ad infinitum. While this is a powerful feature, it tends to cause beginners a bit of a headache until they get the hang of it. This *piping* of information can be a bit of a hassle, especially if your really long "pipes" start leaking bad data somewhere in the middle. *Garbage in, Garbage out.*

■ **As mentioned, shell scripts can be entered into a file or run from the command line.** If you start typing in a multi-line shell script at the shell prompt, bash will "understand" that you are not finished entering the script, and wait until the script is completely typed in before executing it. If a *shell* command entered at a prompt throws you a strange-looking prompt character (e.g., a greater-than sign), type **Control-C** to get things back to normal.

## Pipes

Most programs produce some sort of output. UNIX shells are known for their awesome ability to "chain" this output and input together with the *pipe* character ("|"). For example, consider this simple command:

```
j0pb12:~ johnnylong$ echo shmoo
shmoo
```

In this example, we provide the word "shmoo" to the *echo* command as input, and the command produces the word "shmoo" as output. Consider another command:

```
j0pb12:~ johnnylong$ tr 'o' 'e'
food
feed
mow
mew
```

The *tr* command translates characters. In this example, we are asking *tr* to translate every 'o' character into an 'e.' After entering the command, the shell waits for input. If we type food, the *tr* program translates the characters and produces the word *feed*. Likewise, typing *mow* produces the word *mew*. The *tr* command accepts input, manipulates that input, and produces output. Combining the two examples, we can use the pipe to send the output of the *echo* command into the *tr* program as input:

```
j0pb12:~ johnnylong$ echo shmoo | tr 'o' 'e'
shmee
```

When the word "shmoo" is piped through the *tr 'o' 'e'* command, the output is the word "shmee." These pipes can be used to connect any program that accepts piped input; most UNIX commands do. Some commands require a special switch to read piped data (sometimes referred to as *reading from standard input* or *reading from stdin*), but most UNIX commands accessible from the Terminal are already set up to accept input from another command's piped output without any switches.

# Redirection

There are other ways to manipulate input and output, specifically the use of *redirection*. Similar to using the pipe, redirection is most often used to send output to or read output from a file. Redirection is accomplished through the use of the greater-than (>) and less-than (<) symbols. Consider this variation of our simple *echo* command:

```
j0pb12:~ johnnylong$ echo shmoo > foo.txt
j0pb12:~ johnnylong$ cat foo.txt
shmoo
```

By appending the > sign to the end of the command followed by a file name, the output of the echo command was written to the file *foo.txt*. The *cat foo.txt* command shows that the output was, in fact, written to *foo.txt*. The greater-than symbol is used to send output to a file. A single > symbol will cause the target file to be overwritten. To append to an existing file (or begin writing to an empty file), use *two* > symbols:

```
j0pb12:~ johnnylong$ echo shmoo >> foo.txt
j0pb12:~ johnnylong$ cat foo.txt
shmoo
shmoo
```

Notice that there are no spaces between the >symbols. A space between redirect symbols will produce an error, because output can only be redirected once per command.

```
j0pb12:~ johnnylong$ echo oops > > foo.txt
-bash: syntax error near unexpected token `>'
```

The < symbol is used to read from a file. We won't spend much time discussing the use of the less-than symbol, as it is more common to use a program like *cat* to pipe the contents of a file into another program. These two commands are (practically) identical as written, but the second tends to *look* a bit awkward to a novice shell user:

```
j0pb12:~ johnnylong$ cat foo.txt | more
shmoo
shmoo
j0pb12:~ johnnylong$ more < foo.txt
shmoo
shmoo
```

Either way, both of these commands send the output to the *more* command, which presents output one page at a time, and allows you to scroll back and forth through the file. Redirections can be chained ad-nauseum, and we'll get some wicked chaining going in relatively short order.

# Job Control

If a job runs away from you, you can easily terminate it by pressing **CTRL-C**. For example, this command will cause the shell to sleep for 30 seconds, unless we terminate it with **CTRL-C**:

```
j0pb12:~ johnnylong$ sleep 30
^C
j0pb12:~ johnnylong$
```

UNIX commands (shell scripts included) can also be run as a background process. This enables you to run many different jobs from one Terminal window, each of which can be controlled with special *job control* commands. To run a job in the background, append the *&* symbol to the end of the command:

```
j0pb12:~ johnnylong$ sleep 10 &
[1] 1459
```

The shell responds with two numbers. The first lists the number of the job within the current shell. (Our example displays the number one since this is the first job we've run in the background in this Terminal.) The second number displays the system process ID of this job. Processes can be listed with the *ps* command. After ten seconds our job will complete, although there is no indication of this until the **Return** key is pressed:

```
j0pb12:~ johnnylong$
[1]+  Done                    sleep 10
```

The system informs us that the job has completed successfully. Once a job has been sent to the background, it can be controlled with a variety of commands. For example, the *jobs* command lists the status of the jobs running in the current shell:

```
j0pb12:~ johnnylong$ sleep 50 &
[1] 1469
j0pb12:~ johnnylong$ sleep 60 &
[2] 1470
j0pb12:~ johnnylong$ jobs
[1]-  Running                 sleep 50 &
[2]+  Running                 sleep 60 &
```

To terminate a process from the shell, use the *kill* command followed by a percent sign (%) and the number of the process:

```
j0pb12:~ johnnylong$ kill %1
j0pb12:~ johnnylong$
[1]-  Terminated              sleep 30
```

After killing the process, you may need to press **Enter** again to see the termination message. A background process can also be brought to the foreground using the *fg* command, optionally followed by the job number:

```
j0pb12:~ johnnylong$ sleep 60 &
[1] 1474
j0pb12:~ johnnylong$ fg %1
sleep 60
```

Once a job has been brought to the foreground, it can either be terminated with **CTRL-C** or stopped with **CTRL-Z**:

```
j0pb12:~ johnnylong$ sleep 60 &
[1] 1475
j0pb12:~ johnnylong$ fg %1
sleep 60
^Z
[1]+  Stopped                 sleep 60
j0pb12:~ johnnylong$
```

Once a job has been stopped in this manner, it can be killed with the *kill* command or sent to the background with the *bg* command. Executing the *bg* command without parameters sends the most recent job to the background:

```
j0pb12:~ johnnylong$ bg
[1]+ sleep 60 &
```

It is easy to lose track of what job is running in which state, but using job control can go a long way. Table 2.3 summarizes the basic *job control* commands.

**Table 2.3** Basic Job Control Commands

| Control Character or Command | Description |
| --- | --- |
| & | When placed at the end of a command, this character indicates that the job should be run in the background. |
| CTRL-C | Terminate the current command or shell script. |
| CTRL-Z | Stop (but do not terminate) the current command. It can be resumed or killed. |
| fg | Bring the last stopped or background job to the foreground. Optionally specify a job prefaced with a %. |
| bg | Set the last stopped job to run in the background. Optionally specify a job prefaced with a %. |
| jobs | List the jobs currently running in this shell session. |

# Comments

The pound sign (/)(#) designates the beginning of a comment. When bash encounters a pound sign, any text following it is ignored:

```
#This is a comment in the bash shell
echo "This is written to standard output." #This is a comment
```

# Variables

Variables are set with the equal (=) sign, and recalled with a dollar sign ($). Consider the following example:

```
j0pb12:~ johnnylong$ echo $foo

j0pb12:~ johnnylong$ foo=bar
j0pb12:~ johnnylong$ echo $foo
bar
```

On the first line, we request the value of the variable *foo*, and determine that it is not set. On the second line, the value of *foo* is set to *bar*. On the third line, the value of *foo* is requested again, and this time we discover the variable is set to *bar*. When setting a variable, *don't* use the dollar sign. When checking the value of the variable, *use* the dollar sign. When assigning strings, **spaces matter**. Consider the following examples in Tables 2.4 and 2.5:

**Table 2.4** Setting Variables

| Command/Result | Description |
| --- | --- |
| j0pb12:~ johnnylong$ foo= bar | Broken assignment. Foo is set to *NULL*, |
| -bash: bar: command not found | and the shell attempts to run the command *bar*, which it can not find. |
| j0pb12:~ johnnylong$ foo = bar | Bad command. The shell attempts to run |
| -bash: foo: command not found | *foo* as a command, which it can not find. The equal sign and *bar* are passed to foo as arguments. |
| j0pb12:~ johnnylong$ foo =bar | Bad command. The shell attempts to run |
| -bash: foo: command not found | *foo* as a command, which it can not find. *=bar* is passed to foo as an argument. |

There are quite a few special variables that bash recognizes, some of which are more commonly used within shell scripts. For example:

**Table 2.4** Recognizable Variables

| | |
|---|---|
| $0, $1, $2, etc | These variables hold the values of any arguments passed to a shell script. *$0* is reserved for the name of the script itself. *$1* holds the name of the first argument. For the command *./nappyscript check*, *$0* would contain *"./nappyscript"* while *$1* would contain *"check."* |
| $@ | This variable holds all *of* the parameters passed to a script. A loop like this will echo all arguments:<br>`for i in "$@"`<br>`do`<br>`  echo $i`<br>`done` |
| $# | This variable holds the number of arguments that were passed into a script. When no arguments are provided to a script, *$#* is equal to zero. For each additional argument, *$#* is increased by one. |

# Tests and Return Codes

There are several different ways to compare values in bash. The first and most commonly used is called (appropriately enough) *test*. Like many other bash built-in commands, test can be run from the Terminal prompt, but in the case of the *test* command, it makes more sense to use test in what's known as a list. For example, this command uses test to check for the existence of a directory:

```
j0pb12:~ $ test -d /etc
j0pb12:~ $ test -d /etca
```

This example should let us know whether or not the */etc* directory exists (it does) and whether or not the */etca* directory exists (it doesn't). The reason this seems a bit odd is that *test*, like many other well-coded UNIX commands, produce a *return code* which can be monitored to determine if a command completed successfully. Return codes are not written as ouput to the screen, but they can be monitored to debug a script. One common (and handy) convention is to use return codes in a *list*, which uses the && and || character combinations to control program flow. Consider the following example:

```
j0pb12:~ $ test -d /etc && echo "Exists." || echo "Does not exist."
Exists.
j0pb12:~ $ test -d /etca && echo "Exists." || echo "Does not exist."
Does not exist.
```

The *&&* character combination will execute the next command if the previous command produced a zero return code, indicating that the command executed without error. The | | character combination will execute the next command if the previous command produced a non-zero return code, indicating that the command encountered an error. Although chaining these two character combinations may seem illogical (technically, the | | should be testing the return code of the *echo* command), bash is smart enough in this case to pass the return code straight through the *echo* command. List and test combinations are also a great way to test for arguments in a shell script. If a user must provide arguments to a shell script, this example shows how the number of arguments can be tested in as little as two lines:

```
j0pb12:~ johnnylong$ cat foo
test $# = 0 && echo "Please provide arguments." && exit
echo "Starting program."

j0pb12:~ johnnylong$ ./foo
Please provide arguments.

j0pb12:~ johnnylong$ ./foo 1
Starting program.
```

This script tests the number of arguments provided via the *$#* variable. If no arguments are provided (*$#* is equal to zero), the *test* command returns true and passes control to the *echo* command, which instructs the user to provide arguments. Control then passes through to the *exit* command, which terminates the script. If an argument is provided (*$#* is greater than zero), the *test* command returns false and control flows past the two *&&* tests to the rest of the script. This is certainly useful, but test can be used to check a lot of things, including the examples in Table 2.6.

**Table 2.6** *Test* Command Syntax and Examples

| Test Syntax | Description | Example |
|---|---|---|
| string | Returns True if string exists and is not zero | *test $NOTZERO* |
| -*d* file | Returns True if file is a directory | *test -d /etc* |
| -*e* file | Returns True if file exists | *test -e /tmp/file* |
| -*r* file | Returns True if file exists, and is readable | *test -r /tmp/read* |
| -*s* file | Returns True if file exists and is not zero length | *test -s /tmp/empty* |
| -*w* file | Returns True if file exists and is writable | *test -w /tmp/write* |
| -*x* file | Returns True if file exists and is executable | *test -s /tmp/execute* |
| -*n string* | Exists and is not zero | *test -z $NOTZERO* |
| *string1 = string2* | True if strings are identical | *test $FOO = $FOO* |
| *string1 != string2* | True if strings are not identical | *test $FOO != $BAR* |
| *string1 < string2* | True if string1 comes before string2 (ASCII compare) | *test $ABC < $DEF* |
| *string1 > string2* | True if string1 comes after string2 (ASCII compare) | *test $DEF > $ABC* |
| *num1 -eq num2* | True if integer num1 is algebraically equal to integer num2 | *test 1 -eq 1* |
| *num1 -lt num2* | True if integer num1 is algebraically less than integer num2 | *test 1 -lt 2* |
| *num1 -gt num2* | True if integer num1 is algebraically greater than integer num2 | *test 2 -gt 1* |
| *num1 -ge num2* | True if integer num1 is algebraically greater than or equal to integer num2 | *test 1 -ge 1* |
| *num1 -le num2* | True if integer num1 is algebraically less than or equal to integer num2 | *test 1 -le 1* |

The *test* command can also be used in a sort of shorthand, using brackets ([ ]]). Enclosing *test* command parameters within these brackets runs them through the *test* command as shown in these examples:

```
j0pb12:~ johnnylong$ [ "1" -eq "1" ] && echo "True."
True.
j0pb12:~ johnnylong$ [ "1" -eq "2" ] && echo "True."
j0pb12:~ johnnylong$ [ -d /etc ] && echo "Directory exists."
Directory exists.
j0pb12:~ johnnylong$ [ -d /etca ] && echo "Directory exists."
j0pb12:~ johnnylong$
```

Note that spaces must surround the *[ ]*. Using *[ ]*without surrounding spaces will produce an error. The *test* command is one of the most common *shell* commands; it will be worth your while to learn the nuances of this command.

# The All-Important If, Then, and Else

The lists which utilized the *&&* and *||* character combinations are nice for one-shot program control, but nothing beats *if-then-else* statements, or in bash-speak, *if-then-elif*. Here is a simple parameter checking example:

```
j0pb12:~ johnnylong$ cat foo
if [ $# -eq 0 ]; then
  echo "Give me at least one parameter."
elif [ $# -eq 1 ]; then
 echo "OK, give me two."
else
 echo "Oops, too many."
fi

j0pb12:~ johnnylong$ ./foo
Give me at least one parameter.

j0pb12:~ johnnylong$ ./foo 1
OK, give me two.

j0pb12:~ johnnylong$ ./foo 1 2
Oops, too many.
```

Note the use of spaces around the *[ ]*. These must exist or the test will produce an error. The *if* statement tests the return code of the *test* statement, and if it evaluates as true, will execute the line or lines following the first *then* statement. If the statement evaluates as false, the script continues to the *elif*, which is shorthand for *else, if*. If the *else, if* statement evaluates as true, the program will execute the line or lines following the *then* statement. If *both* the *if* and *elif* statements evaluate as false, the *else* statement is executed. There can be multiple *elif* statements, but there can only be *one else* statement, which should be the last selection before the *fi*, which marks the end of the *if* clause.

# Loops

There are quite a few different loops, and they are all robust. We take a look at the most basic implementations of both *for, while*, and *until*. The first use of for operates on a provided list of words. Consider the following example:

```
j0pb12:~/temp johnnylong$ cat for_list
for i in "abc" "def"; do
  echo $i
done

j0pb12:~/temp johnnylong$ ./for_list
abc
def
```

This script runs through the *for* loop twice, each time assigning a value to the *$i* variable. The first time through the loop, *$i* is set to *abc*, and the second time through the loop, *$i* is set to *def*. Each time through the loop, the content of the $i variable is printed to the screen with the *echo $i* command. There is a different way to produce the same results in a potentially more powerful way:

```
j0pb12:~ johnnylong$ cat foo
for i in `echo abc def`; do
    echo $i
done

j0pb12:~ johnnylong$ ./foo
abc
def
```

This script assigns *abc* and *def* to variable *$i* and writes it to the screen, with the exact same results as the first example. There's a specific convention used here(not yet discussed), but it is very powerful; the use of the grave (`) symbol. This symbol, which is located below the *esc* key and to the left of the *1* key on most Mac keyboards, triggers the launch of a *subshell*. Once the command enclosed in *graves* is executed, the output of that command is sent to the top-level shell, where that output is operated on, one space-delimited word at a time. Put another way, the output of the command in graves replaces the command itself in the script. For example, changing the *sub-shell* command to *ls* would send the output of the *ls* command through the *for* loop:

```
j0pb12:~/temp johnnylong$ cat poo
for i in `ls`; do
  echo $i
done


j0pb12:~/temp johnnylong$ ls
file1    file2    file3    poo


j0pb12:~/temp johnnylong$ ./poo
file1
file2
file3
poo
```

Notice that this example "fed" the output of the *ls* command through the *for* loop. The *output* of the *ls* command replaced the command itself in the script, one word at a time. Although this seems useless, a script like this can be easily modified to perform an action on each and every file:

```
j0pb12:~/temp johnnylong$ ls
file1 file2 file3 poo


j0pb12:~/temp johnnylong$ cat file*


j0pb12:~/temp johnnylong$ cat poo
for i in `ls`; do
if [ $i != "poo" ]; then
   echo "This file owned by a Mac Hacker" >> $i
fi
```

```
done


j0pb12:~/temp johnnylong$ ./poo


j0pb12:~/temp johnnylong$ cat file*
This file owned by a Mac Hacker
This file owned by a Mac Hacker
This file owned by a Mac Hacker
```

The local directory contains three files: *file1*, *file2*, *file3*, and *poo*. The first three files are empty and the file *poo* contains our script. The script runs the *ls* command, and runs each word output from the *ls* command through the *for* loop, assigning that word to the *$i* variable. If the name of the current file (held in *$i) is not* poo, the phrase *"This file owned by a Mac Hacker"* is appended to that file. We'll use this technique later in this section.

Our *for* loop could be modified to operate on a sequence of numbers by changing the *subshell* command to something such as *"echo 1 2 3,"* or by providing a *for* loop like *for i in 1 2 3; do*, but a second variation of the *for* loop accounts for this:

```
j0pb12:~/temp johnnylong$ cat for_loop
for (( i=1; $i <= 3; i=i+1 )); do
echo $i
done


j0pb12:~/temp johnnylong$ ./for_loop
1
2
3
```

This script uses a different type of *for* loop, which accepts no more than three expressions. The first expression is run once, when the *for* loop is first executed. The second expression is analyzed each time it goes through the loop, to determine if the expression evaluates to false. If this expression returns false, then the *for* loop's body is bypassed and control passed to the expression following the *done* marker. The third expression is executed each time the loop is executed. In our example script, the variable *$i* is first set to *1*, and the second expression is evaluated. It is determined that *$i* is less than or equal to 3, so the body of the *for* loop is executed, echoing the value of *$i*. Once the body of the loop is completed, the *for* loop increments *$i* by one, and the loop repeats until *$i* is greater than 3, at which point control is passed to the *done* marker, which is located at the end of this script. This loop becomes even more powerful if more complex expressions are used, especially those which spawn subshells.

The *while* loop is also extremely useful, and is a bit more simple than the *for* loop. Consider this example:

```
j0pb12:~/temp johnnylong$ cat while_loop
while [ "$i" != "abc" ]; do
  read i
done


j0pb12:~/temp johnnylong$ ./while_loop
def
ghi
abc
j0pb12:~/temp johnnylong$
```

A *while* loop will execute as long as the expression evaluates as true. In this example, the loop will run as long as *$i* is not equal to *abc*. The body of the *while* loop reads characters from the keyboard, assigning each to *$i*. As long as *abc* is not entered at the keyboard, the loop will continue to run. We can also emulate the behavior of a *for* loop, as long as we can increment a number. Incrementing a number is fairly simple thanks to the *let* command:

```
j0pb12:~/temp johnnylong$ x=1
j0pb12:~/temp johnnylong$ echo $x
1
j0pb12:~/temp johnnylong$ let x=x+1
j0pb12:~/temp johnnylong$ echo $x
2
j0pb12:~/temp johnnylong$
```

This example sets *$x* equal to *1*, and displays it to the screen with the *echo* command. The *let* command is then used to set *$x* equal to the current value *plus one*. Notice that the second *x* in the *let* command does not use the *$x* reference. However, it probably should since *setting* a variable does not use the *$*, but *referencing* a variable should use the *$*. The *let* command does not require the *$*, making it one of the easiest ways to increment a variable.

Using *let*, we can emulate a *for* loop with a *while* loop:

```
j0pb12:~/temp johnnylong$ cat ./while_loop
i=0
```

```
while [ "$i" -le "3" ]; do
  echo $i
  let i=i+1
done


j0pb12:~/temp johnnylong$ ./while_loop
0
1
2
3
```

Notice that the *$i* variable must be set to a value first, and that it is incremented inside the loop with the *let* command. The *while* loop executes as long as the expression (in this case *"$i" -l "3"*) evaluates as true. Conversely, the *until* loop will execute as long as the leading expression evaluates as false. Here's what the simple counter script would look as an *until* loop:

```
j0pb12:~/temp johnnylong$ cat until_loop
i=0
until [ "$i" -gt "3" ]; do
  echo $i
  let i=i+1
done


j0pb12:~/temp johnnylong$ ./until_loop
0
1
2
3
j0pb12:~/temp johnnylong$
```

Notice that the *$i* variable is again defined before the loop is executed, and that it is incremented *inside* the loop. This is similar to the *while* loop, and unlike *until* loops in other programming languages, the expression is evaluated at the top of the loop.

Loops can also be *nested*, meaning they can run inside other loops:

```
j0pb12:~/temp johnnylong$ cat ./nested_loop
for (( i=1; $i <= 3; i=i+1 )); do
  echo "i: $i"
  for (( x=1; $x <= 2; x=x+1 )); do
    echo "  x: $x"
```

```
   done
done

j0pb12:~/temp johnnylong$ ./nested_loop
i: 1
  x: 1
  x: 2
i: 2
  x: 1
  x: 2
i: 3
  x: 1
  x: 2
```

In this example, *$i* is incremented between increments of *$x*. This type of loop can be very powerful, especially if you keep track of all your variables.

# Harnessing Mac's UNIX Commands

The Mac's BSD shell is just that; it's a *shell*. While it offers a great deal of flexibility; however, the shell exists to execute commands and produce output. Without commands to actually execute, the shell is worthless. In this section, we will look at some of the most popular commands and explore how they can be used to get the most from your Mac.

## *Cat*

We have already used the *cat* (concatenate) command quite a bit, however, two other options are real gems. The *-v* option displays any control characters as printed text, and the *-t* option displays control characters as printed text *and* displays tabs as ^I characters. These options come in very handy when you need to process a file that has these nasty things embedded in them. Table 2.7 lists some of *cat's* more interesting options.

**Table 2.7** *Cat's* More Interesting Options

| Option | Description |
|--------|-------------|
| -n | Number output lines |
| -v | Display control characters as printed text |
| -t | Like -v, but also display tabs as ^I characters |

# Grep

The *grep* command is so commonly used that it has become geek-speak for "find." The *grep* command locates lines in a file that match a specific pattern. For example, to locate the *ssh* service in the */etc/services* file, use this command:

```
j0pb12:~/temp johnnylong$ grep ssh /etc/services
ssh            22/udp    # SSH Remote Login Protocol
ssh            22/tcp    # SSH Remote Login Protocol
sshell         614/udp   # SSLshell
sshell         614/tcp   # SSLshell
#                       Kazuhito Gassho
            Gassho.Kasuhito@exc.epson.co.jp
```

Notice that *grep* located several instances of *ssh*, including one instance that appeared in a name, *Kazuhito Gasso*. If we were interested in only locating lines that referred to the *ssh* service itself, we could narrow our search quite easily by appending a space after the search string. This example locates *ssh* followed by a space:

```
j0pb12:~/temp johnnylong$ grep "ssh " /etc/services
ssh            22/udp    # SSH Remote Login Protocol
ssh            22/tcp    # SSH Remote Login Protocol
```

Another way to search for a specified string is using metacharacters, specifically the caret (^) and the dollar sign $, which represent the beginning and end of a line, respectively. If you know the string you are looking for is at the beginning of a line, precede the search string with the *carat*. This example locates the string *ssh* at the beginning of a line:

```
j0pb12:~/temp johnnylong$ grep "^ssh" /etc/services
ssh            22/udp    # SSH Remote Login Protocol
ssh            22/tcp    # SSH Remote Login Protocol
sshell         614/udp   # SSLshell
sshell         614/tcp   # SSLshell
```

Notice that this search did not return the line containing *Kazuhito Gassho's* name, since the string *ssh* did not appear at the beginning of the line. The *grep* command can also be used to display strings that do not contain a particular string by applying the *-v* switch. This example returns no results, since *every* line of the */etc/services* file contains a *pound sign*:

```
j0pb12:~/temp johnnylong$ grep -v "#" /etc/services
j0pb12:~/temp johnnylong$
```

The *grep* command can be chained together like other UNIX commands through the use of the pipe (|) character. This example first searches for *ssh* in the */etc/services* file, and then strips out all lines that contain either the string *sshell* or *Gassho*:

```
j0pb12:~/temp johnnylong$ grep ssh /etc/services | grep -v "sshell" | grep -v "Gassho"
ssh             22/udp      # SSH Remote Login Protocol
ssh             22/tcp      # SSH Remote Login Protocol
```

Although this is much less elegant than a search for *^ssh*, no one said shell scripting had to be pretty. In many cases, it is simply a case of "whatever works." As you use bash, you will undoubtedly be stricken by its elegance, and your *shell* commands will most likely become more streamlined, but there is no replacement for ugly, down and dirty, "whatever works" practice. Table 2.8 lists some of the more popular switches used by the *grep* program. If you need some practice with redirection and pipes, begin your journey by playing around with *grep's* options. It will be time well spent.

**Table 2.8** Common *grep* Options

| Option | Description |
| --- | --- |
| -a | Search *binary* files as if they were text. |
| -A *num* | Print *num* lines of text *after* the matched line. |
| -B *num* | Print *num* lines of text *before* the matched line. |
| -c | Do not print search results; only print the number of lines that matched. |
| -H | Print the filename for each match. This is helpful when searching large numbers of files. |
| -i | Ignore the case of the search. Treat upper and lowercase the same. |

**Continued**

**Table 2.8 continued** Common *grep* Options

| Option | Description |
|--------|-------------|
| -R | Search each directory and file matching the search string recursively. This is helpful when you are not exactly sure where the file is that contains the search string. |
| -v | Return lines that do not match the search string. |

## Notes From the Underground...

### The Power of Regular Expressions

A *regular expression* is a pattern that matches a set of strings. Regular expression allow you to search for *patterns* of text as opposed to specific strings of text. Most UNIX commands that process text support regular expressions, including *grep*, *sed*, and *awk*. Regular expressions are also used in many programming languages such as PERL. Although we cannot do regular expressions justice in this limited space, if you plan on doing any heavy-duty text searching, you will need to get a handle on them. See the *grep man* page for more information about regular expressions, and practice with *grep*, which accepts properly-formed regular expressions as standard search strings.

# Sed

Stream Editor (*Sed*) performs powerfully on-the-fly text replacement. Sed is so insanely powerful and flexible that entire books have been written about it. When combined with regular expressions, *sed* can do incredible things. One use of *sed* allows you to replace bits of text with other bits of text. This simple example reads input from the console, replacing the word *Nate* with *Naytin*:

```
j0pb12:~/temp johnnylong$ sed 's/Nate/Naytin/g'
Fred
Fred
Joe
Joe
Nate
Naytin
```

This is similar to an example we saw earlier using the *tr* command, which is a character replacement utility. It is designed to replace every instance of one character with a different character. *Sed's* syntax is awkward at first glance, so let's examine its syntax from the previous example.

The format of the basic use of *sed* is fairly straightforward. First, enclose the entire command in quotes. This informs the shell that the entire quoted phrase is not to be expanded on by the shell. Remember, bash sees spaces as *delimiters*. To preserve spaces within *sed's* arguments, enclose them in, single quotes (*'*) for strong protection from the shell or double quotes (*" "*) for partial protection from the shell. Within the quotes, *sed* expects some action. In this case, we want to substitute (or replace) text, so we supply the *s* parameter. The *substitute* parameter requires a *search string* as well as a *replacement string*, separated by forward slashes. The search string will be replaced by the *replacement text*. The last parameter to the substitute function is optional. If left blank, *sed* will only replace the first occurrence of the search string. By setting this last parameter to *g*, we are doing a *global* substitution, meaning we want to replace *all instances* within each line. So, in a nutshell, the search and replace function of *sed* looks like this:

```
's/search_string/replace_string/'
```

A global replacement (replacing every occurrence on each line) would look like this:

```
's/search_string/replace_string/g'
```

*Sed* can also be used on a file by supplying a filename:

```
j0pb12:~/temp johnnylong$ cat test.txt
See Jake.
See Jake run.
See Jake come back.

j0pb12:~/temp johnnylong$ sed 's/See/I saw/g' test.txt
I saw Jake.
I saw Jake run.
I saw Jake come back.
```

Input to *sed* can be piped in from another program:

```
j0pb12:~/temp johnnylong$ grep "back" test.txt | sed 's/See/I saw/g'
I saw Jake come back.
```

*Sed* is very powerful, and although we only scratch the surface, the search and replace functionality is very powerful, as you will see in practice later in this section.

# Awk

*Awk* is a strange and wonderful beast. Powerful, flexible, and just *awk*ward enough to keep the amateur geeks at bay, *awk* is a program that combines all of the best features of *grep* and *sed*, and adds some unique capabilities. In short, *awk* searches a file and performs an action or series of actions on each matched string. Although we used *sed* to do search-and-replace in the last example, *awk* can handle this as well, although the format may appear awkward at first glance. Here's the *awk* version of the last *sed* example:

```
j0pb12:$ awk '/back/ { sub("See","I saw"); print $0 }' test.txt
I saw Jake come back.
```

Like bash, *awk* accepts multiple commands and can be written into a script, which *awk* reads when provided with the *-f* option. However, in this example, *awk* is used in a single-line mode, as each of the examples in this section will be. Notice that the *awk* command is broken into two major parts. The first part is the argument list, which is enclosed in single quotes. This protects the arguments from bash expansion. The second part of the command is the file name that *awk* will act on, in this case *test.txt*. As always, the file name can be removed, and input can either be read from the console or piped in from another command. The arguments to *awk* look are examined in more detail.

The first section, */back/,* is an optional search string. When this is present, *awk* will perform its actions only on lines that contain this string. The actions follow the search string, and are enclosed in curly ({}) brackets. There are two distinct actions (separated by a semicolon) performed on every line that contains the word *back*. The first action, *sub*, substitutes the string *See* with the string *I saw*. The second action, *print $0*, prints the whole line now that substitutions have been made on it. So, a basic *awk* command looks like this:

```
awk '/search string/ { action_1; action_2; action_n }' filename
```

The search string works much like *grep*, and in the simplest examples, *grep* can be used in its stead. This type of use would rely on piping *grep*'s output into *awk* and would negate *awk*'s filename requirement:

```
j0pb12:~/temp johnnylong$ grep back test.txt | awk '{ sub("See","I saw");
print $0 }'
I saw Jake come back.
```

Search and replace functions can be performed any number of ways, but one of the features that sets *awk* apart is its ability to work with *fields* within a line. A *field* is a string that is delimited, or separated, by other characters or strings. This line can be separated into fields any number of ways:

```
The new song I sing with every breath, breathes sight in
```

If a space is used as a delimiter, then each distinct word is a field. Field one would be *the*, field two would be *new*, field three would be *song,* and so on. If a comma (,) is used as a delimiter, field one would be the phrase *The new song I sing with every breath* and field two would be the phrase *breathes sight in*. If a comma is used as a delimiter, however, a space precedes the second field, since the line is written with a space following the comma. To make things even stranger, if the character *s* is used as a delimiter, field one would be *The new* (followed by a space), field two would be *ong I* (followed by a space), field three would be *ing with every breath breathe* (followed by a space), and so on. Delimiters do not have to be a single character either. They can be words, phrases, or control character combinations. The default field delimiter in *awk* is a space, but it can be changed using the *-F* argument (but delimiters are only useful if we can reference distinct fields within a line. *Awk* handles this through the use of special variables. The variable *$0* refers to an entire line, from beginning to end. The end of a file is marked by a *line delimiter*, or *record separator*, which is set to *newline* by default. The *$1* variable is used to reference the first field in a line, *$2* refers to the second field, and so on. Therefore, knowing that the default field delimiter is a space, this command will print the first word of every line in a file:

```
j0pb12:~/temp johnnylong$ cat breathe.txt
The new song I sing with every breath, breathes sight in

j0pb12:~/temp johnnylong$ cat breathe.txt  | awk '{print $1}'
The
```

As discussed in the previous paragraph, the delimiter can be changed with *awk's -F* parameter. These examples break up a line into various chunks, using different delimiters:

```
j0pb12:~/temp johnnylong$ cat breathe.txt
The new song I sing with every breath, breathes sight in

j0pb12:~/temp johnnylong$ cat breathe.txt  | awk -F',' '{print $1}'
The new song I sing with every breath
```

```
j0pb12:~/temp johnnylong$ cat breathe.txt   | awk -F's' '{print $1}'
The new

j0pb12:~/temp johnnylong$ cat breathe.txt   | awk -F's' '{print $2}'
ong I
j0pb12:~/temp johnnylong$ cat breathe.txt   | awk -F's' '{print $3}'
ing with every breath, breathe

j0pb12:~/temp johnnylong$ cat breathe.txt   | awk -F'th' '{print $1}'
The new song I sing wi
j0pb12:~/temp johnnylong$ cat breathe.txt   | awk -F'th' '{print $2}'
 every brea
j0pb12:~/temp johnnylong$ cat breathe.txt   | awk -F'th' '{print $3}'
, brea
```

Notice that in the last three examples, *awk* ignores the *Th* at the beginning of the sentence. This is because *awk*, like most UNIX programs, is case sensitive. *Th* is wholly different than *th*. Thanks to delimiters and the power of *awk*, we can do some real heavy lifting.

# Pulling It Together: A *bash* Mini-project

To see some of these techniques in action, we will work on a mini-project. Let's take a look at ripping apart an iTunes exported song list file, which is bulky and all but unusable in its standard form. To generate a song list, select *Export Song List…* from the iTunes File menu. Set the file type to Plain Text (see Figure 2.46).

**Figure 2.46** iTunes Song List Export

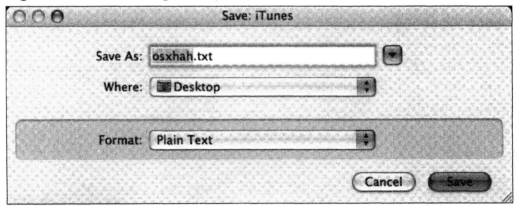

The exported song list file is a real mess, as revealed by the word count (*wc*) command, and the *cat -v* output:

```
j0pb12:~/Desktop johnnylong$ wc -l osxhah.txt
       0 osxhah.txt
```

```
j0pb12:~/Desktop johnnylong$ cat -v osxhah.txt
Name     Artist  Composer        Album    Grouping        Genre   Size     Time
Disc Number  Disc Count      Track Number    Track Count     Year     Date
Modified    Date Added   Bit Rate       Sample Rate    Volume Adjustment
Kind    Equalizer   Comments        Play Count     Last Played    My
Rating        Location^M
```

The first problem with this output file is that the *wc* command lists the file as being zero lines long, due to the lack of UNIX line delimiters. Secondly, there are many useless fields in the file. Third, there are goofy **CONTROL-M** characters (^*M*) all through the line, which are carriage returns. Operating systems end lines in different ways. Windows uses a carriage return followed by a line feed (a throwback to 1960's teletypes), while UNIX streamlines this to a line feed. Most Macs use only a carriage return. When dealing with text files on any platform, this inconsistency is the first thing you will need to overcome, since it can wreak havoc on most UNIX commands. For example, the *cat* command (issued *without* the -*v* option) will list the contents of this file, wrapping up with a line that looks like this:

```
j0pb12:~/Desktop johnnylong$ s:01 Little Green Men.mp3
```

In an attempt to print the carriage return to the screen, the Terminal got confused and wrote part of the file on the same line as the shell prompt. Further, attempting to delete this character with *awk, sed* or *tr* can also create problems, since there is no obvious way to type a **Control-M** (or any other control character) into the shell. This command looks good on paper:

```
j0pb12:~/Desktop johnnylong$ cat osxhah.txt | tr -d '^M'
```

This command would *delete* (the -*d* option to *tr*) any ^*M* characters from the file, but typing this command (along with an actual ^*M*) into the terminal results in a bit of shell goofiness:

```
j0pb12:~/Desktop johnnylong$ cat osxhah.txt | tr -d '
>
```

Remember that the ^*M* is a carriage return. The *bash* shell thinks you hit the **Return** key, and since you did not provide a closing ', assumes you are still typing a *shell* command, and provides a handy subshell to continue your command. **CTRL-C** will take you out of this subshell, but the problem still remains: what about the control characters? Fortunately, control characters can be dealt with fairly easily, thanks to *escape sequences*. An escape sequence is a combination of characters (or keystrokes) that represent a character that is normally not printable (or typeable). Table 2.9 lists some of the most commonly used escape sequences.

**Table 2.9** Common Escape Sequences

| Escape Sequence | Description |
| --- | --- |
| \a | Alert (bell) |
| \b | Backspace |
| \f | Form feed |
| \n | New line |
| \r | Carriage return (aka ^M) |
| \r\n | Carriage return followed by line feed |
| \t | Horizontal tab |
| \\ | Backslash |
| \' | Single quote |

Notes From the Underground…

## Mastering Control Characters With CTRL-V

There is another way to represent a control character in most shells—the direct way. The **CTRL-V** key enters a sort of escape mode, which waits for you to type a control character and then prints it to the screen as a single character. For example, pressing **Control-V** followed immediately by **Control-M** in *bash* will print ^M to the Terminal. However, this is not simply the caret (^) followed by a capital *M*, this is a control character in printed form. You can see proof of this by pressing the **Backspace** key immediately after pressing **Control-M**. One backspace deletes both the caret and the capital *M* at once. This can come in handy when you know what a control character looks like, but cannot locate an escape sequence for it. Be warned, however, that not all programs handle these control character representations in exactly the same way. Some will be happy to accept these representations, while others will balk. *Vi, tr, awk* and *grep* are all happy to accept these representations as control characters.

So, the "shorthand" for the nasty ^M carriage return is simply \r. We can easily turn this "Mac" file into a "UNIX" file with this quick *tr* command:

```
j0pb12:~ $ cat osxhah.txt | tr '\r' '\n' > osxhah-unix.txt

j0pb12:~ $ wc -l osxhah-unix.txt
      10 osxhah-unix.txt
```

This replaced every occurrence of an ^M with a UNIX new line. Notice that the *wc -l* command now recognizes ten distinct lines in the file, one for each of the nine songs in the play list and one header line. Likewise, we can turn this "Mac" file into a "Windows" file with this quick *tr* command:

```
j0pb12:~ $ cat osxhah.txt | tr '\r' '\r\n' > osxhah-windows.txt
j0pb12:~ $ wc -l osxhah-windows.txt
       0 osxhah-windows.txt
```

However, the Windows version of this file contains no UNIX-recognized line breaks, and will be incompatible with our UNIX commands. So, we can first convert our song list file to a UNIX-friendly file, or we can simply inform *awk* about the goofy line delimiters (or as *awk* calls them, *record separators*) in the original file. While we have already seen that field separators are defined via *awk's -F* option, record separators are defined in a slightly different way, via the *-v* option and the *RS* variable name. For example, to properly process our carriage-return delimited file, we could use this command:

```
j0pb12:~ $ awk -v RS='\r' '{print $0}' osxhah.txt | wc -l

10
```

By setting the proper record separator, printing each line, and counting the number of results, we can see that *awk* is now recognizing distinct lines. We can verify this by printing the first field (*$1*) of each record:

```
j0pb12:~ $ awk -v RS='\r' '{print $1}' osxhah.txt
Name
Knocked_Down
Fireproof
Echelon
Wildfire
Me
A
Chapter
A
Little
j0pb12:~/Desktop johnnylong$
```

Obviously, *awk* now properly recognizes line breaks, but judging from the name of the songs listed, there may be a problem with the *field delimiters. Awk* uses a space by default, but viewing the file through *cat -t* reveals that *tabs* (not spaces) are being used to delimit fields:

```
j0pb12:~/Desktop johnnylong$ cat -t osxhah.txt
Name^IArtist^IComposer^IAlbum^IGrouping^IGenre^ISize^ITime^IDisc
Number^IDisc Count^ITrack Number^ITrack Count^IYear^IDate Modified^IDate
Added^IBit Rate^ISample Rate^IVolume
Adjustment^IKind^IEqualizer^IComments^IPlay Count^ILast Played^IMy
Rating^ILocation^M
```

When executed with this option, *cat* displays control characters as printed equivalents, and tabs as the ^*I* character. Setting the record separator as \r and the field separator as \t (tab), we begin to see quite a bit of progress in wrangling the song list file:

```
j0pb12:~ $ awk -F'\t' -v RS='\r' '{print $1}' osxhah.txt
Name
Knocked_Down
Fireproof
Echelon
Wildfire
Me Against Me
A toast to my former Self
Chapter 2
A Shadow On Me
Little Green Men
```

Now, it's taken quite a bit of page space to describe this process, but once you get the hang of thinking in terms of *record* and *field* separators, *awk* can be wielded for insanely powerful results. The nasty song list file can now be tossed around with very little effort. For example, we can poke through the headers to find the ones we're interested in:

```
j0pb12:~/ $ awk -F'\t' -v RS='\r' '{print $1}' osxhah.txt | head -1
Name
j0pb12:~/ $ awk -F'\t' -v RS='\r' '{print $2}' osxhah.txt | head -1
Artist
j0pb12:~/ $ awk -F'\t' -v RS='\r' '{print $3}' osxhah.txt | head -1
Composer
```

The *head -1* command is used to show only the first line of the output file. Therefore, to see only the artist and the name of the song, in that order, separated by a colon, we can use a quick *awk* command:

```
j0pb12:~/ $ awk -F'\t' -v RS='\r' '{print $2": "$1}' osxhah.txt
Artist: Name
Disciple: Knocked_Down
Pillar: Fireproof
Pillar: Echelon
P.O.D.: Wildfire
Project 86: Me Against Me
Project 86: A toast to my former Self
Project 86: Chapter 2
Project 86: A Shadow On Me
Project 86: Little Green Men
```

Notice that we've re-ordered the fields (artist printed first, followed by song title) and that a colon and a space were inserted after the artist name by simply inserting them in the print statement, surrounded by quotes. Re-ordering fields is a no-brainer with *awk*, and inserting text is simple as well, thanks to the *print* statement. Changing *awk's print* statement to '*{print $1": "$2}*' would print the song title first, followed by the artist name.

Simple text insertion is nice, but we can do so much more that simple text-based output. We could, for example, print each line as basic HTML, displaying the artist name in bold text, and inserting an HTML break (*<BR>*) after each line (see Figure 2.47). The backslash character has been used to break a single line of *bash* into two, which is more visually appealing parts.

## Figure 2.47 iTunes Song List To Ugly HTML With *awk*

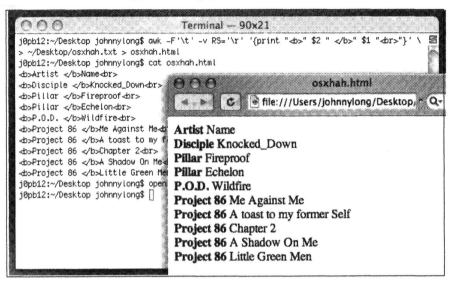

This *awk* command used the *print* statement to print both static text and *awk* variables. Static text is enclosed in double-quotes while *awk* variables are not. This *awk* command did a great job printing the *<b>* tag, the artist name, the song title, and the trailing *<br>* tag, but the output is ugly. A table would look nicer, but the format of a table is a bit more complex, as shown in this skeleton of an HTML table:

```
<HTML>
<TABLE BORDER=1>
<TR><TD>Artist </TD><TD>Name </TD></TR>
</TABLE>
</HTML>
```

To create a table, we need to insert the *<TR>*, *</TR>*, *<TD>*. *and </TD>* tags on each line of output, and we need to print the *<HTML>* and *<TABLE>* tags at the beginning and the *</TABLE>* and *</HTML>* tags at the end of the HTML. We could build an HTML file by echoing tags into a file, appending the *awk* script's output to that file, and appending the closing tags, using commands like *echo* alongside *awk,* but this is tedious. *Awk* can handle this behavior with the *BEGIN* and *END* functions. The *BEGIN* function executes once, before *awk* starts processing the input file, and the *END* function executes once after the input file has been processed. This would allow us to print the "head" and "tail" of our HTML file with ease. The script itself would look like this:

```
'BEGIN {print"<HTML><TABLE border=1>"}


{print "<tr><td>" $2"</td><td>"$1"</td></tr>"}


END {print "</table></HTML>"}'
```

This script (like all *awk* scripts) can be run on one line, and the output written to a file, as shown in Figure 2.48:

**Figure 2.48** iTunes Song List To HTML Table With *awk*

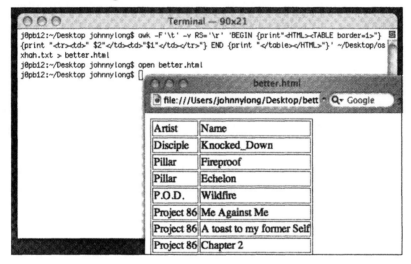

Having performed this task from the command line, a single shell script can be written (or cut and pasted) that accepts the name of an output file, and automatically opens it in Safari:

```
j0pb12:~/Desktop johnnylong$ cat convert_songlist.sh
# Build a table-based HTML file based on iTunes song list


# If no output file is supplied, call it "out.html"
test $# -eq "0" && OUTPUT_FILE=out.html || OUTPUT_FILE=$1


echo "Writing to $OUTPUT_FILE..."


# Record Separator = \r, Field Separator = \t
# Output HTML Table
```

```
awk -F'\t' -v RS='\r' '\
BEGIN {print"<HTML><TABLE border=1>"} \
      {print "<tr><td>" $2"</td><td>"$1"</td></tr>"} \
END   {print "</table></HTML>"}' ~/Desktop/osxhah.txt > $OUTPUT_FILE

echo "Writing to $OUTPUT_FILE..."

open $OUTPUT_FILE
```

Of course, there's no end to the amount of automation you can employ, including AppleScripting the iTunes file export, but at some point, it's best to leave well enough alone and move on to more pressing (or interesting) automation tasks. And while there are certainly other ways to produce this song list output, the skills presented apply well to many different tasks, and show how UNIX tools can be used together to obtain great results.

# Curl

*Curl* is a tool designed to transfer data from a server using various protocols including HTTP, HTTPS, FTP and others. It can run without user interaction as long as the parameters required to complete the transaction are supplied at the command line. The basic use of *curl* requires the name of a remote file and the *-o* option to save the file as a supplied name, or the *-O* option to download the file using the name used on the remote server. This example downloads an HTML file from a remote Web server:

```
j0pb12:~ $ curl -O http://gimbo.org.uk/archives/2004/01/mac_os_x_for_ha.html
  % Total    % Received % Xferd  Average Speed   Time    Time     Time
Current

                                 Dload  Upload   Total   Spent    Left
Speed
100  8331    0  8331    0     0   1683      0 --:--:--  0:00:04 --:--:--
2306

j0pb12:~ $ head -5 mac_os_x_for_ha.html
<!DOCTYPE html PUBLIC "-//W3C//DTD XHTML 1.0 Transitional//EN"
"http://www.w3.org/TR/xhtml1/DTD/xhtml1-transitional.dtd">

<html xmlns="http://www.w3.org/1999/xhtml">
  <head>
  <title>Gimboland: Mac OS X for hackers</title>
```

*Curl* has many cool features, including the ability to download groups of files with a similar name. This example downloads two JPEG images (*01.jpg* and *02.jpg*) from the Syngress.com Web site:

```
j0pb12:~ $ curl -O http://www.syngress.com/vegas/[01-02].jpg
```

```
[1/2]: http://www.syngress.com/vegas/01.jpg -| 01.jpg
--_curl_--http://www.syngress.com/vegas/01.jpg
 % Total    % Received % Xferd  Average Speed   Time    Time     Time
Current
                                Dload  Upload   Total   Spent    Left
Speed
100  308k  100  308k    0     0  40983      0  0:00:07  0:00:07 --:--:--
43476
```

```
[2/2]: http://www.syngress.com/vegas/02.jpg -| 02.jpg
--_curl_--http://www.syngress.com/vegas/02.jpg
100  468k  100  468k    0     0  40107      0  0:00:11  0:00:11 --:--:--
34639
```

*Curl* interpreted a portion of the URL (*[01-02].jpg*) as referring to two specific files, downloading and saving them accordingly. This type of expansion can be performed on any part of a URL, and can use alphabetic characters to walk though a series of letters, allowing you to download a large number of related files with a single command.

# Lynx

*Lynx* is a command line Web browser that can be installed via various package management utilities. See the Chapter 5, *Penetration Testing*, for more details. Like *curl, lynx* can be used to access Web-based content with relative ease. *Lynx* has several unique and interesting features, including the ability to *display* a Web page as it might appear in a browser. This can make it easy to extract, or *scrape*, data from the Web page. For example, a typical Google results page is fairly uncluttered (see Figure 2.49).

**Figure 2.49** Google Results Pages are Prime For Scraping

However, if you are interested in getting to the results line of this page to determine the number of hits for this search term, a *curl*-saved HTML file can be very difficult to search:

```
j0pb12:~/ $ curl
"http://www.google.com/search?&safe=active&q=%22OS+X+For+Hackers%22" -A lynx
-s -o output.html
j0pb12:~/Desktop johnnylong$ grep Results output.html
<table width=100% border=0 cellpadding=0 cellspacing=0><tr><td
bgcolor=#3366cc><img width=1 height=1 alt=""></td></tr></table><table
width=100% border=0 cellpadding=0 cellspacing=0 bgcolor=#e5ecf9><tr><td
bgcolor=#e5ecf9 nowrap><font size=+1> <b>Web</b></font> </td><td
bgcolor=#e5ecf9 align=right nowrap ><font size=-1>Results <b>1</b> -
<b>10</b> of about <b>151</b> for <b><b>&quot;
```

The results of this *grep* statement (cut for brevity) are difficult to parse through, but the displayed version of the page (accessible with *lynx's -dump* option) makes the job a snap:

```
j0pb12:~/ $ lynx -useragent lynx -dump \
"http://www.google.com/search?q=%22OS+X+For+Hackers%22" | grep Results
    Web  Results 1 - 10 of about 145 for "[10]OS [11]X For [12]Hackers".
```

By pasting the Google query from the browser into a *lynx* command, we can get to the *Results* line very quickly. Putting this into some creative *awk* commands, we can get the total results string:

```
j0pb12:~/Desktop johnnylong$ lynx -useragent lynx -dump \
"http://www.google.com/search?q=%22OS+X+For+Hackers%22" | \
grep Results | awk '{print $2": "$8}'
Results: 145
```

The *lynx* dump output is also handy, as it displays a list of referenced links ; which is easily accessed with a *grep* statement that displays everything (at least 10000 lines) after the word *References* in the output file:

```
j0pb12:~/Desktop johnnylong$ lynx -useragent lynx -dump \
"http://www.google.com/search?q=%22OS+X+For+Hackers%22" | \
grep -A 10000 References

References


   1. http://www.google.com/webhp?hl=en
   2. http://images.google.com/images?q=%22OS+X+For+Hackers%22&sa=N&tab=wi
   3. http://groups.google.com/groups?q=%22OS+X+For+Hackers%22&sa=N&tab=wg
   4. http://news.google.com/news?q=%22OS+X+For+Hackers%22&sa=N&tab=wn
   5. http://froogle.google.com/froogle?q=%22OS+X+For+Hackers%22&sa=N&tab=wf
[cut]
```

A quick *awk* statement, a *grep* to chop out the Google links, and a *sort* (with *-u* for *unique* lines) will show only the unique non-Google links. This type of script can be used to siphon off the outbound links from pretty much any Web page:

```
j0pb12:~/ $ lynx -useragent lynx -dump \
"http://www.google.com/search?q=%22OS+X+For+Hackers%22" | \
grep -A 10000 References | awk '{print $2}' | \
grep -v "google.com\|cache" | sort -u

http://gimbo.org.uk/archives/2004/01/mac_os_x_for_ha.html
http://www.bookpool.com/sm/1597490407
http://www.bookpool.com/ss/140?su=osx
http://www.comcol.nl/idxd.php?anr=51823
http://www.compman.co.uk/htmlcat/1597490407_OS_X_for_Hackers_at_Heart.asp
http://www.elx.com.au/item/1597490407
http://www.oreilly.com/catalog/1597490407/
http://www.oreillynet.com/cs/catalog/view/au/1918
http://www.syngress.com/catalog/?pid=3430
http://www.woodslane.com.au/woodslane/searchresults.asp?isbn=1597490407
```

If you see something interesting in the browser view of a Web page and are interested in extracting data from it, *lynx's -dump* option may be the easiest way to scrape that information.

# Bridging the Gap From *bash* to AppleScript

Now that we have seen the capabilities of AppleScript and the power of the UNIX shell *bash*, let's harness the power of the two combined. AppleScript can be executed from the shell with the help of the *osascript* command (see Figure 2.50).

**Figure 2.50** osascript Executing AppleScript From the UNIX Shell

```
                        Terminal — 82x9
j0pb12:~ johnnylong$ osascript
tell app "Safari"
  activate
  make new document
  set the url of the front document to "http://www.project86.com"
end tell
j0pb12:~ johnnylong$
```

The *osascript* command accepts lines of AppleScript. After entering the AppleScript, pressing the **Control-D** key executes the script. This particular script will launch Safari, create a new window, and connect to *www.project86.com*. Although this may seem primitive and awkward when compared to the Script Editor's slick interface and interaction, this process can be streamlined by wrapping both the AppleScript and the *osacript* command inside a shell script. By taking advantage of UNIX redirections, we can feed multiple lines of AppleScript into *osascript*. Consider the following shell script:

```
1.      osascript <<EOF
2.      tell app "Safari"
3.      activate
4.      make new document
5.      set the url of the front document to "http://www.project86.com"
6.      end tell
7.      EOF
8.      echo "All done!"
```

The first line of this script will take all the following lines (up to the EOF line) and feed them to *osascript*, which will execute them. After the AppleScript is finished loading, "All done!" is written to the console. This seems rather simplistic, but what we have done is significant: we have bounced back and forth from AppleScript to UNIX shell script within a single *bash* shell script. We could bounce between AppleScript and shell many times in the same script, but this is meaningless unless we can pass parameters between the two. Passing shell parameters into our AppleScript program is relatively easy via the standard *$1* shell variable. Remember that *$1* in the UNIX shell refers to the first parameter passed to the script. By changing line 5 in the above script, we can instruct Safari to load a user-supplied URL from the command line:

```
5.    set the url of the front document to "$1"
```

Our script will load either the page provided on the command line (see Figure 2.51) or a blank page. This works because the UNIX shell script expands all variables (e.g., *$1*, *$2*, *$#*, and so forth) to their real values before feeding them into *osascript*.

**Figure 2.51** Parameter-aware *osascript*

# Using Bash, AppleScript, and Automator Together!

Each of the automation solutions we have discussed has its strong points. Automator presents extremely polished-looking user interface dialogs with drag-and-drop simplicity, but is limited to performing the actions coded by software developers. AppleScript provides excellent control over many different applications and is very powerful, but presents a steeper learning curve and makes user interface details more difficult to obtain. *Bash* scripting is extremely powerful and is limited only by the programmer's imagination and the capability of installed programs, but can be very frustrating for non-technical users, presenting a *very* steep learning curve. One of the best ways to get the best of both worlds is to integrate all three of these solutions, allowing an automation environment that is relatively easy to master, well-polished from a user's perspective, and quite powerful.

This section explores ways that *bash*, *AppleScript*, and *Automator* can be integrated, allowing you to do all sorts of cool tricks. We will discuss a few tidbits that will help you automate tasks, whip up handy front-ends for command-line software, and pass data back and forth between these three automation solutions.

# Overcoming Automator's Lame Display Dialogs

One of the frustrating limitations of Automator is its apparent inability to simply display interactive messages to the screen. AppleScript's *display dialog* command, on the other hand, is more powerful and flexible. Thanks to the *Run AppleScript* action, we can use AppleScript dialogs within Automator (see Figure 2.52).

**Figure 2.52** Generating An AppleScript Dialog From Automator

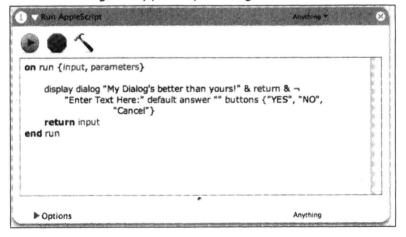

Of course, what good is a dialog if it doesn't interact with anything? We'll need a way to pass data into an Automator action, and a way to pass data out of an Automator action.

# Exchanging Data With AppleScript

Since we'll be using Automator as the framework for our automation tasks, we'll need to discuss how, exactly, to pass data between Automator, AppleScript and *bash*. Figure 2.53 shows how data can be passed from an Automator action into AppleScript.

**Figure 2.53** Sending Data From Automator to AppleScript

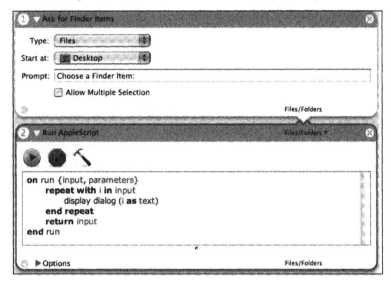

The first action in this workflow prompts the user for Finder items using Automator's slick dialog. The AppleScript in the second action catches the filename as the *input* variable and displays it in a dialog window, as shown in Figure 2.54. The *return input* line passes the filename onto the third action.

**Figure 2.54** Simple AppleScript Dialog Box

This file-naming convention may seem foreign to most, because the file name is written in a Unique, Universal, and Uniform character enCoding *(UNICODE)* format. The format is rather straightforward, describing the file as the volume name of the disk, the full path, and the file name, respectively, separated by colons. AppleScript recognizes this as a valid file name, and a line such as *tell application "Finder" to open i* inserted after the *display dialog* command in this script will open the selected file using the default application. Of course Automator honors this naming convention as well, and a third action like the one shown in Figure 2.55 would open the file with the default application as well.

**Figure 2.55** A Third Action Readily Accepts UNICODE

In summary, AppleScript uses the input variable to capture data from an action, and the return command to pass *data into* the following action. *Return* statements can also be used to pass multiple values in just about any format. A command such as *return "1" & "," & "2"* would pass the string *"1,2"* onto the following action. The following action would then be required to break this data apart into meaningful strings.

# Exchanging Data With *Bash*

Passing data into a *bash* script is relatively easy, but *bash* isn't too happy about a UNICODE naming convention. *Bash* would be much happier with a Portable Operating System Interface (POSIX)-formatted file name. Thankfully, this conversion is relatively simple (see Figure 2.56).

**Figure 2.56** UNICODE Filename Translation to POSIX

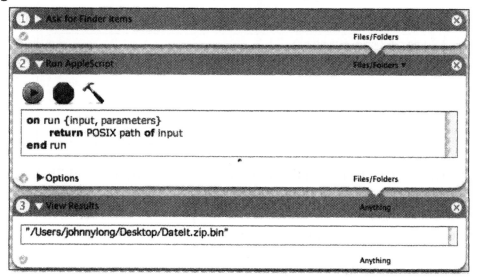

This workflow's first action prompts the user to select a file. The second action's AppleScript then converts the filename into a POISX format and passes it to the next action with *return POSIX path of input*. A *Run Shell Script* action could accept this filename as shown in Figure 2.57.

**Figure 2.57** The Handoff To *Bash*

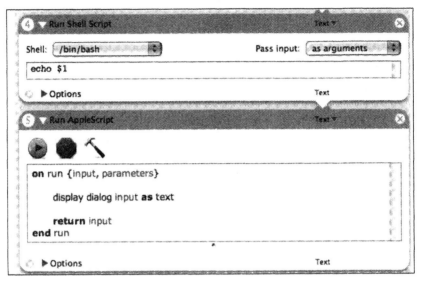

When the *Pass Input* dropdown is set to *as arguments*, the Run Shell Script action accepts the input as any standard shell script; through *$ variables*. Since *$1* is the first argument, the fourth action simply echoes this value. In a standard shell, this would be displayed to the screen, but embedded in an action, any output written from a shell will be forward to the next action as *text*. The fifth action displays this value to the screen with a standard dialog. Although this seems crude (and admittedly a bit pointless), the combination of Automator, AppleScript and *bash* is extremely powerful. In the next sections we'll have some fun as we automate some cool tasks, and put a new face on same previously bland ones.

# Ethereal Auto-Launcher

In the *OS X For Pen Testers* chapter, we discuss *fink* and describe how it can be used to install powerful tools like the Ethereal packet analyzer. Ethereal "sniffs" packets on a network and analyzes them, presenting them in a graphical interface for analysis. Once XWindows and *fink* is installed, Ethereal can be installed with two simple commands: *fink install gtk+2* and *fink install ethereal*. However, once Ethereal is installed, it can be a bit of a pain to actually launch. First, XWindows must be launched. After XWindows successfully launches, Ethereal must be launched with a command like */sw/bin/ethereal*, but to streamline the process it's best to determine which interface to sniff from. This requires the use of a command like *ifconfig* to determine available interfaces. Ethereal could then be launched in auto-capture mode with a command like */sw/bin/ethereal -k -i en1* to capture data from interface *en1*. To make matters even more complex, Ethereal should be run as root through the *sudo* command.

This is all quite a bit tedious, but a bit of AppleScript entered into Script Editor (Figure 2.58) can accomplish the same task. When saved as an application, this script makes Ethereal's launch a simple double-click affair.

**Figure 2.58** Ethereal Auto-launcher Written in AppleScript and *bash*

```
1.     tell application "Finder"

2.     activate

3.     open application file "X11.app" of folder "Utilities" of folder
"Applications" of startup disk

4.     end tell


5.     set available to do shell script "ifconfig | grep UP | awk -F':'
'{print $1}' "


6.     display dialog ("Available Interfaces:" & return & available as text)
& return & "Pick one!" default answer "en1"


7.     set interface to text returned of result


8.     tell application "X11" to activate
9.     do shell script "export DISPLAY=:0; /sw/bin/ethereal -k -i" &
interface with administrator privileges
```

The first section of this script began as a recording. With Script Editor's record mode engaged, the XWindows (X11) application was launched, and after the extraneous Finder lines were removed, produced lines 1 through 4, which launches the X11 application.

Line 5 runs *ifconfig*, capturing all *UP* interfaces, extracts the interface number (thanks to the *awk* tricks learned earlier), and places the results in the variable available.

Line 6 displays the available interfaces (Figure 2.59), prompting the user to select an interface, and in line 7, the result is stored in the variable *interface*.

Lines 8 activates the X11 application, and line 9 runs Ethereal with the *-k* (auto capture) and *-i* (select interface) options, providing the name of the interface just as the user entered it. To avoid having to use *sudo* to become root, *with administrator privileges* runs to command as an Administrator, assuming the user types the correct Administrative password.

**Figure 2.59** Ethereal Auto-launcher Interface Selection

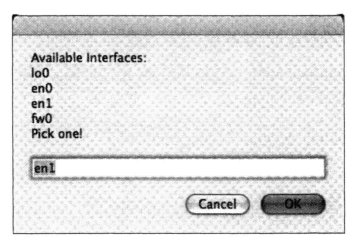

## Password-protected Zip and Unzip

Although Mac OS X has a *zip* and *unzip* command installed in */usr/bin*, they do not support password-protected zip files. Double-clicking a password-protected zip file in Finder produces the error message shown in Figure 2.60.

**Figure 2.60** OS X Dislikes Password-protected Zip Files

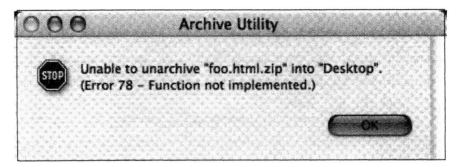

However, thanks to the package-management utilities discussed in Chapter 5, *OS X For Pen Testers*, a password-capable version of the zip utilities can be installed with a simple command such as *fink install zip-ssl*. This will install a version of both *zip* and *unzip* in the */sw/bin* directory. Using the *-P* (password) option, the file *foo.html* could be stored in a password-protected zip with a command like */sw/bin/zip -P PASSWORD foo.html.zip foo.html*. The file could then be extracted with a command such as */sw/bin/unzip -o -P PASSWORD foo.html.zip*. Although these commands can be run from a Terminal prompt, the combination of Automator, AppleScript, and *bash* allows us to create an application (or Finder plug-in) to accomplish this task. The application will be framed in Automator, so a logical first action is the "Get Selected Finder Items," which will pass the selected finder items into the workflow. Our goal is to create a Finder plug-in, allowing right-click access to the application, and this action is well suited for capturing the selected items.

The first obstacle to overcome is determining whether or not the selected Finder item is already a zip file. If it is, the script should present the user the option to either *zip* or *unzip* the file. This is accomplished with AppleScript:

```
1.      on run {input, parameters}
2.          set file_name to POSIX path of (input as text)
3.          set operation to "Zip"

4.          if (file_name) ends with ".zip" then
5.              display dialog "This is a zip file! What should I do?" & return
& "Clicking Unzip will overwrite existing files!" buttons {"Unzip", "Zip",
"Cancel"}
6.              set operation to the button returned of result
7.      end if
```

The first line (inserted automatically when the *Run AppleScript* action is selected) grabs the input, in this case the file name, from the first action. The second line stores this value as *file_name* after first converting it to a POSIX file, which our later *bash* script can better handle. The third line sets the variable *operation* to *Zip*. We will use this variable to keep track of whether the user wants to *zip or unzip* the selected file. Line four checks to see if the file name ends with *.zip*. If it does, line five displays the dialog shown in Figure 2.61, informing the user that a zip file was selected and prompting him or her to select *Zip*, *Unzip*, or *Cancel*. Notice the use of return to indicate a line break in the dialog box. Line six sets the variable operation to the name of the clicked button, which we will use to select between the *zip* and *unzip* programs. If *Cancel* is selected, the workflow will terminate.

**Figure 2.61** Prompting the User To Select a Zip Operation

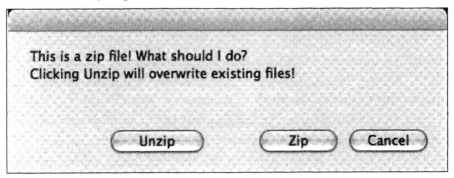

The next task is to determine what password to use to zip or unzip the file. This is handled with a bit more AppleScript, all of which will be housed in a single Automator action:

```
1.    display dialog "Enter password for" & file_name & ": " & ¬ return &
return default answer ""

2.    set zip_password to the text returned of result

3.    return (file_name & "," & zip_password & "," & operation) as list

4.    end run
```

The first line presents the dialog shown in Figure 2.62, which prompts the user for a password. This password is stored in the variable *zip_password* in line two. Line three uses *return* to form a string that passes all of the collected data into the next action. Notice the use of the *&* character to build a return string. If the user selected *the /tmp/foo.zip* file, clicked the *Unzip* button, and entered a password of *PASSWORD*, the return string would look like *{/tmp/foo.zip,PASSWORD,Unzip}*. The curly braces will not appear in the actual data string. This string will be used by the next action in the workflow, which will do the real magic.

**Figure 2.62** The Password Prompt

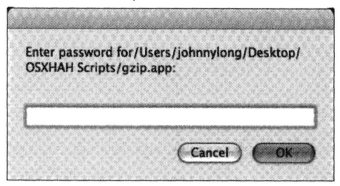

Inserting View Action is a great way of debugging a workflow; This action does not affect the data that flows through it, so it should be used often. After inserting View Action, the first three actions of the workflow can be seen in Figure 2.63.

**Figure 2.63** The Beginning of a Powerful Workflow

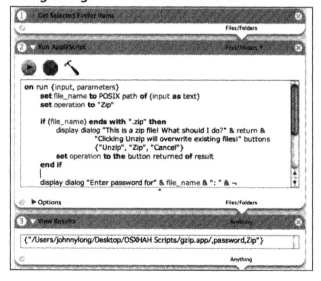

Once the file has been selected, an operation (whether *Zip* or *Unzip*) has been selected, and a password has been entered, the workflow must now delve into a *Run Shell Script* action, which will do the heavy lifting. Since the last action bunched together all the data, the first task for the shell script is to unpack the data. Since the data is delimited by commas, this can be done in three quick *awk* commands, one for each variable:

```
1.      file_name=`echo $1 | awk -F"," '{print $1}' | sed 's/\/$//'`
2.      password=`echo $1 | awk -F"," '{print $2}'`
3.      operation=`echo $1 | awk -F"," '{print $3}'`
```

Each of these lines assigns a variable, which is the result of running a bit of shell script. Notices the use of the *grave* symbol around each shell command. As we discussed earlier, this indicates that the *result* of each script is to be assigned to each variable in turn. Since *$1* holds the entire parameter passed from AppleScript, we can use *awk* to break this into distinct pieces. For example, if $1 contains */tmp/foo.zip,PASSWORD,Unzip* we can use the comma as a delimiter (*-F","*) and view the parameter as three distinct strings. *Awk's $1* would contain */tmp/foo.zip*, *$2* would contain *PASSWORD*, and *$3* would contain *Unzip*. These strings would then be assigned to *bash's* *$file_name*, *$password*, and *$operation*, respectively. The *file_name* gets one bit of additional massaging, as any trailing *forward-slash* (remember that *$* in a string represents an end-of-line, therefore *$/*, or *\/$* in a sed string) is removed from the name. This is extremely handy, since it allows the user to select a *folder* as a file name, and the application can zip the contents of the folder without a problem. This one blob of *sed* expands the usefulness of the application. With the variables effectively captured in *bash,* it's time to do the actual *zip* and *unzip.* Continuing with the *bash* script:

```
1.      if [ $operation = "Unzip" ]; then

2.          /sw/bin/unzip -o -P $password "$file_name" 2>&1 && echo
"...Completed!" || echo "...Error!"

3.      else

4.          /sw/bin/zip -r -P $password "$file_name".zip "$file_name" 2>&1 &&
echo "...Completed!" || echo "...Error!"

5.      fi
```

First, the script checks to see if the user selected an *Unzip* operation in line one. If so, the script executes (line 2) a properly formatted *unzip* command, providing the overwrite option (*-o*), the password option (*-P*) with the password filled in, and the name of the zip file to extract. The error messages are sent to the "screen" (*2>&1*) so that the user can view any output and errors, and ...*Completed!* is written if the command succeeds (*&& echo*

"...*Completed*"). If the command fails, ...*Error!* is written to the screen ( | |
*echo* "...*Error!*"). Likewise, the *zip* command line is executed in line four if the
user had not selected to *Unzip*. The recursive (-*r*) option is provided to allow
for zipping of directories (and bundled applications), and the name of the zip
file is created by adding *.zip* to the end of the original file name.

Once this script completes, a lot of stuff is written to the "screen," but
since this is an Automator workflow, the text is simply forwarded to the next
action. Since it is not a bad idea to debug the workflow, a *View Results* line
would be handy, followed by a *Run AppleScript* action to display the results,
which would look similar to the dialog shown in Figure 2.64

**Figure 2.64** Password Protected Zip Output

The completed workflow is shown in Figure 2.65, complete with *View
Results* actions that show the progression of the workflow.

**Figure 2.65** Completed Password-protected Zip Workflow

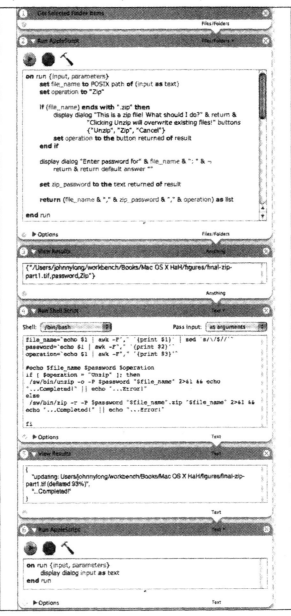

This workflow encompasses many of the techniques we have discussed in this chapter, and makes quick work out of an otherwise complex programming task. We have done little in the way of error checking, although little effort is required. Automator's "Get Selected Finder Items" action forces users to select a valid file. AppleScript's *Zip/Unzip* dialog allows for only two choices (not including the cancel option process), and the *bash* script makes quick work of oddball characters in a file name due to the fact that the characters are enclosed in double quotes. While there are certainly things that can wrong with this script, it is easy to assemble, has a decent enough GUI, and when saved as a Finder plug-in (as shown in Figure 2.66), the application is never more than a mouse-click away.

**Figure 2.66** Password-enabled Zip Finder Plug-in

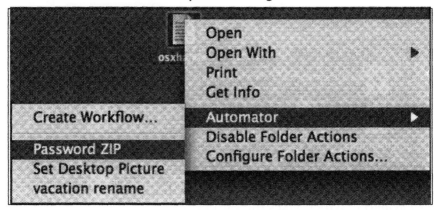

# Basic *nmap* Front-end

The *nmap* program by Fyodor, available from *www.insecure.org*, is the industry-standard port scanner. Although *nmap* has many excellent features, in its most basic configuration it can be used to determine which ports are listening on a remote machine. Nmap can be installed in a variety of ways, as discussed in Chapter 5, but once installed, it can be used to scan the address 192.168.1.1, by entering the command */sw/bin/nmap 192.168.1.1*. A very simple front-end for *nmap* can be built with the workflow (see Figure 2.67).

**Figure 2.67** A Basic *nmap* Front-end

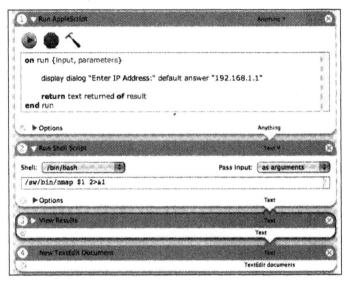

This workflow displays an AppleScript dialog (as shown in Figure 2.68), which prompts for *nmap* parameters. Whatever is typed into this dialog is sent to *nmap* as arguments, and the results are sent through *View Results* to *New TextEdit Document,,* which takes the output text and sends it to a new TextEdit document, which is automatically opened (see Figure 2.69). This document can then be saved or deleted as needed.

**Figure 2.68** Prompt For *nmap* Parameters

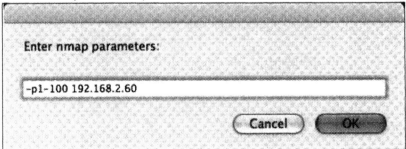

**Figure 2.69** *nmap* Report

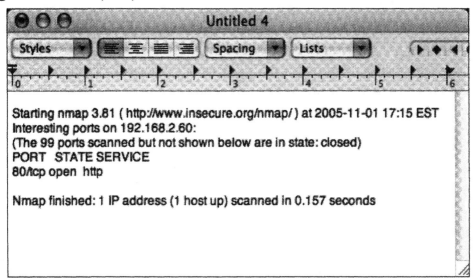

This basic workflow can be used to automate all kinds of command-line programs and is very versatile. This workflow also emphasizes how powerful and simple it can be to combine Automator, AppleScript, and the *bash* shell.

# Summary

Automator provides simple drag-and-drop automation capabilities, and is ideal for automating many simple tasks. With a slick-looking interface and pleasing, user-friendly dialogs, Automator is a great choice, especially for the user with only basic automation needs. Automator actions are provided by software developers, although advanced users with programming knowledge can create custom actions.

AppleScript is a very powerful, easy-to-read language designed to automate Mac tasks. GUIs for most applications can be controlled from AppleScript, and most application functionality is accessible with AppleScript. To fully engage the power of AppleScript requires some diligence, and a programming background is recommended.

The *bash* shell is extremely powerful, and any advanced user will find it to be an extremely versatile method of executing tasks and performing administrative activities. The *bash* shell was designed by techies for techies; thus, the syntax and structure of *bash* shell scripting may be foreign to most beginners.

The combination of these three technologies provides a wealth of capabilities to the upstart and seasoned user alike. By combining AppleScript functions and shell (*bash, PERL, PYTHON*) programs and scripts into the workflow provided by Automator, Apple has provided its users with a powerful and extensible automation solution.

# Solutions Fast Track

## Using Automator

- ☑  Simple Drag-and-drop automation creator
- ☑  Uses actions put together into a workflow to create applications
- ☑  Limited to software vendor supplied actions

## Understanding AppleScript

- ☑  Powerful, flexible scripting language
- ☑  Advanced use requires a familiarity with programming

## Bash Scripting

☑ Powerful, flexible, dangerous for beginners

☑ Created *by* techies *for* techies

☑ Basic usage requires little more than perusing man (manual_ pages

☑ Relies on many system commands such as PERL, awk, sed, and grep to derive it's power.

# Links to Sites

- developer.apple.com/documentation

- www.apple.com/applescript/guidebook/sbrt/index.html: AppleScript Guidebook: Essential Sub-Routines

- www.dougscripts.com/itunes/

- macscripter.net/faq ; the Mac Scripter AppleScript FAQ

- *http://bbs.applescript.net/*;  the Mac Scripter Bulletin Board System (BBS)

# Frequently Asked Questions

The following Frequently Asked Questions, answered by the authors of this book, are designed to both measure your understanding of the concepts presented in this chapter and to assist you with real-life implementation of these concepts. To have your questions about this chapter answered by the author, browse to **www.syngress.com/solutions** and click on the **"Ask the Author"** form.

**Q:** How can I get a hold of new Automator actions?

**A:** Software developers create actions and bundle them with Mac OS X applications. You should check in with your software developer to find out when new actions are released. Actions will appear in Automator when an application containing them is added to the system.

**Q:** Why do I get a quick message box flashing on the screen when I run an application I developed?

**A:** In most cases, this occurs when running an application outside of Script Editor. Run the application in Script Editor to ctch the message.

**Q:** Why does an application I created have a has a non-standard icon, and why is it not working outside Automator?

**A:** Automator has bugs. Seriously, Automator is a relatively new application, with lots of cool things happening behind the drag-and-drop interface. With all Automator's doing, it's no wonder it flakes out every now and again. Keep a watch out for updates to Automator, and until all the bugs are worked out, plan on seeing weird stuff every so often.

# Chapter 3

## OS X in a Microsoft Environment

### Solutions in this chapter:

- Accessing Network File Systems
- NTLM Authentication
- Connecting to a Windows PPTP Server
- Zen of Running Windows Boxes from a Mac

☑ Summary

☑ Solutions Fast Track

☑ Frequently Asked Questions

# Introduction

Macintosh and Windows systems today are a lot friendlier with each other than they were in the days of yore. The first version of Mac OS that I used in a corporate environment was 7.6.1. Back then, you could turn on Apple file sharing on your NT server and that was about it. There were third-party apps to access Apple files shares from Windows, and vice versa, but built-in support was limited.

With OS X, Apple was able to introduce the Samba project into their operating system, taking advantage of the years of work the Samba team has done to make UNIX and Windows play nice on file sharing, printing, and authentication.

This chapter examines the tools, hacks, and general knowledge that have been found useful using OS X in Windows centric environments. Keep in mind that a lot of the interoperability OS X has gained comes from open source projects that were originally started on Linux or BSD derivatives. A lot, although not all, of what is discussed in this chapter can be applied to Linux and the BSDs as well.

It's unavoidable that if you work in Windows shop there are going to be times when you need to use a Windows PC. Hopefully this chapter will reduce frequency of those times.

This chapter briefly touches on some complex protocols and systems, most of which have books dedicated to explaining them. With that in mind, when a new protocol or system is introduced there will be a brief explanation of how it works and then move on to getting you bootstrapped and working. It is highly encourage that you to let your curiosity motivate you to explore these topics more in depth. Being able to perform tasks and getting work done is only part of the battle; having a strong fundamental understanding of how things work will take you to the next level and give you the ability to discover new tricks of the trade on your own.

## Who Should Read this Chapter?

This chapter covers a wide variety of topics. Some of the topics are basic survival skills while some involve nitty-gritty network details. If you are a power user feel free to skip around if you are all ready familiar with some of the subject matter. At the same time, if you are a networking newbie don't let the terms *IP address* and *Active Directory* scare you away. The solutions in this chapter focus on getting you up and running.

# Windows Terms You Should Know

If you are reading this, chances are you're a dedicated Mac user. There is terminology in this chapter that you might not be familiar with. As the chapter progresses, the terms and technology will be explained as they are encountered.

One thing that should be covered up-front is the concept of *Active Directory* and Windows *domains*. These terms are used quite a bit; therefore, it is important that you know what they mean.

*Active Directory* is a Microsoft architecture for managing computers, printers, users, groups and much more. The backbone of Active Directory is servers called *domain controllers* (DCs). Domain controllers contain all the information about resources in the Active Directory. This includes but is not limited to Windows XP workstations, servers, printers, user accounts, and security privileges. In addition, Active Directory provides centralized authentication for all of these objects. Once you have an account in the Active Directory a system administrator can assign you access to any object in the Active Directory. You can be granted privileges to print to one printer, access a co-workers computer, log into various websites, all with a single username and password stored in the Active Directory.

Windows computers can operate without Active Directory. These computers are said to be running in *workgroup* mode or *standalone* mode. The main difference is that you only need one account in Active Directory, but if you have a group of computers in workgroup mode, you will need to grant access and create accounts on each separate machine. As you can imagine, the latter can get tedious as the number of machines you manage grows.

In Windows shops you will hear the word domain mentioned a lot. Previous to Active Directory, in the days of Windows NT 4, the architecture for integrating Windows computers was called a domain. Think of the NT domain as the predecessor to the Active Directory. However, it can be confusing because the term is still used in Active Directory. Domains are subsets of the Active Directory. If you have an account in Active Directory, it belongs to a domain, and you will need to know what the domain name is because it is usually required for authenticating to Windows systems from a Mac.

Figure 3.1 illustrates a very simple Active Directory network with four servers and two clients. Two of the servers are domain controllers, which provide authentication for people logging into Windows workstations and provide access to resources on Windows servers. When a user logs into his or her Windows machine, the domain controller is contacted and confirms that the user supplied proper login credentials. For the configuration used in all of the examples, login access to the OS X machine is handled by the local account on the computer, however access to file shares residing on Windows servers is handled by the domain controllers. The file servers are where the actual network file systems being connected to reside.

Long story short, if you intend to use the tools in this chapter in a Windows Active Directory environment, three things you should definitely know are your:

- Username
- Password
- The name of the domain your account belongs to

If you are using an environment without Active Directory and your Windows computers are in workgroup mode, you will just need your username and password.

What about Apple? Do they have an equivalent to this Active Directory thing? In fine Apple fashion of late, they have taken an existing open source project (the OpenLDAP directory server) and integrated it into OS X for centralized authentication and directory services. Combine this with Netinfo, which allows you to centrally control configuration aspects of OS X computers, and you have something that is on par with Active Directory. Apple calls this product *Open Directory*. Open Directory does not have anywhere near the install base that NT domains or Active Directory does, but it is available as part of OS X.

**NOTE**

It is possible to integrate OS X boxes further into Active Directory than just providing access to file and print shares. This is a huge subject in itself. A good starting point for more information is Apple's website (www.apple.com/itpro/articles/adintegration/).

**Figure 3.1** Active Directory Network

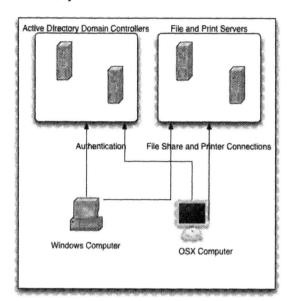

# Accessing Network File Systems

Network file systems are the main vehicles to share documents, spreadsheets, and even sometimes databases on computer networks. If you are accessing file shares on a Windows server, you are most likely using SMB protocol.

SMB stands for Server Message Block, and it is a protocol for sharing files and printers over a network. Windows computers run Microsoft's implementation of SMB. Computers running OS X, or some other UNIX-style operating system usually use Samba (www.samba.org) to implement the SMB protocol. The Samba software suite allows your Mac to access file shares residing on a Windows server, as well as to share your files with Windows clients. In addition, you can access printers shared on a Windows server and share printers with Windows clients as well.

The most basic way to get access to network file systems is to use the *Finder*. With the Finder window open, the command + k hotkey will connect to a server window. This functionality can also be found under the **Go** menu in the Finder.

To connect to a share on a Windows machine (as shown in Figure 3.2) use the following URL syntax in the **Server Address** field: smb://server-name/sharename.

**Figure 3.2** The Finder's Connect to Server Window

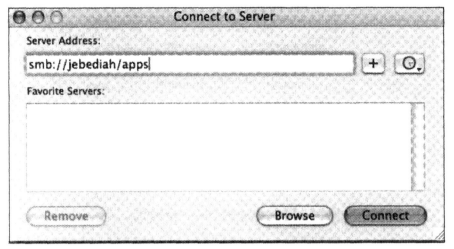

For this example, we are connecting to a server named *Jebediah* and a share called *apps*. All of these examples will access the servers that are connected by their names. However, it is worth noting that you can also use a computer's IP (Internet Protocol) address when connecting to network file systems. In fact, if you have problems connecting to a file server, trying the IP address instead of the name can be a good trick for troubleshooting the problem. If it works when you use the IP address but not when you use the name, then DNS (Domain Name System) resolution is a likely source of your problem.

If you are having problems connecting both via IP address and via computer name, there are some things you should check:

- Is there a firewall running on the machine you are attempting to connect to?

- Can you ping the computer you are attempting to connect to?

- Can you access the file share from another computer?

While these are not all the techniques that can be used to troubleshoot connectivity problems, they are a good start to isolating what could be causing the problem. If this is your first time connecting to the server or if you have never saved your login in the OS X keychain you will be prompted to authenticate. If the server you are connecting to is an Active Directory, when you submit your username and password the server will talk to a domain controller in the domain you specified to check your login credentials. This is illustrated in Figure 3.4. If the server is not in an Active Directory, its check its local authentication database.

**Figure 3.3** Connecting and Authenticating to smb://jebediah/apps

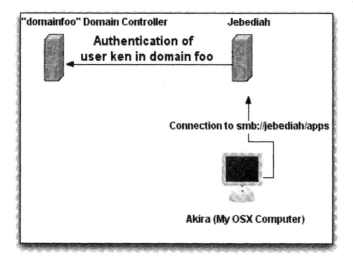

**Figure 3.4** The Finder's SMB Authentication Window

If you authenticate correctly you should now be presented with a finder window that shows you the remote windows file share.

The next few sections will cover different ways to automate connecting the network file systems you may use on a daily basis. For all of these examples we are going to assume that you want to map three shares on a server named *Jebediah*. These three shares are *backups*, *intranet*, and *apps*. Of course, you can change these to match the server and share names on your network.

# Mounting Network File Systems via AppleScript

If you connect to more than one or two file shares on a regular basis, using the Finder to connect to these shares can grow old quick. So let's try and automate this a little bit by using AppleScript. Launch the *scripteditor* application in *Applications/AppleScript* and enter in the following code:

```
Tell application "Finder"
     Try
             Mount volume "smb://ken:badpassword@jebediah/apps"
             Mount volume "smb://ken:badpassword@jebediah/backups"
             Mount volume "smb://ken:badpassword@jebediah/intranet"
     End try
End Tell
```

**Figure 3.5** AppleScript Editor Window with Code to Mount Network File Shares

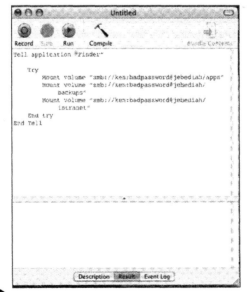

The code above is telling the Finder to mount three windows file shares. The breakdown of the URL you will use is as follows:

- smb is the protocol you are using, thus the **smb://** entry.
- ken:badpassword is the username and password you are using separated with a colon (:).
- Jebediah is the server name.
- The three shares you are mounting are apps, backups, and intranet.

If you were to click **Run** in the scripteditor with this code, you would probably not have much luck, unless you happen to be on my network and **badpassword** was the correct password. When you run this script on the network with this password, three file shares appear on the desktop and you are able to get access to the resources.

To get this running in your environment replace the respective parts with information that matches your environment and give the script a test run to make sure it works. To debug any problems you may be having, you can test the URLs first by entering them at the **Connect to server** prompt you used at the beginning of this section.

Hard-coding your username and password into the script is not a good idea; it makes it easier for someone to find your password and it makes your script unusable to other people unless they edit it with their information. OS X comes with a *keychain,* which can store your usernames and passwords for you so you don't have to leave them lying around in scripts.

So instead, let's remove the usernames and passwords and do it like this:

```
Tell application "Finder"

    Try
            Mount volume "smb://jebediah/apps"
            Mount volume "smb://jebediah/backups"
            Mount volume "smb://jebediah/intranet"
    End try
End Tell
```

If this is your first time connecting to these shares, you will be prompted for your username, password, and domain. If you are on a Windows network with a domain or Active Directory, put the domain name in the respective field; otherwise, feel free to leave it with the default value. Enter your username and password, and make sure to enable the **remember this password in my keychain** option so that every time you run this script in the future the keychain will do authentication work for you. In the last example, we are only connecting to network file systems that reside on a single server. However, it should be noted that this is not a limitation—you can specify multiple servers even in different domains and the keychain will keep track of this for you.

While this chapter is primarily focused on Windows, it's worthwhile mentioning that you can use these types of scripts to mount almost any network volume. FTP (File Transfer Protocol), NFS (Network File System), Web-Dav just replace the "smb" prefix with the prefix for the protocol you want to use.

# Mounting Network File Systems via Terminal

Apple says OS X is powered by UNIX, so let's dig in to its UNIX roots and delve into the command line. The Terminal app can be found in Utilities subfolder of the Applications folder. In the terminal, let's mount some SMB file shares using the *mount_smbfs* command. The mount_smbfs command is used to mount SMB (Windows) file shares. You will need to do this as the root user, or use the *sudo* command. The first time you use sudo you will be asked for your password; sudo will remember your password for five minutes.

**NOTE**

The *sudo* command allows you to execute a command as another user. In most cases it is used to execute commands as the root user. On most UNIX variants the super user account, which has access to the entire system, is called *root*.

The first step is to create the directories that you will use as mount points using the **mkdir** command. Mount points are where the file shares get mapped in the file system. Even using the first AppleScript example the files shares get mounted by finder in the *Volumes* directory. You can see mounted file systems (both local and network) by executing the mount command from the terminal window.

```
Mkdir apps
Mkdir backups
Mkdir intranet
Sudo Mount_smbfs -W MYDOMAINNAME //ken@jebediah/apps ./apps/
Sudo Mount_smbfs -W MYDOMAINNAME //ken@jebediah/backups ./backups/
Sudo Mount_smbfs -W MYDOMAINNAME //ken@jebediah/intranet ./intranet/
```

The next step is to mount the remote files systems using the *mount_smbfs* command. The first option, specified by **–W**, is the workgroup or domain name. Following that you will see a syntax that is somewhat different from the AppleScript example:

```
//Username@ServerName/FileShare ./MountPoint/
```

It is also worth mentioning that mounting network file systems via this method does not use the OS X keychain, therefore you must always enter your password after running these commands. One solution is to use the syntax //UserName:badpassword@ServerName/ShareName, but this is involves more typing from the command line when you want to mount a share. If you want to put this in a script then you have your passwords floating around in plain text—again, not a good practice.

# Using a .nmbrc or nsmb.conf File to Store Login Information

The .nmbrc file and nsmb.conf are used to store information about your Windows environment so that the Samba client, in this case mount_smbfs, can access it and not have to bug you for it.

The nsmb.conf file is located in the /private/etc directory on your computer. This is considered the system-wide configuration file for the Samba client. Anything you put in here will affect all users of your computer.

The .nmbrc file is a file you can create in your home directory that contains information that only is used when you are logged in and using the computer. It should be noted that values set in the system-wide /private/etc/nsmb.conf file will override values set in the .nmbrc file.

You can take a lot of typing out the mount_smbfs command by putting information in the /etc/nsmb.conf file or in the .nsmbrc file in your home directory. Which method you use is up to you, but it is recommended that you use the .nsmbrc file in your home directory so if someone else needs to use your machine you are not giving them the system-wide ability to log in with your credentials. In addition, if you use FileVault to secure your home directory then anything kept in this file is protected by FileVault as well since it is stored in your home directory.

Here is a look at the sample configuration:

```
[default]
workgroup=MYDOMAINNAME
[JEBEDIAH:KEN:BACKUPS]
password= $$174464421213a0f1ce1f5ec
[JEBEDIAH:KEN:APPS]
password= $$174464421213a0f1ce1f5ec
[JEBEDIAH:KEN:INTRANET]
password= $$174464421213a0f1ce1f5ec
```

Under the default key you can set a global value for your domain or workgroup name, and for each share a key with the syntax [Servername:Username:Sharename]. In that key you can set a value for the password. Looking at the password, you will see it is not a plain text password, but an encrypted string. To generate that encrypted string you use the *smbutil* command, as shown in this example:

```
akira:~ ken$ smbutil crypt badpassword
$$174464421213a0f1ce1f5ec
```

It should be noted that the encrypted string returned by the smbutil command is not very secure and is merely a way to make the password non-human readable to prevent shoulder surfing. If someone has access, it is very simple for him or her to deduce your password. Therefore, you should make sure that this and any files containing sensitive information have restrictive file permissions. You can make this file readable and writable by only you (or in this case me) by using the *chmod* command:

```
Chmod 700 .nsmbrc
```

Since you created the file you should already be the owner. The chmod example shown makes the file readable, writable, and executable only by the owner, which in this case is your account, *ken*.

You can verify this with the *ls* command:

```
ls -la .nsmbrc
-rwx------   1 ken  ken  193 Jul 28 22:37 .nsmbrc
```

Now the *mount_smbfs* command can get the domain, username, and password out of the .nsmbrc file, reducing your command line to work to:

```
akira:~ ken$mount_smbfs //jebediah/backups  ./backups
akira:~ ken$mount_smbfs //jebediah/apps  ./apps
akira:~ ken$mount_smbfs //jebediah/intranet ./intranet
```

# Microsoft Distributed File System

Connecting to shares via Microsoft's distributed file system (DFS) is not currently supported in OS X. However, it's worth mentioning what it is, as it's very likely you will run into it.

MS DFS allows you to take a name space such as your domain name in Active Directory and use that as a way to reference file shares on your network without needing to the know the server name.

For example, if you are on a Windows network with a domain of foo.com, you might be able to access the distributed file system by going to smb://foo.com/dfs, in which case you could see which file shares are available to the users in the foo.com domain. The nice thing about DFS is that you never need to know the name of the servers on which the shares reside. Let's say you want to access on a share on the DFS called *biz-dev*. You can go to smb://foo.com/dfs/biz-dev, while the actual share might live on a server named *Lisa*. This way the system administrator can move shares around to different servers behind the scenes and keep it transparent to the users. In addition, DFS supports replicating shares to multiple servers for redundancy.

That being said, if someone gives you a DFS link to network file system you will need to find out the name of the server that the share resides on and use the traditional smb://servername/sharename syntax to access it.

# NTLM Authentication

NTLM stands for Windows NT LAN Manager. It is a challenge- and response-based authentication protocol that is used frequently in the Windows world (for more information, visit http://msdn.microsoft.com/library/default.asp?url=/library/enus/secauthn/security/microsoft_ntlm.asp)

Some common places to find NTLM authentication are:

- Web pages residing on IIS (Internet Information Service) Web servers

- Microsoft Proxy Server

- Microsoft Internet Security and Acceleration Server

- Accessing SMB network file systems

Microsoft IIS Web servers are often configured to use NTLM authentication because it is more secure that the traditional basic authentication in the HTTP (Hypertext Transfer Protocol) specification, which sends your username and password over the wire or wireless in plain text.

Microsoft Internet Security and Acceleration Server is a firewall and proxy server (www.microsoft.com/isaserver/). It is used as your main gateway to the Internet. It is not uncommon to require end users to authenticate before allowing any sort of outbound Internet access.

Fortunately , most browsers support NTLM authentication, including Safari and Firefox. This is quite an improvement over the days when Internet Explorer was the only option you had of you wanted to access to a site or proxy server using NTLM authentication. While this is great for end users, it can be more of a pain for the geek in us who may want to use something other a graphical browser to access a Web page.

# Accessing NTLM-Protected Web Servers via the Command Line

Web browsers are great for people looking at Web pages. However, when you write to script to automate a task (such as retrieving data from a website) on a routine basis, you are better off using command line tools.

In this situation you have access to a routinely updated file on an IIS Web server using NTLM authentication. Every so often you can fire up Safari or Firefox open the URL in your Web browser and save the page to your local machine. The sysadmin in you knows there has to be an easier way so you decide to automate this with a cron job that executes the following:

```
curl http://windoze-server/foo.html > foo.html
```

*Curl* is a tool that can retrieve data from a URL. It supports quite a few protocols; HTTP, HTTPS GOPHER, TELNET, and LDAP (Lightweight Directory Access Protocol).

In this case you are concerned with HTTP. The example tells curl to grab the file residing at http://windoze-server/foo.html and redirect the output to a local file named foo.html.

Upon first looking at foo.html after running the job you will notice that the file does not contain the data you am looking for, but rather the HTML (Hypertext Markup Language) from an IIS 401 "Access Denied" page, telling you that you don't have access to view the page. "Ah, no problem," you think to myself, "the Web server must have authentication turned on for this HTML file since it's sensitive data". You can use curl's built-in HTTP authentication support.

```
curl --user ken:badpassword http://windoze-server/foo.html > foo.html
```

Now you tell curl that you would like to use basic HTTP authentication, since that is what the majority of Web servers are configured to use. Pass your username and password separated by a colon as an additional argument.

When you inspect your file the next time the job is run and it contains the same error page. You check the timestamp on the file and it was definitely updated since the first time the job ran. After a phone call to your Windows system administrator, you find out that all of your IIS Web servers use NTLM authentication.

After a quick read through the curl manpage... viola, curl supports NTLM authentication:

```
curl --ntlm --user ken:badpassword http://windoze-server/foo.html > foo.html
```

Now I can successfully access http://windoze-server/foo.html.

# Using an NTLM-Protected Proxy from the Command Line

So it's your first day at your new job. You come in with your trusty Mac, plop it down on your desk and attempt to start surfing the Web. Everything looks in order, you are getting an IP address via DHCP (Dynamic Host Control Protocol), your default gateway is set, and DNS resolution seems to work. So you call your system administrator and explain your predicament. "Ah," he says, "You probably don't have a proxy server configured in your Web browser. It's a lot easier for us to log all the websites you go to if everyone is using a centralized proxy server." The system administrator gives you the hostname to their proxy server, you plug it into your trusty Web browser, and now you are prompted for authentication. After entering your username and password you are happily surfing the Internet.

Then you notice that your trusty command line tool curl cannot reach websites on the Internet. Pesky NTLM authentication has done it again. This time, though, it's not just one site on an IIS Web server that you can't get to. The proxy server, your gateway to the World Wide Web wants to authenticate you for all your Internet access. Well luckily, curl supports proxy servers that require NTLM authentication as well:

```
curl  --proxy http://corporate-proxy:8080 --proxy-user ken:badpassword --
proxy-ntlm http://google.com
```

So let's look at this curl command. The **--proxy** flag is the URL for your local proxy server that big brother demands you route your Web traffic through. Next is your login in the username:password format. Third is the **--proxy-ntlm** flag, which tells curl to attempt NTLM authentication. Last, but not least is the URL you are trying to access. Who thought going to www.google.com could be so much work! For a simple overview of the differences between these two previous examples refer to Figure 3.6

**Figure 3.6** Talking to a Web Server vs. Proxy Server

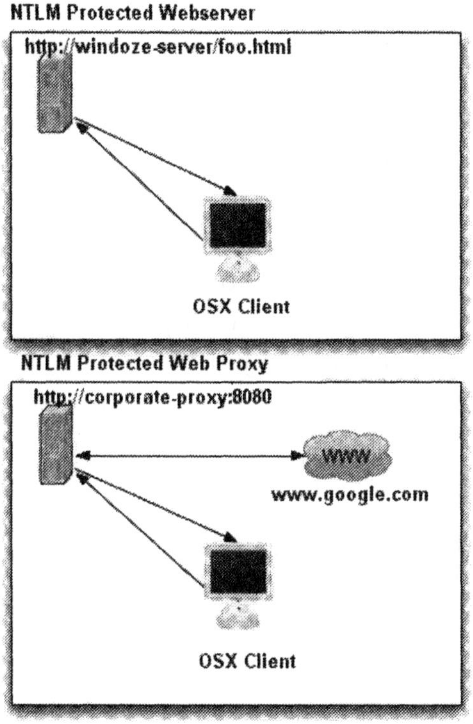

# Using a Local Proxy
# to Handle NTLM Authentication

Using scripts and command line tools like curl are handy for a lot of things. If you find yourself using them often in an environment where you have to authenticate via NTLM you can quickly grow tired of always having to specify your proxy server, username, and password. In addition, you may want to use a script or a tool that does not support NTLM authentication to gain access to these resources.

A situation that I ran into this was in security auditing of Web applications. In your case you wanted to use a homegrown script that checks for vulnerabilities in a website. However, my script did not know how to speak NTLM authentication, therefore I couldn't get it to access the site in question.

A similar situation I experienced was one in which I was on a network where getting out to the Internet required NTLM authentication as mentioned in the previous section, and I wanted to access the Internet from a non-NTLM aware application.

The solution I chose was setting up a proxy server that handles this part of the connection for you. A proxy, in simplest terms, is something that handles your requests for you. Large networks sometimes use proxy servers for caching frequently accessed information on the Internet. These are usually referred to as *caching proxies*. In this case you are going to look at a proxy server that is designed to do one thing: accept your Web requests and forward them on to a NTLM protected resource and handle the authentication for you.

NTLM Authorization Proxy Server (http://ntlmaps.sourceforge.net/) is an open source program that will do just that you. To get started, download the source code and open the tar archive. As of this writing, the latest version is ntlmaps-0.9.9.5.

```
tar -xvf ntlmaps-0.9.9.5.tar
```

If you look in the directory that was created (in this example, ntlmaps-0.9.9.5), you will find a file called server.cfg. This is the main configuration file for the proxy. In this example, there two example configurations. The first is used to access a website requiring NTLM authentication. Open the server.cfg file in your favorite text editor and change the following values:

- **PARENT_PROXY** should be blank, because you are connecting directly to a Web server.

- **NT_DOMAIN** should be set to the domain your account is in.

- **USER** should be set to your account username.

- **PASSWORD** can be left blank and you will be prompted for it when starting the server, or you can place it here if you are comfortable with storing your password in a text file.

Here is what mine looks like:

```
[GENERAL]
LISTEN_PORT:5865
PARENT_PROXY_PORT:8080
PARENT_PROXY_TIMEOUT:15
ALLOW_EXTERNAL_CLIENTS:0
FRIENDLY_IPS:
HOSTS_TO_BYPASS_PARENT_PROXY:
```

```
DIRECT_CONNECT_IF_POSSIBLE:0
URL_LOG:0
MAX_CONNECTION_BACKLOG:5
 [CLIENT_HEADER]
Accept: image/gif, image/x-xbitmap, image/jpeg, image/pjpeg,
application/vnd.ms-excel, application/msword, application/vnd.ms-powerpoint,
*/*
User-Agent: Mozilla/4.0 (compatible; MSIE 6.0; Windows NT 5.1; SV1)
 [NTLM_AUTH]
NT_HOSTNAME:
NT_DOMAIN:domainfoo
USER:ken
PASSWORD:badpassword
LM_PART:1
NT_PART:0
NTLM_FLAGS: 06820000
NTLM_TO_BASIC:0
 [DEBUG]
DEBUG:0
BIN_DEBUG:0
SCR_DEBUG:0
AUTH_DEBUG:0
```

Now you are ready to start the server. To do this you execute the following command from within the ntlmaps-0.9.9.5 directory:

```
/usr/bin/python main.py
```

The proxy server should now be up and running (similar to Figure 3.7). In this scenario you will use the NTLM proxy to handle NTML authentication. It will authenticate using the username and password in the configuration file. It will do this all behind the scenes so the Web client that you are using doesn't need to know NTLM at all. With the proxy server listening on port 5865 of your local machine, you will fire up curl and tell it to use the proxy server with the –x flag:

```
curl  -x localhost:5865 http://windoze-server/foo.html
```

Now you are able to access the site without being asked for your credentials because the proxy server took care of that for you.

**Figure 3.7** Connecting to an NTML-Protected Website with NTLMAPS

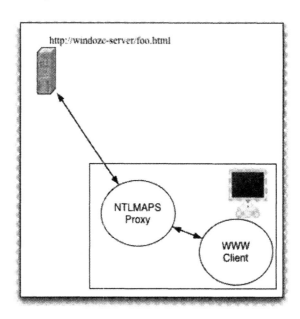

For the second example (Figure 3.8) you want to use a proxy server that requires NTLM authentication such as the MS proxy server or MS ISA server. The only thing you need to change from your previous configuration file is the **PARENT_PROXY** and **PARENT_PROXY_PORT** values. Set these to match the host or IP address and port number for the proxy server you wish to connect through. For example, **PARENT_PROXY:corporate-proxy** and **PARENT_PORT: 8080**.

To follow with your previous examples, using the local NTLM proxy to go through an NTLM protected Web proxy, you could do the following:

```
curl  -x localhost:5865 http://google.com
```

**Figure 3.8** Connecting to an NTLM-Protected Web Proxy with NTLMAPS

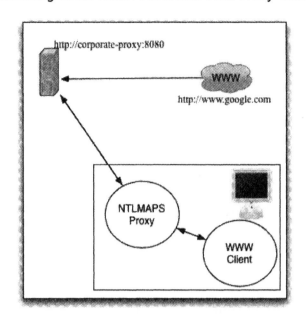

There are many things you can tweak in the server.cfg file. This section does not cover all of them, but the config file is fairly well commented. Some that you may find useful are:

- **LISTEN_PORT** the port that ntlmaps will listen on for connections.

- **ALLOW_EXTERNAL_CLIENTS** if set to 1, will allow clients other than your machine to use the proxy server you setup. The default is 0, which only allows your local machine.

- **URL_LOG** if set to 1, will log URLs accessed through the proxy server to a file named url.log. Its default setting is 0, which will not log anything.

- **HOSTS_TO_BYPASS_PARENT_PROXY** will take a list of hosts or IP addresses that, when requested, will not be accessed through a parent proxy if one is configured.

**User-Agent** allows you set the type of browser the site or proxy you're connecting to sees you as. This is handy for masking the fact that you are using curl or some other tool. Its default is set to impersonate Internet Explorer 6.0.

So there you have it. As you can see, proxy servers are not just for caching Web requests; they can be used to fool upstream servers and to compensate for lack of functionality on the client's end.

# Connecting to a Windows PPTP Server

PPTP (Point to Point Tunneling Protocol) is often not regarded as the most secure VPN (virtual private network) technology, primarily because of the potential attacks that exist against MS-CHAP and MS-CHApv2 authentication protocols used by PPTP. However, it's easy to set up on the server side, it comes with Windows 2000 and 2003 server, and it has native support in both Windows and OS X clients, as well as open source clients for Linux and the BSDs. All of these factors have helped give it a large install base among small- and medium-sized businesses.

Configuring a PPTP connection is fairly simple. You will need two pieces of information: your login credentials, which are almost always the same as your active directory/domain login, the IP address or host name of the PPTP server. With this you can fire up the Internet Connect application located in your Applications folder and do the following:

1. Choose the **VPN** option.

2. Select **Edit Configurations** from the drop-down list and create a new configuration by choosing **Other**.

3. Enter a description for the configuration, the IP address or hostname of the server you are connecting to, and your login and password. If you are using RSA Secure ID or Client Side Certificates you will need more information from the system administrator running the VPN server (see Figure 3.9).

4. Click **OK** to save the configuration and then click **Connect**.

**Figure 3.9** Internet Connect PPTP Configuration Window

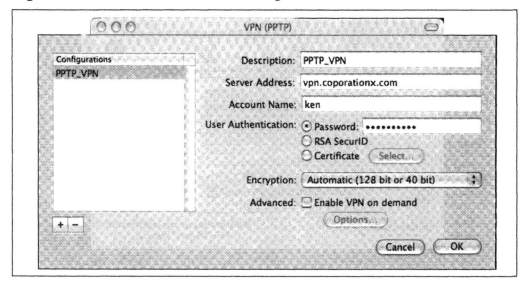

When you establish a PPTP connection your computer will create a virtual network interface named ppp0. This can be seen by executing the command **ifconfig -a** from the terminal.

The default behavior is to change your default route to that of the PPTP connection. This means that all traffic, regardless of its destination, will be routed through the VPN. For example, if you try to access www.google.com, that request gets sent through the VPN connection and not your local Internet gateway. This is usually done by design as a security precaution. It helps to prevent someone from attacking your machine via your local Internet connection and then gaining access to your corporate network via the VPN connection. This is not foolproof; if the attacker is on the same local network as you then he or she can still attack your computer and potentially access the VPN network if he gains control of your computer. However, if he is attacking from a remote network coming in via your local Internet connection, any responses back to him will get routed out the VPN connection with a different source address. A lot of this will depend on your VPN server and networks configuration as well.

The remainder of this section discusses some ways to achieve *split tunneling* so you can route your Internet access where you like, and also ways to determine where your DNS requests get resolved. If you are connecting to a corporate VPN server, be sure to review your company's security policy, as some of the things you are going to look at may violate the security policy and therefore should not be done in those circumstances.

# Split Tunneling

So you are happily connected to your PPTP server and able to access machine remotely via the PPTP VPN. However, you may not want to route your general Internet requests over the PPTP VPN for a variety of reasons. For one, perhaps your local Internet connection is much faster than the connection on the remote end of the VPN. Therefore the VPN is going to be a bottleneck. Maybe the VPN server is in London and you are in the US, and you don't want to make a round trip from the US to London and then back to the US again just to look at a website. Maybe you just don't want other people on the VPN network to be able to see which websites you are looking at.

It's important to ensure that when a PPTP connection is established the default route is not changed. You can view your current default route by executing the netstat command from the terminal. The first route you see in the netstat output is your default route.

```
akira:~ ken$netstat -rn | more
Routing tables


Internet:
Destination  Gateway          Flags    Refs     Use   Netif
default       192.168.0.1      UGSc     40       6     en1
```

In this case the default route is 192.168.0.1, which is the gateway on the local network. If you connect to your PPTP VPN you should see this change:

```
akira:~ ken$netstat -rn | more
Routing tables


Internet:
Destination  Gateway          Flags    Refs     Use   Netif
default       10.1.1.100       UGSc     40       6     en1
```

Now that you are connected to the VPN, the default route has changed to that of your VPN connection. The IP address here is relative to your network and VPN configuration. Yours will almost definitely be different. The thing to pay attention to is the change in this route.

This new default route is telling the kernel all packets not destined for a local network address should get sent out the VPN connection. In order to change this you need to do two things. You need to disable the VPN connection from setting a new default route, and you need to add routes for the networks you want to access on the VPN network.

On your machine you have the following configuration:

**192.168.0.0/24**  The local network.

**192.168.0.10**  The IP address of the machine.

**192.168.0.1**  The default gateway to the Internet.

**10.1.1.0/24**  The address range used on the VPN network you are connecting to.

Your PPTP connection has a name in the Internet Connect application (**PPTP_VPN**). Follow these steps to disable the setting of a default route with the PPTP connection:

1. Create a text file in /etc/ppp/peers/ that matches the name of your VPN.

2. Add a line that says **nodefaultroute**.

The next time you launch your PPTP connection it should be without the default route.

Now that you have eliminated the default route, you need to add a static route so the computer knows which traffic to send out the VPN connections. In this case, the remote network you are connecting to over the VPN is 10.1.1.0/24. In the /etc/ppp/ directory there is a script called **ip-up**. This script is executed when the VPN connection is established. It is a shell script, therefore you can add some commands to setup the route for the VPN network:

```
/sbin/route -n add -net 10.1.1.0 $IPREMOTE >> /tmp/ppp.log 2>&1
```

This script runs the route command to add a route for the 10.1.1.0/24 network with a gateway of **$IPREMOTE**, which is an environment variable containing the IP address of the VPN interface that is created.

When you connect to the VPN, the following happens:

1. The tunnel is established and the interface ppp0 gets an IP address from the VPN server.

2. The nodefaultroute option in the PPTP_VPN file ensures that your default gateway to the Internet is not changed.

3. The ip-up script sets the route for the remote VPN network so that traffic destined for the VPN is routed accordingly.

Next let's move on to routing DNS requests for the VPN network.

# Routing DNS Requests

DNS is a large network of servers on the Internet that translate names of servers to IP addresses and vice versa. When you ask your browser to take you to google.com, it queries a DNS server to find out which IP address google.com resides at.

This is important to know because the machines you want to access on your VPN network are not in the Internet's DNS system. They are in an internal DNS system that is only accessible from your private network. Most network administrators do not publish internal hostnames in the Internet DNS because the machines are not accessible from the Internet and it can also potentially give away sensitive information about the private network.

This presents a problem because you want to be able to use DNS servers on the Internet to perform name lookups for Internet hosts, and you want to use your internal DNS servers to perform name lookups for host names on the VPN network.

Which DNS servers to use are typically set a couple of different ways. The most common is through the DHCP protocol. The DHCP protocol allows a computer to connect to a new network, send out a broadcast request, and have network settings assigned to it. These generally include IP address, subnet mask, default gateway, and which DNS servers to use. You can also manually set your DNS servers via the Network System Preferences.

When following the previous PPTP split tunneling configuration, you need some way to tell your computer to use different DNS servers for DNS requests for machines on the VPN network. You can do this on a domain-by-domain basis. In this case all of the machines you want to access on the VPN network are in the corporationx.com domain. That means any name lookups for *.corporationx.com should use your internal DNS servers. Not a problem. To do this you create a text file in /private/etc/resolver called corporationx.com.

In /private/etc/resolver/corporationx.com you are going to add a couple of lines telling your computer which DNS servers to use when resolving any name followed by corporationx.com. This file will follow the syntax as resolv.conf, which stores the IP addresses of DNS servers you use by default. The syntax for this file is simple:

```
Nameserver 10.1.1.100
Nameserver 10.1.2.100
```

The string nameserver is followed by the IP address of the DNS server. You can get away with having just one DNS server listed, but most networks have at least two for redundancy. If the first one does not respond it will attempt to query the second.

So now all of your DNS requests for corporationx.com will be sent to the DNS servers mentioned above. The rest will go to the DNS servers your machine is configured to use by default.

# Zen of Running Windows Boxes from a Mac

Hate it or love it, the majority of system administrators are responsible for at least some Windows servers, if not a lot. Unlike OS X and other UNIX-like operating systems, most of the built-in tools for running Windows servers are specific to computers running Windows.

While are there always going to be times when you need to jockey up to Windows box for some reason or other, you can spend most of your time on a Mac. I personally have been running large amounts of Windows servers from either OS X or Linux for quite a few years.

## MS Remote Desktop Client

Remote Desktop, formerly known as Terminal Services, provides you with a remote graphical terminal into a Windows computer via the remote desktop protocol (RDP). In the days of NT 4 there was a Terminal Services Edition that was a separate distribution of Windows NT with the added bonus of Terminal Services. In Windows 2000, Microsoft made Terminal Services part of the OS and has now included it in Windows XP. As of Windows XP and 2003 Server, Terminal Services is now referred to as Remote Desktop (www.microsoft.com/mac/otherproducts/otherproducts.aspx?pid= remotedesktopclient).

Some of the features of Remote Desktop are:

- Ability for users on non-Windows computers to access Windows-only applications.

- Ability to disconnect your session, leave all applications running and reconnect at a later time.

- Shared clipboard between your local remote session for cutting and pasting.

- Using the MS Remote Desktop client for Mac, you can have the local file systems on your Mac available as network drives in your Remote Desktop session when connecting to computers running Windows XP or 2003 Server.

Some of the cons of Remote Desktop are:

- On Windows XP you may only have one login session active. If you log in via Remote Desktop you will lock out anyone sitting at the console of the machine.

- On 2000 and 2003 Server, administration mode only allows two concurrent connections; all subsequent login attempts will be denied.

- While in 2000 and 2003 Server application mode, you need to have a client access license for each computer connecting via Remote Desktop.

Ultimately, Remote Desktop is your best friend if you are required to support Windows computers. Being able to log in remotely to a Windows machine when debugging a problem is priceless; it's a really a wonder that I survived running NT 4 boxes without it.

# Opening Remote Desktop Connections from the Command Line

One of the things that separates Mac OS X from other UNIX-style operating systems is its fantastic GUI (graphical user interface). However, having my roots in the command line, I like to have the option to do things the old fashioned way, so I spent some time looking around for a way to launch the Remote Desktop client from the command line and I came across Mac OS X's *open* command

Open is a command line tool that takes a filename, directory name, or URL as an argument. If you were execute the command **open somefile.txt**, open would determine via launch services that the file should be opened with text editor and it will launch a text editor session with that file. In addition, you can also force open to use certain applications using the -a flag. However, in this situation, the default will work.

The first thing you need to do to be able to open a Remote Desktop connection from the command line is to configure a Remote Desktop connection via the Microsoft client and save the connection as a file (see Figure 3.10).

**Figure 3.10** Configuring a Remote Desktop Connection to Save as a File

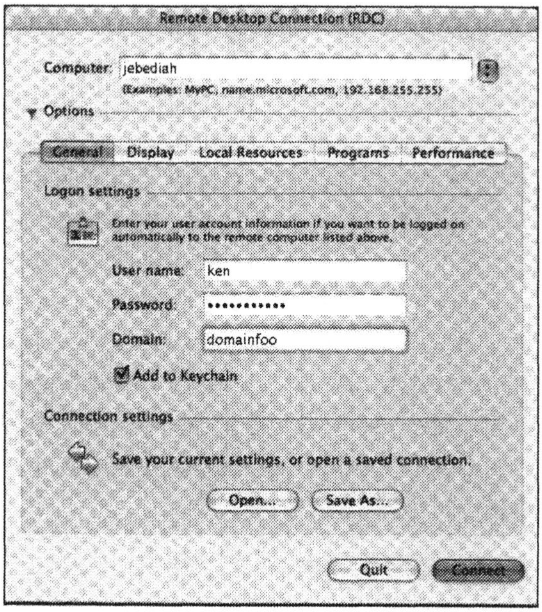

In this example, you am connecting to a computer named *jebediah* and putting in your username, password, domain name, and saving it to the keychain. This allows you pop into a Remote Desktop connection without having to enter your login credentials each time. The next step is to save the connection as a file by clicking **Save As**. You are going to save your connection in a subdirectory of your home directory named RemoteDesktop with a filename of jebediahRDC.

Now from a terminal window in the RemoteDesktop directory, you can type **open jebediah** and, poof, you are automatically logged into your server, no mouse clicks required. Unfortunately, though, this method does not allow you run concurrent Remote Desktop sessions.

```
akira:~ ken$ open jebediahRDC
```

## Opening Concurrent Remote Desktop Sessions

One of the downfalls of the Microsoft Remote Desktop client for Mac (unlike the Windows client) is that it does not allow you to run multiple Remote Desktop sessions. If you have a session open and you click on the Remote Desktop icon hoping to fire up another connection, it will bring your existing one to the foreground. I don't know about you, but I am usually logged into quite a few machines while at work and I find this unacceptable.

Luckily, someone has a written a tool that helps work around this limitation. The tool is called Rdcmenu and is available from www.xutils.com/rdc-menu/. After downloading Rdcmenu and opening the .dmg, just drag the application to the applications folder and launch it. When you open the application for the first time it will prompt you to point it to the location of the Remote Desktop client. This is usually in the Applications/Remote Desktop Connection folder. After that, access the **Preferences** tab and select the option to have the Remote Desktop icon displayed on the menu bar. You should now notice a new icon on your menu bar. You should also choose the option to have Rdcmenu launched (Figure 3.11) at login since you use it all the time. At this point you can now click on the icon in the menu bar and launch as many concurrent Remote Desktop sessions as you would like, computer resources permitting.

**Figure 3.11** RDC Menu in the Menu Bar

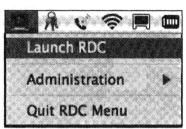

**NOTE**

If you have another Remote Desktop session open, Rdcmenu has a tendency to stick new ones behind your foreground window instead of putting them in the foreground where you can see them.

# Making Local Resources Available on the Remote Windows Computer

Another feature of the Microsoft Remote Desktop client is the ability to make your local disk drives and printers available to your Remote Desktop session. This means that while in your Remote Desktop session you can access files on your local machine and copy or move data back and forth without having to manually connect to the remote machine via the Finder. In addition, you can also have access to printers that are set up on your local machine.

**NOTE**

Accessing local resources is a convenient feature, however it should be noted that while these resources are available via the Remote Desktop session, other people that have access and sufficient privileges on the Windows computer can potentially access the data on your local machine.

To enable this feature click **Options** and select the **Local Resources** tab. In the **Local devices** section, enable the **Disk Drives** and/or **Printers** options to enable the desired access (Figure 3.12). Click **Connect**. You will see a warning similar to the one shown in Figure 3.13 if you selected to share disk drives. This local resource sharing feature only works when connecting to computers running Windows XP or Windows 2003 server.

**Figure 3.12** Enabling Local Resources for Remote Desktop

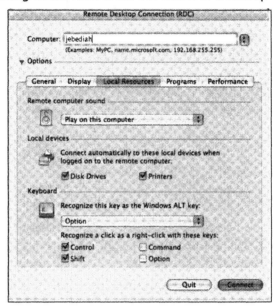

**Figure 3.13** Local Resource Sharing Warning

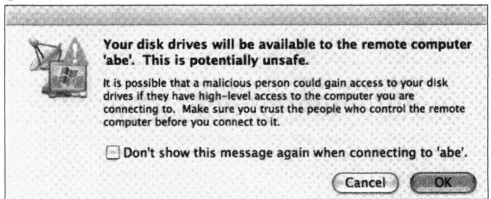

The next time you login via Remote Desktop, you should see a screen similar to the one shown in Figure 3.14. At the bottom of the explorer window the hard drive on your OS X computer (Akira) mapped as a local drive.

**Figure 3.14** Making Your Local Hard Drive Available in a Remote Desktop Connection

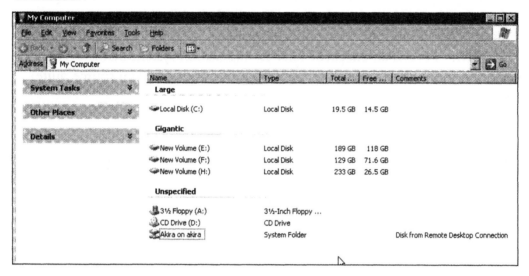

# Rdesktop—The Open Source Remote Desktop Client

Rdesktop is an open source remote desktop client. If you come from a Linux or BSD background you might already be familiar with it, as it is the only option for remote desktop connectivity on those platforms. Why use yet another remote desktop client when Microsoft already provides one? The reason I prefer it is because it provides much more flexibility running it from the terminal. I really like to cut down on the amount of time my hands spend on the mouse or trackpad, so anytime a good command line tool is available I will use it over a GUI tool.

Rdesktop, being rooted in UNIX, does not use Apple's graphical interface, Aqua. It uses the X11 windowing system, which is a staple on most UNIX systems. Luckily, Apple ships an X11 implementation with Tiger, which runs rather nicely with Aqua. It can be found on the OS X installation CDs or DVDs.

The installation of Rdesktop you are going to perform also has the requirement of the X11 Software Development Kit or SDK. This can be found on the OS X developer's disk. During the installation process you will be compiling Rdesktop from source code. The compiler will need to use some of the source code in the X11 SDK to successfully build.

Why build from source? While you may find some pre-built packages for Rdesktop on the Internet, most of them are out of date and are missing some of the features of the newer versions. But don't fret! Building software from source is not as hard as it sounds, especially with tools like the Darwin Ports.

Darwin Ports is an excellent software installation system that is derived from the FreeBSD ports tree. It makes building software from source quite painless

## Installing Rdesktop

If you have X11, the X11 SDK, and Darwin Ports installed, building Rdesktop is easy.

At the terminal, enter **port install rdesktop**. You will need to be connected to the Internet during this process because Darwin Ports will fetch the source code and build it for you. Port install should be run as root or run via the sudo command to ensure it has proper access to install Rdesktop.

```
akira: ken$ sudo port install rdesktop
--->   Fetching rdesktop
--->   Attempting to fetch rdesktop-1.3.1.tar.gz from
http://voxel.dl.sourceforge.net/rdesktop
--->   Verifying checksum(s) for rdesktop
--->   Extracting rdesktop
--->   Configuring rdesktop
--->   Building rdesktop with target rdesktop
--->   Staging rdesktop into destroot
--->   Packaging tgz archive for rdesktop 1.3.1_0
--->   Installing rdesktop 1.3.1_0
--->   Activating rdesktop 1.3.1_0
--->   Cleaning rdesktop
```

Once you have completed the installation of Rdesktop, enter **rdesktop.** You should see a list of command line options:

```
akira: ken$ rdesktop
rdesktop: A Remote Desktop Protocol client.
Version 1.3.1. Copyright (C) 1999-2003 Matt Chapman.
See http://www.rdesktop.org/ for more information.

Usage: rdesktop [options] server[:port]
   -u: user name
   -d: domain
   -s: shell
   -c: working directory
   -p: password (- to prompt)
   -n: client hostname
   -k: keyboard layout on server (en-us, de, sv, etc.)
   -g: desktop geometry (WxH)
   -f: full-screen mode
   -b: force bitmap updates
   -e: disable encryption (French TS)
   -E: disable encryption from client to server
   -m: do not send motion events
   -C: use private colour map
   -D: hide window manager decorations
   -K: keep window manager key bindings
   -S: caption button size (single application mode)
   -T: window title
   -N: enable numlock synchronisation
   -a: connection colour depth
   -r: enable specified device redirection (currently: sound)
   -0: attach to console
   -4: use RDP version 4
   -5: use RDP version 5 (default)
```

# Setting Up Terminal to Use Your X11 Server

By default, X11 is installed in Applications/Utilities. Navigate there in the
Finder and open X11. It will start up and open a window called xterm.
Xterm is the UNIX equivalent to the OS X terminal. X11 is a separate
graphical environment from the standard Mac GUI, Aqua. Rdesktop requires
X11 to run properly, and it has to know how to talk to X11. This is done

with an environment variable called $DISPLAY. Enter the following in the xterm window:

```
echo $DISPLAY
```

This will show you the value of the $DISPLAY variable. It should be set to :0.0. Any application that uses X11 will check the value of $DISPLAY to figure out which X11 server, and which X11 screen to display it on.

So now if you were to run Rdesktop or any X11 application from within xterm, it would get the value of variable and use it to talk to the X11 environment. The look and feel of the OS X terminal is better than xterm. Well, no problem. You can run X11 applications from the terminal as long as you set this environment variable from within terminal. At the terminal, enter:

```
echo $DISPLAY
```

Notice it has no setting, so let's take care of that:

```
export DISPLAY=:0.0
echo $DISPLAY
```

Now Rdesktop will know how to communicate with X11 when you invoke it from a terminal. However, once you close the terminal window, this setting is lost. Setting it every time you launch a new terminal window is a pain, so let's add it to the file that is read every time you start a terminal window.

When you start a new terminal window, you are in a shell. The shell is your command line interface into the computer; it interprets your commands and then figures out what to do with them. The standard shell in OS X is *bash*. You can confirm that you are in the bash shell by checking the $0 environment variable:

```
echo $0
-bash
```

When you start a new terminal and bash is launched, it looks for a file in your home directory called .bash_profile (notice the . at the beginning). You can add the line **export $DISPLAY=:0.0** to your .bash_profile and it will be executed every time you launch a new terminal. Here is an example of a .bash_profile:

```
export PATH=$PATH:/Users/ken/bin:/usr/local/bin:/sw/bin:/opt/local/bin
export DISPLAY=:0.0
```

In your .bash_profile you are setting your PATH variable, which is where bash checks for executable files. If you attempt to execute a command that is not in one of the directories in your PATH variable, bash won't be able to find it.

Last but not least is your DISPLAY variable telling it how to connect to your X11 server. To make this change go into effect immediately, you can source the file by typing the following:

```
. .bash_profile
```

Notice the first dot, then a space and then the name of your .bash_profile file. This will read the file, set the variables, and you are ready to go. The next time you open a terminal window this will happen behind the scenes and you will not have to set the DISPLAY variable. Now you can launch X11 apps from the terminal.

## Using Rdesktop

In order to use Rdesktop you need to make sure the X11 server is running. You can find the launcher, as shown in Figure 3.15, for X11 in the utilities subdirectory of your applications directory.

**Figure 3.15** X11 Launcher

To use Rdesktop you have to give it some information; minimally, you need to tell it the server you are connecting to. In this case you want to connect to a Windows server name HOMER.

```
akira: ken$ rdesktop homer
```

Now you can log into a Windows computer as you would using the Microsoft Remote Desktop client. In addition to server name, Rdesktop will accept various command line arguments. For a list, just run Rdesktop without any arguments. Some of the ones that are quite handy are:

- **f** full-screen mode
- **d** desktop geometry, set the geometry of the Rdesktop window, such as 1024x768
- **u** username, the username to log in with
- **d** domain, the domain to log in with
- **p** password, the password to log in with

The following command should log you into a server named homer, with a 1024x768 window and because you are providing all of the authentication information on the command line, it will log you right into the Windows box with your account.

```
rdesktop -d 1024x768 -u ken -p password -d corporationx homer
```

# Using Shell Scripts to Speed up Rdesktop Logins

Let's try and speed up the Rdesktop logins a little bit. One of my favorite things about using Rdesktop is the lack of mouse usage required to open a session in comparison to the Microsoft RDC client and RDC menu.

So let's take the command line approach and speed it up a little more. Let's create a UNIX shell script that handles most of the typing for you. You have a shell script called homer.sh. When run, it will log you into homer, but with much less typing. This script is pretty simple; the first line tells it where to find the shell you want to use, in this case /bin/sh. The next line calls the rdesktop command. Notice that you put the full path to the command. This does two things. First, if for some reason the person does not have that directory in the $PATH environment variable they will not be able to simply type **rdesktop**; this insures it will work in that situation. Second, there may be multiple versions of Rdesktop installed. This ensures you are using the one I want.

```
#!/bin/sh
/opt/local/bin/rdesktop -u ken -d domainfoo -p badpassword homer
```

So now if you were to run homer.sh from the terminal it should open up an Rdesktop session to homer. Well this is nice. However, creating and maintaining a shell script for each server you want to connect to can be tedious. So let's make this script a little more universal and useful. By using the basename command and symbolic links, I can use one file for multiple servers. The following changes have been saved as rdc.sh:

```
#!/bin/sh
/opt/local/bin/rdesktop -u ken -d domainfoo -p badpassword `basename $0`
```

*basename $0*, when used in this script, will use the value of *basename $0*, as the server to connect to. In order to make use of this script you need to create symbolic links to this file, and name the links the same as the servers you connect to:

```
ln -s rdc.sh homer
ln -s rdc.sh jebediah
```

Now when you run the homer symbolic link from the command line, it will run rdc.sh and basname $0 will return homer as its value since that is how you invoked it. The beauty of this solution is that you can make a change to rdc.sh (such as a password or username change) once and it will affect all of your connections.

Let's take this one step further. If your OS X users use the same login on their OS X machines as they do on Windows boxes, you can make this script even more portable by using the whoami command to tell the script who is logged in and thus which username to use:

```
#!/bin/sh
/opt/local/bin/rdesktop -u `whoami` -d domainfoo -p badpassword `basename
$0`
```

These may seem like little hacks, but combined with command autocompletion in your UNIX shell, they can make logging into Windows fast and mouseless.

# Virtual Network Computing

Virtual network computing is an invaluable tool originally written at AT&T Labs in the UK. VNC allows you to remotely view and operate another computer as if you were sitting in front of its keyboard and monitor. VNC is a client server application. You run the VNC server on the machine you wish to connect to, and you run the VNC client on your local computer.

How is VNC different from Remote Desktop? VNC acts as a remote keyboard and mouse for the system you are connecting to. Remote Desktop creates a virtual session for you when you log in. For instance, if are you using VNC across a network and someone is looking at the monitor attached to that computer, they will see everything you are doing. Is this bad? Maybe. However, if you attempt to help someone remotely troubleshoot a problem, you might want him or her to see what you are doing or vice versa. In addition, you can have multiple users connect to VNC session in a view only mode, while one person does all the work. This can be useful for demonstrations of administrative tasks to remote users.

Another difference that is worth mentioning is that VNC does not use Windows authentication; it uses its own password stored in the registry. Furthermore, VNC is also cross-platform; you can run the client and server on almost any operating system out there.

There are countless times that I have been asked to remotely troubleshoot a problem, and the majority of these times, having the remote user install VNC on their computer has helped tremendously to provide a hands-on view of the problem they are having.

That being said, VNC should not be taken lightly. This small yet powerful tool can pose some serious security problems as well. The free version of VNC does not support encrypted connections and only uses a password to protect access to the VNC server. For those wanting a more secure implementation there is a Personal Edition and an Enterprise Edition that offer strong encryption and use of existing user accounts for authentication.

The best way to avoid these problems is to not use the software; however that does not help much. When using VNC over untrusted networks it is important to make sure you are using the latest version, which should hopefully include any fixes to security flaws in the software. In addition, you should use a firewall to ensure that you only allow access to the VNC server from authorized networks or IP addresses. You should also try to use VNC on demand, instead of running it on a computer all the time. Ask someone to install it and turn it only when you need it.

Now to move on to setting up VNC. There is more than one implementation of VNC available. The version maintained by the original authors is available from RealVNC (www.realvnc.com). In these examples you are going to use the VNC implementation called TightVNC (www.tightvnc.com). TightVNC is under active development and in my opinion seems to be the better choice if you are looking for a good free VNC package. If you are willing to pay for more Enterprise features, check out the Enterprise and Personal editions of VNC that RealVNC has to offer.

## Installing VNC on Windows

On the TightVNC website, you can find the latest version for Windows. As of this writing the latest version is 1.2.9 and the installer is tightvnc-1.2.9-setup.exe. To install TightVNC you will need to answer a couple of questions, including where to install the software. The default location should suffice for most people. Next you must decide which components to install. At a bare minimum you need the server, but you can also install the client and documentation if you wish. Last, but not least, is whether you wish to install the VNC server as a Windows service and if the installer should start the service (Figure 3.16). If you are familiar with the terminology, running as a service is the equivalent to running as a UNIX daemon, while running VNC from the system tray is the equivalent to running a process in the foreground. If you choose to install the VNC server as a service, the server can run when you're not logged into the machine, which is usually desirable. Otherwise, someone will have to be logged into the computer with the VNC server running as an application. If the person decides to log off, the VNC server will no longer be running. It is recommended that  you enable both of these options so the VNC server will be installed as a service, and the service will be started after the installation is finished.

**Figure 3.16** Configuring VNC to Run as a Service and Start Automatically Upon Reboot

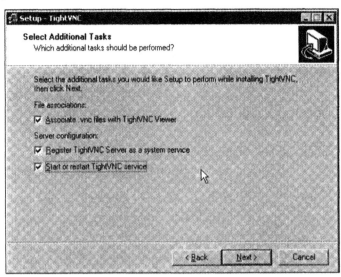

Once the installer finishes installing and starting the service, it will prompt you with a warning that there is no password set for the VNC server. After clicking through the warning you will be given an option to inspect the VNC server settings and set the password, as shown in Figure 3.17.

**Figure 3.17** Configuring a Password for the VNC Server

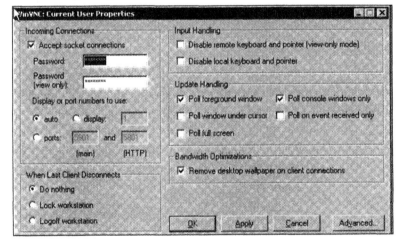

# Connecting the VNC Server from OS X

Now comes the easy part. TightVNC has a java-based client that should run on any platform that has a Java virtual machine. To top it all off, the TightVNC server installation serves this java client from a built in Web server. So once you have a server installed on your Windows machine, all you need to do is access the Web server from your browser to run the VNC client. By default, the Web server runs on port 5800. If your Windows machine has an IP address of 10.16.1.55, so the URL you use to access it is http://10.16.1.55:5800.

After you enter your password (Figure 3.18) and click **OK**, you are presented with the desktop of your remote Windows machine (Figure 3.19). You are now accessing the computer as you would from the keyboard and monitor attached to it. Although the response time is not the same, it gives you full access to the remote machine. From here you can install software, change Control Panel settings, configure a Web server, anything you could do when logged into the machine physically.

**Figure 3.18** VNC Login Page

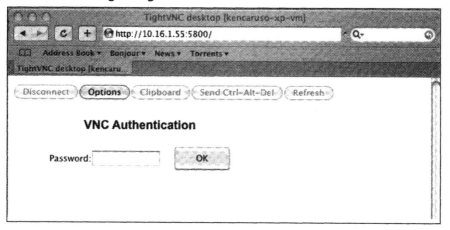

**Figure 3.19** Remote Windows Desktop using VNC

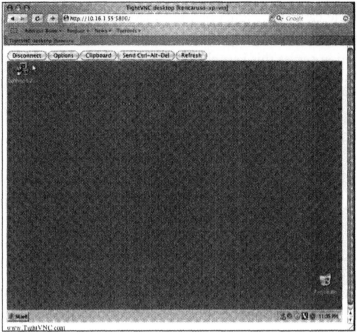

# Synergy—Using a Mac and PC from one Keyboard/Mouse

It is a common scenario to see someone with both a Mac and a Windows box on his or her desk. To use two separate machines you are usually left one of two choices; either have two keyboards and mice at your desk, or use a keyboard/video/mouse switch to switch between the two computers when you need to. *Synergy* is an open source program that can facilitate this experience

Synergy allows you to control multiple computers, each with their own monitor, from one keyboard and mouse. It even connects them virtually so that when your mouse moves off the edge of one screen it jumps to the screen on the other computer and vice versa. It does this by creating a connection over the network, which it uses to send keyboard and mouse movements.

Synergy is open source and runs on OS X, Windows, and most versions of UNIX. In theory you could have a collection of screens on your desk all connected to machines of different operating systems and roam between the desktops from a central keyboard and mouse.

Synergy is a client server application; the server is the machine that has the master keyboard and mouse. The clients are the machines whose desktops you wish to connect to the master. You tell Synergy how your screens are laid out and it sets up the connections accordingly.

In the example, you have two computers. akira.local is a Macintosh, which will act as the master, and kenspc is a Windows machine, which will be a client you can control using the mouse and keyboard on your Mac.

# Installing and Configuring Synergy

To get started on setting up Synergy you will need to download both the OS X version and the Windows version to the respective machines. As of this writing the latest version on the Synergy website (http://synergy2.source-forge.net) is 1.2.4-1. There is a binary package available for OS X and an installer for Windows.

On your Mac, open up the tarball you downloaded. In the tarball there should be the synergys and synergyc binaries; these are the server and client, respectively. In addition there should also be the synergy.conf file. This is the configuration file that drives the UNIX and OS X versions of synergy. The Windows version comes with a GUI for configuration.

**Figure 3.20** A Directory Listing of the Synergy Directory

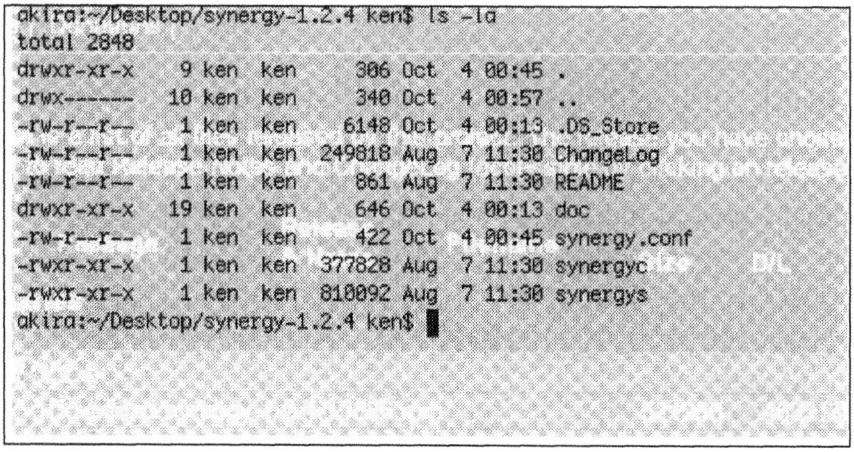

```
akira:~/Desktop/synergy-1.2.4 ken$ ls -la
total 2848
drwxr-xr-x    9 ken  ken     306 Oct  4 00:45 .
drwx------   10 ken  ken     340 Oct  4 00:57 ..
-rw-r--r--    1 ken  ken    6148 Oct  4 00:13 .DS_Store
-rw-r--r--    1 ken  ken  249818 Aug  7 11:30 ChangeLog
-rw-r--r--    1 ken  ken     861 Aug  7 11:30 README
drwxr-xr-x   19 ken  ken     646 Oct  4 00:13 doc
-rw-r--r--    1 ken  ken     422 Oct  4 00:45 synergy.conf
-rwxr-xr-x    1 ken  ken  377828 Aug  7 11:30 synergyc
-rwxr-xr-x    1 ken  ken  810092 Aug  7 11:30 synergys
akira:~/Desktop/synergy-1.2.4 ken$ 
```

Let's take a look at the sample the given config files:

```
section: screens
        moe:
        larry:
        curly:
end


section: links
        moe:
                right = larry
                up    = curly


        larry:
                left  = moe
                up    = curly
then
        curly:
                down  = larry
end
section: aliases
        curly:
                shemp
end
```

The configuration above is for three screens, but for this example configuration you are going to simplify things and use only two.

There are three basic sections in the Synergy configuration file. The first is *screens*, where you specify the hostnames of machines that you wish to connect to each other. In the *links* section, you describe how the screens are physically laid out in respect to each other. In this case, your Windows machine, kenspc is to the right of your Mac, akira.local. The last section is *aliases*, where you can configure aliases for screen names if you like.

```
section: screens
        akira.local:
        kenspc:
end


section: links
```

```
    akira.local:
            right = kenspc
    kenspc:
    left  = akira.local
    end

section: aliases
        # This is where you put aliases for screen and hostnames
end
```

> **NOTE**
>
> The *.local* entry in the code above is appended to the computer name as part of Bonjour, Apple's zero-config implementation. Synergy detects your machine's name as *akira.local* and thus expects you to reference it by that name in the configuration file.
>
> Also note that there is a description for each computer. You would think that saying, "kenspc is on the right" would be enough for it to figure out that akira.local is on the left, but that is not the case. If you were to leave the *kenspc:* section out of *screens:* your mouse would make it over to the other machine, but not know how to get back to your Mac.

Now let's start the Synergy server with your new configuration file. In the terminal, access the directory where the Synergy files are located and type the following command to start the server:

```
./synergys -f -c synergy.conf
```

```
INFO: synergys.cpp,1034: Synergy server 1.2.4 on Darwin 8.2.0 Darwin Kernel
Version 8.2.0: Fri Jun 24 17:46:54 PDT 2005; root:xnu-
792.2.4.obj~3/RELEASE_PPC Power Macintosh
DEBUG: synergys.cpp,1043: opening configuration "synergy.conf"
DEBUG: synergys.cpp,1054: configuration read successfully
DEBUG: COSXScreen.cpp,1067: screen shape: 0,0 1280x854 on 1 display
DEBUG: COSXScreen.cpp,138: starting watchSystemPowerThread
DEBUG: CScreen.cpp,38: opened display
NOTE: synergys.cpp,500: started server
```

```
DEBUG: COSXScreen.cpp,1148: started watchSystemPowerThread
INFO: CServer.cpp,1031: screen "akira.local" shape changed
```

If everything worked you should see something similar to the output shown here. You used two command line arguments when invoking the Synergy server. The first is -f, which tells the server to run in the foreground instead of in daemon mode. Running it in the foreground for now allows you to see any error messages that may pop up and make troubleshooting any problems you run across easier. Once the configuration is tested you can get rid of the -f option and run it in daemon mode. The second flag, -c, is to tell Synergy which configuration file to use. This can come in handy if you have multiple monitor layouts that you use and want to keep a separate configuration file for each one.

Now on to the Windows side. The Synergy installer only gives you a couple of options, one for the location to install the software and the second allowing you to choose if you want the documentation installed. The defaults will work just fine.

Once Synergy is installed and you start it up, you will be presented with a fairly simple GUI, as shown in Figure 3.21. Since you are acting as a client all you need to do is put in the hostname or IP address of the master you want to connect to.

**Figure 3.21** Synergy Configuration Screen for Windows

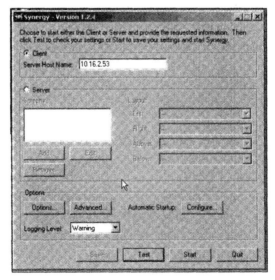

You can use the **Test** button to test the connection beforehand. Once everything checks out OK, click **Start** and you should be ready to go. Synergy will minimize to the taskbar, go to your OS X machine and move the mouse on the screen toward your Windows machine, ta-da!

As mentioned earlier, Synergy is supported on multiple operating systems, so you could have many different machines, all with screens on your desk talking to each other. The configuration file also understands top and bottom as well as left and right, so feel free to stack away.

# Talking to Windows From the Terminal

This section goes over some basic ways to establish command line-based connectivity to Windows machines. You will do this by installing OpenSSH on a Windows box, as well becoming more familiar with some of the command line tools that come with Samba.

How far to take this is left as an exercise for the reader. This section will show some basic examples, which you can then use as a base to continue increasing your Mac to Windows command line foo.

Windows has a ton of built-in and third-party command line tools that allow you to do almost everything you can through the GUI—everything from adding domain accounts to importing a registry key using the Regedit program. In addition, if you combine command line access with a Windows scripting language that can access things like WMI (Windows Management Instrumentation), you can do a lot of cool things all from the command line and all from the comfort of your Mac.

# SSH

OpenSSH is software project maintained by the OpenBSD project. OpenBSD is a project that focuses on building highly secure software such as their core BSD-based operating system. The OpenSSH suite of tools, including the SSH client and server, come with OS X.

In the days of yore, UNIX geeks used tools such as Telnet, FTP, and rlogin for remotely logging into computers and transferring data. These tools worked great with one caveat; they lacked encryption. The result was that someone using these tools was at risk of someone eavesdropping on their network traffic and intercepting crucial information such as usernames and passwords.

OpenSSH is built of programs that replace these encrypted tools with ones that use OpenSSL, an open source implementation of SSL and TLS (transport layer security). So now you have ssh, which replaces Telnet, sftp, which replaces FTP, and scp which replaces rcp. Practically all UNIX-like operating systems now ship with an implementation of SSH, although not all use OpenSSH.

So great, these awesome tools came with OS X, but how do they help me with MS Windows? Well these tools have been ported to Windows as well (http://sshwindows.sourceforge.net). Here you will find a binary distribution of OpenSSH compiled for Windows. As of this writing the latest version available is 3.8p1-1 20040709.

With OpenSSH installed on a Windows machine, it will be possible to log into a Windows command line shell using your OS X terminal and run commands on the remote Windows box.

---

**NOTE**

Windows XP and 2003 Server come with a Telnet server that will afford you some of the functionality of SSH. However, Telnet does not use encryption and thus poses a lot of security risks. In addition, the Microsoft Telnet server has a limit on how many concurrent Telnet logins you can have. Finally, SSH has the ability to allow you to create encrypted tunnels for almost any TCP (Transmission Control Protocol)-based application.

---

## Installing SSH on Windows

Installing OpenSSH on Windows is not quite as cut-and-dry as most Windows software, but with a little elbow grease you can get through it. One thing to keep mind is that OpenSSH is written for UNIX-like operating systems, which Windows is far from. So there is a little tomfoolery that has to happen to get OpenSSH working.

1. Download the latest version from the sshwindows website (http://sshwindows.sourceforge.net) and put it on the Windows machine you wish to install it on.

2. Expand the zip file to a new folder and execute the setup program setupssh.exe.

3. Select the installation location; for most people the default location, C:\Program Files\OpenSSH, should suffice. You will briefly see a Windows shell window open up as the installer generates an SSH host key for your system.

4. You will now see a dialog box telling you that you have to create a password and group file in order for OpenSSH to work properly; click **OK**.

5. To open a Windows command shell, click **Start | Run**, then type **cmd** and press **Enter**.

6. Change your working directory to C:\Program Files\OpenSSH\bin by typing **cd c:\Program Files\OpenSSH\bin**.

7. If your Windows computer is in a domain, enter the following commands:

```
mkgroup -d >> ../etc/group
mkpasswd -d >> ../etc/group
```

If your Windows computer is *not* in a domain, enter the following:

```
mkgroup -l >> ../etc/group
mkpasswd -l >> ../etc/group
```

8. Start the OpenSSH server from the command line by typing **net start opensshd**.

You should now see a message telling you that the service started.

What did you just do? OpenSSH is written for UNIX, that is not going to change. Therefore, it looks for usernames, passwords, and group membership in the places where they would normally be on a UNIX box—the passwd and group files. Since Windows does not have these files, you use the mkgroup command and the mkpasswd command to export some of this information into these files to make it work.

When you use the -d flag with mkpasswd and mkgroup you are getting the user and group information from the Windows domain or Active Directory. When you use the -l flag you are getting this information from the local machine's account database.

So now OpenSSH is up and running and awaiting your connections. To connect the Windows computer via SSH, fire up a terminal window (Figure 3.22)and run the command below, replacing the username and computer name with your information. In this example your username is *ken* and the computer you are connecting to is *frink*:

```
Ssh ken@frink
```

**Figure 3.22** Terminal Window for Connecting Windows Computer via SSH

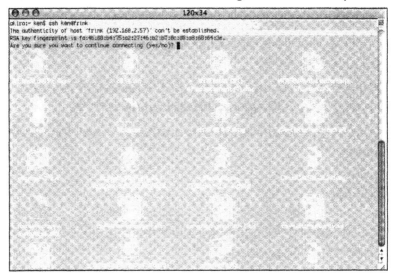

The first time you connect you will be asked to verify the fingerprint of the SSH server's public key. If you like to live on the edge you can just say **yes** to this, however this check happens to ensure that you are in fact connecting to the server you intended and no one is attempting to intercept or interfere with your SSH connection. You can compare the fingerprint presented to the fingerprint on the server by using the *ssh-keygen* command on the Windows machine in the C:\Program Files\OpenSSH\bin directory like so:

```
Ssh-keygen -l
```

When prompted, point to the servers public host key. If you are in the bin directory the location would be ..\etc\ssh_host_dsa_key.pub, or if you are using RSA the location would be ..\etc\ssh_host_rsa_key.pub. This will show you the fingerprint of the host key and after verifying that the two match you can safely say **yes** and your local machine will cache the fingerprint for comparison during later connections.

When prompted for a password, enter the password for your Windows account and you will be greeted with a Windows command prompt like the one shown in Figure 3.23.

**Figure 3.23** Windows Command Prompt

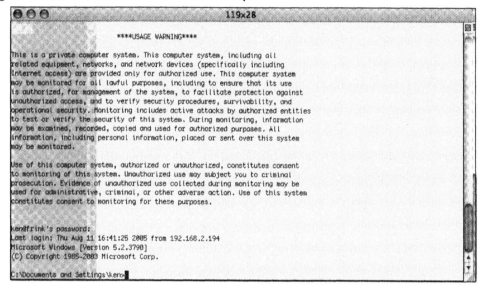

## Starting and Stopping a Service

So now you that you can login to your windows box through SSH, let's put it to use for a simple administrative task; stopping and starting a service. Services include things such as IIS and the Microsoft DNS server.

To see a list of services running on your windows box type **net start** at the Windows command prompt. You will probably see a fairly long list of services, similar to those shown in Figure 3.24. If you remember from the VNC section, you installed the VNC server as a service. Well now that you are done with the VNC server, you want to shut it down so it's not running and posing a potential security threat to your system. After you run *net start*, you see that Windows refers to the VNC service as *VNC Server*.

To stop the server, type **net stop "VNC Server."** The next time you need VNC you can log in again via SSH and start the VNC server back up by using **net start "VNC Server."**

**Figure 3.24** List of Services

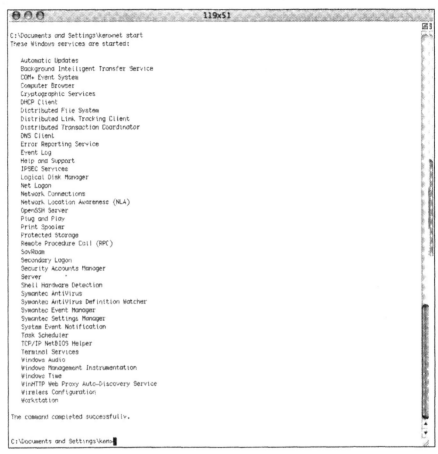

```
C:\Documents and Settings\ken>net start
These Windows services are started:

    Automatic Updates
    Background Intelligent Transfer Service
    COM+ Event System
    Computer Browser
    Cryptographic Services
    DHCP Client
    Distributed File System
    Distributed Link Tracking Client
    Distributed Transaction Coordinator
    DNS Client
    Error Reporting Service
    Event Log
    Help and Support
    IPSEC Services
    Logical Disk Manager
    Net Logon
    Network Connections
    Network Location Awareness (NLA)
    OpenSSH Server
    Plug and Play
    Print Spooler
    Protected Storage
    Remote Procedure Call (RPC)
    SavRoam
    Secondary Logon
    Security Accounts Manager
    Server
    Shell Hardware Detection
    Symantec AntiVirus
    Symantec AntiVirus Definition Watcher
    Symantec Event Manager
    Symantec Settings Manager
    System Event Notification
    Task Scheduler
    TCP/IP NetBIOS Helper
    Terminal Services
    Windows Audio
    Windows Management Instrumentation
    Windows Time
    WinHTTP Web Proxy Auto-Discovery Service
    Wireless Configuration
    Workstation

The command completed successfully.

C:\Documents and Settings\ken>
```

# Windows Command Line Tools

Windows has a myriad of command line utilities available. The majority of them should work through an SSH session without any problems. In this section you are going to briefly touch on some simple examples of things that are used frequently.

If you are familiar with DOS and its available commands then you can hit the ground running with such tasks as copying and deleting files. If not, here a couple of quick examples that will get you going:

- Copying a file named *textfile.txt* from the C: drive to the *ken* directory on the D: drive:

```
Copy c:\textfile.txt d:\ken\textfile.txt
```

- Deleting a file named *textfile.txt* that resides in the *ken* directory on the D drive:

```
Del d:\ken\textfile.txt
```

- Copying a file named *textfile.txt* to a share called *fileshare* on a computer named *barney*:

```
Copy c:\textfile.txt \\barney\fileshare\
```

In addition to the DOS commands, Windows occasionally surprises you with something like *netstat*. Netstat is a tool that all UNIX administrators consider invaluable. Netstat displays information and statistics about network connections. On most UNIX operating systems it has a wide range of options for retrieving and display network statistics. However, on Windows it's a little simpler with only nine different command line flags available. To get a full list of options you can type **netstat –h**. Here are a couple of options you can use:

- Show a list of all connections, listening ports and update it every 10 seconds:

```
Netstat -a 10
```

- Show a list of all connections, listening ports and show the executable associated with each one:

```
Netstat -ab
```

**NOTE**

www.sysinternals.com is a great resource for UNIX-style command line utilities that can be used on Windows.

**NOTE**

The Windows 2003 Server Resource Kit comes with many additional command line utilities that are very useful for system administration. These utilities are available for download from Microsoft. Check out the Windows 2003 server home page for more info at http://www.microsoft.com/windowsserver2003.

## Samba Command Line Utilities

We briefly talked earlier about what the Samba project is. Under the hood it's what is actually doing the work of connecting to Windows file shares and printers. However, the tools in the Samba suite are capable of much more than that. They can be used for discovering what computers are in an Windows environment and also for managing some aspects of a Windows environment without ever having to interactively log into a Windows machine. In the majority of previous examples, you were interactively connecting to a Windows computer via protocols like SSH and Remote Desktop. In the following examples you will run commands on your local computer to discover and perform administrative tasks on remote windows computers.

### Findsmb

The findsmb tool is a perl script that comes with Samba. It discovers computers responding to SMB queries on a given network. This tool is useful for discovering what machines are on a network and collecting information about their operating system versions. It is fairly simple with only two command line options. If invoked without any options, it looks on the local network of the machine it is run on and displays a list of computers with information about their workgroups or domains and their operating systems. You can specify a broadcast address as an argument if you want to query a network other than your local network.

Let's look at the output from the findsmb command:

```
IP ADDR          NETBIOS NAME     WORKGROUP/OS/VERSION

--------------------------------------------------------------------

192.168.2.53    JEBEDIAH        [DOMAINFOO] [Windows 5.0] [Windows 2000 LAN
Manager]
```

In this case you only have one Windows machine on your local network, named *Jebediah*. It tells you the domain the computer belongs to, as well the operating system version and the SMB implementation it is running. Taken from the man page for findsmb you might see something like this on a more mixed network:

```
IP ADDR          NETBIOS NAME    WORKGROUP/OS/VERSION

--------------------------------------------------------------------

192.168.35.10   MINESET-TEST1   [DMVENGR]
192.168.35.55   LINUXBOX       *[MYGROUP] [Unix] [Samba 2.0.6]
192.168.35.56   HERBNT2         [HERB-NT]
192.168.35.63   GANDALF         [MVENGR] [Unix] [Samba 2.0.5a for IRIX]
192.168.35.65   SAUNA           [WORKGROUP] [Unix] [Samba 1.9.18p10]
192.168.35.71   FROGSTAR        [ENGR] [Unix] [Samba 2.0.0 for IRIX]
192.168.35.78   HERBDHCP1      +[HERB]
192.168.35.88   SCNT2          +[MVENGR] [Windows NT 4.0] [NT LAN Manager
                 4.0]
192.168.35.93   FROGSTAR-PC     [MVENGR] [Windows 5.0] [Windows 2000 LAN
                 Manager]
192.168.35.97   HERBNT1        *[HERB-NT] [Windows NT 4.0] [NT LAN Manager
                 4.0]
```

As you can see, findsmb also identifies UNIX computers running Samba.

## Net

In the Windows world there is the *net* command. You used it earlier in this chapter for stopping and starting a Windows service. It supports other functions such as mapping network file systems and viewing server statistics. The Samba suite comes with a net command as well. It was originally intended to mimic the Windows version, however it has grown to do much more. For a complete description of everything that can be done with net command, reading the man page is definitely in order. Some of these cover some of the options that you have found useful for administering Windows systems.

When invoking the net command the first argument is almost always the protocol you want to use to execute commands on the Windows server. All of the examples will use RPC, which stands for Remote Procedure Call. RPC is a protocol for executing commands on a remote system over a network. Some commands will require you to authenticate with a domain account, and some with an administrator-level domain account. You can specify username and password from the command line the following format:

```
-U username
```

If you give just the username you will be interactively prompted for a password. You can specify the password by appending **%** to the username and then appending the password. For example:

```
-U username%password
```

The first example you will use is the *info* option for the net command. This option does not require any authentication to run. You are going to query a domain controller on your network named *lisa* with the command **net rpc info**. Net is the base command and *rpc* tells it to use RPC for communications. *Info* is the option you want to run and the *−S* flag specifies the server you want to talk to.

```
akira:~ ken$ net rpc info -S lisa
Domain Name: DOMAINFOO
Domain SID: S-1-5-21-3004504114-827126951-3990820360
Sequence number: 1
Num users: 210
Num domain groups: 0
Num local groups: 40
```

There is some interesting information in the output of the net rpc info command, but for the most part it's not all that useful day-to-day. How about getting a list of users in the domain that the server *lisa* is a domain controller for? Notice that you are authenticating with the domain administrator account now:

```
akira:~ ken$ net rpc user -S lisa -Uadministrator%badpassword
Administrator
anonymous
BACKUPUSER
chris
```

```
DesktopBackupAccount
ken
```

The actual list has been truncated for the sake of brevity, but you should have a complete list of users in the domain, assuming the machine you queried is a domain controller. If it is not a domain controller, but rather a standalone server or a member server in your domain, you should get a list of all of the local accounts on that server.

So how about a fairly common task such as adding a user account? You can do that too:

```
akira:~ ken$ net rpc user add ken-test-account -S lisa
-Uadministrator%badpassword
```

Removing an account?

```
akira:~ ken$ net rpc user delete ken-test-account -S lisa
-Uadministrator%badpassword
```

In these examples you are specifying *rpc* as your protocol, the user option, then the action you wish to perform (add or delete), the name of the account , the server you wish to perform the action on, and your login credentials. The net command is a great utility to add to your toolbox, and best of all it and the rest of the Samba suite come as stock equipment on OS X.

# Summary

This chapter covers tools ands techniques for communicating with Windows hosts from your computer running OS X. A good chunk of interoperability between Windows and OS X comes from open source tools such as the Samba project.

You can mount Windows network file shares via the finder, AppleScript, and even via the terminal in favorite command shell.

NTLM authentication is used frequently in the Windows world. There are programs such as curl, Safari and Firefox that support it natively on OS X. For times when it is not supportive you can use an NTLM proxy to handle authentication for non-NTLM aware applications.

OS X has built-in support for PPTP, a VPN solution pioneered by Microsoft and common in Microsoft Shops. Using your Mac you can remotely connect to networks using PPTP. With some simple hacks you can achieve split tunneling to choose which network traffic gets routed over the PPTP VPN, as well specifying which DNS servers you wish to use for certain DNS requests.

Remote Desktop is a great tool for accessing Windows systems from OS X. In addition to Microsoft's Remote Desktop client for OS X, there is also an open source implementation called rdesktop. VNC is a slightly different approach to remotely access systems. VNC provides a remote console on the actual desktop of the machine you are connecting to and is available for most operating systems.

Synergy is an open source project which allows you to control multiple machines of varying operating systems all from a single computer. You can have OS X and Windows computers in front of you and seamlessly move your mouse from one to the other, utililizing a network connection to send your mouse and keyboard commands.

OpenSSH is commonly found on Unix systems, however both the client and server have been ported to Windows. With an OpenSSH server installed on Windows you can remotely log in via the terminal and run commands on your Windows Systems.

The Samba suite comes with a command called net, which allows you to issue commands to Windows machines via RPC. Things like password resets and account creation can easily be accomplished on OS X using the net command.

# Solutions Fast Track

## Accessing Network File Systems

- ☑ Mount network filesystems through the finder by using the smb:// url prefix.

- ☑ You can use a simple AppleScript to automate the mounting of your network filesystems.

- ☑ The mount_smbfs command allows you to mount Windows shares via the terminal.

- ☑ The .nmbrc or nsnmb.conf files can be used to make using mount_smbfs easier.

## NTLM Authentication

- ☑ NTLM is a Microsoft protocol for authentication.

- ☑ Safari, Firefox and curl all support NTLM authentication.

- ☑ NTLMAPS is an open source proxy server that supports NTLM.

- ☑ Non-NTLM aware apps can use NTLMAPS to handle authentication for them.

## Connecting to a Windows PPTP Server

- ☑ You can configure PPTP connection via the Internet Connect application.

- ☑ Create a file in /etc/ppp/peers/ that has the same name as your PPTP connection and specify "nodefaultroute" in that file to disable the changing of your default route.

- ☑ You can specify DNS servers for a particular domain by placing a file in /private/etc/resolver that is named the same as the domain and contains the DNS server for that domain

# Zen of Running Windows Boxes from a Mac

☑ Microsoft remote desktop client supports a shared clipboard between your local remote computers

☑ Microsoft remote desktop client supports sharing your local hard drive to the remote windows computer

☑ If you save a remote desktop connection as a file you can use the "open" command to launch it from the command line

☑ RDC Menu is a remote desktop launcher that supports concurrent remote desktop connections

☑ Rdesktop is an open source remote desktop client that can be installed via the darwing ports: suod port install rdesktop

☑ Installing VNC server on a Windows computer allows you to connect to the desktop of that machine from OS X

☑ Installing syngery on OS X and windows allows you to control both desktops from one keyboard and mouse

☑ Install OpenSSH server on Windows to login to windows computers using the ssh client on OS X

☑ SSH into a windows computer and use "net start" and "net stop" to start and stop services

☑ findsmb discovers windows machines on your network

☑ The samba "net" command can be used to issue RPC commands to windows

# Frequently Asked Questions

The following Frequently Asked Questions, answered by the authors of this book, are designed to both measure your understanding of the concepts presented in this chapter and to assist you with real-life implementation of these concepts. To have your questions about this chapter answered by the author, browse to **www.syngress.com/solutions** and click on the **"Ask the Author"** form. You will also gain access to thousands of other FAQs at ITFAQnet.com.

**Q:** How can I get a list of available file shares on a server?

**A:** When connecting with the finder use smb://servername without appending a share name, it will show you a list of available shares.

**Q:** Can I have more than one VPN connection?

**A:** The Internet Connect application allows you to have multiple VPN connections, however it will only let you use one at a time.

**Q:** Remote desktop seems slow. Can I tweak it for performance?

**A:** Yes the Microsoft remote desktop client has settings under the options menu that allow you to adjust for performance vs. appearance

**Q:** Do I need special access rights to remote desktop into a windows machine?

**A:** Yes, the account you wish to login with has to be granted rights to use remote desktop

**Q:** Is there a way to copy files to a Windows machine without connecting to network file shares?

**A:** If you install the OpenSSH server on windows you can use the "scp" (secure copy) command to copy files to and from a Windows machine using an encrypted channel.

**Q:** How can I reset my password on a Windows system from OS X?

**A:** You can remote desktop into a windows machine and go to **Start | Settings | Windows | Security** and then click on the change password button. You can also use the samba "net" command to do with out logging into windows.

**Q:** Where can I find more information on the Samba "net" command?

**A:** The man page is a good place to start. Type "man net" from the terminal. Also check out the documentation on the samba website: www.samba.org

# WarDriving and Wireless Penetration Testing with OS X

## Solutions in this chapter:

- WarDriving with KisMAC
- Penetration Testing with OS X.
- Other OS X Tools for WarDriving and WLAN Testing

☑ Summary

☑ Solutions Fast Track

☑ Frequently Asked Questions

# Introduction

WarDriving and wireless local area network (WLAN) penetration testing are fun (and in the case of penetration testing, often lucrative) activities that are great to do with your Mac. OS X has excellent wireless support and there are several tools available to make these tasks both easier and more fun.

The first part of this chapter describes the steps necessary to configure and utilize the KisMAC WLAN discovery tool to successfully WarDrive. The preferences, options, and views available with the KisMAC interface are presented in order to help you gain an understanding of how to use KisMAC. While KisMAC is covered in great detail, this chapter does not provide how-to steps for WarDriving (iGPS choice, antenna theory, location selection, etcetera). If you are interested in information about WarDriving in general, check out the publication *WarDriving: Drive, Detect, Defend* from Syngress Publishing, Inc. The second part of this chapter describes how the information obtained during a WarDrive and details the methods that a penetration tester can further utilize KisMAC to successfully penetrate a customer's wireless network.

# WarDriving with KisMAC

KisMAC, available for free download from http://kismac.binaervarianz.de/, is quite possibly the best WarDriving and WLAN discovery and penetration testing tool available on any platform. Most WarDriving applications provide the capability to discover networks in either active mode or passive mode. KisMAC provides the capability to do both. On other platforms, WarDriving tools such as Kismet for Linux or NetStumbler for Windows provide only the capability to discover WLANs. KisMAC is unique in that it also includes the functionality a penetration tester needs to attack and compromise found networks. Those tools, platforms, scan types, and attach capabilities are better illustrated in Table 4.1.

**Table 4.1** Prominent Wireless Discovery Tools and Capabilities

| Tool | Platform | Scan Type | Attack Capability |
| --- | --- | --- | --- |
| NetStumbler | Windows | Active | No |
| Kismet | Linux | Passive | No |
| KisMAC | OS X | Active/Passive | Yes |

# KisMAC Startup and Initial Configuration

Once KisMAC has been downloaded and installed it is relatively easy to use. The first thing you need to do is load KisMAC. This is a simple single click operation on the KisMAC icon. Habitual WarDrivers will probably want to add KisMAC to their toolbar (Figure 4.1).

**Figure 4.1** KisMAC

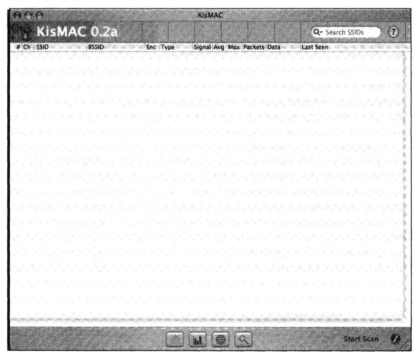

Before you can do anything you need to set your KisMAC preferences and understand the KisMAC interface.

# Configuring the KisMAC Preferences

The KisMAC interface is very straightforward. However, because KisMAC is so robust, there are a lot of different configuration option available. The first thing you need to do is open the **Preferences** window via the KisMAC menu bar (**KisMAC | Preferences**). This section covers six of the eight available preferences (Figure 4.2):

- Scanning
- Filter
- Sounds
- Driver
- Traffic
- .kismac

**Figure 4.2** The KisMAC Preferences

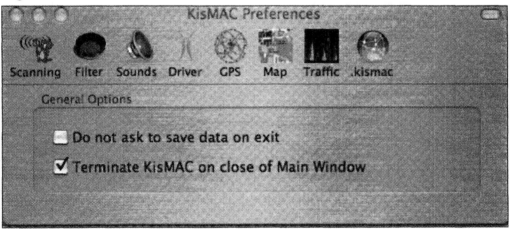

The GPS and Map options are covered later in this chapter, in the section entitled, "Mapping with KisMAC."

# Scanning Options

There are two Scanning Options available (as shown in Figure 4.2), both of which relate to actions KisMAC should take when closing:

- Do not ask to save data on exit.
- Terminate KisMAC on close of Main Window.

These are very straightforward options. By default when you close KisMAC, you will be prompted to save your data file unless you enable the first option. It is a good idea to leave **Do not ask to save data on exit** disabled. Disabling this option will require you to manually save your data before closing KisMAC and can result in the accidental loss of data. The second option controls whether or not KisMAC will end when you close the main window. This is more a matter of personal preference. If this option is disabled then KisMAC will be closed but remain loaded, and will continue to display in the toolbar.

## Filter Options

The Filter options (Figure 4.3) allow you do designate specific MAC (media access control) addresses that you do not want included in your results. Entering a MAC address and clicking **Add** enables this functionality. This is especially useful for removing wireless networks that you control, such as your home network or other boxes you are using for an attack, from your results. Additionally, if you are doing a penetration test, it is likely that you want only traffic from your target in your data sets.

**Figure 4.3** The Filter Options

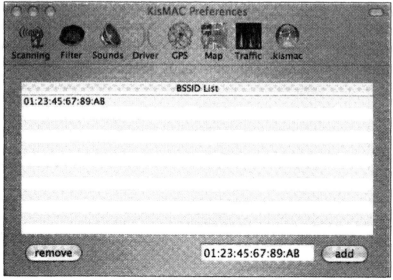

# Sound Preferences

Unlike its Linux counterpart, Kismet, which requires a third-party application such as Festival, KisMAC has built-in functionality for speaking the SSID (Service Set Identifier) of found networks (Figure 4.4). This can be useful and fun when you are driving and don't have the ability to look at the screen to see the names of found networks.

**Figure 4.4** KisMAC Sound Preferences

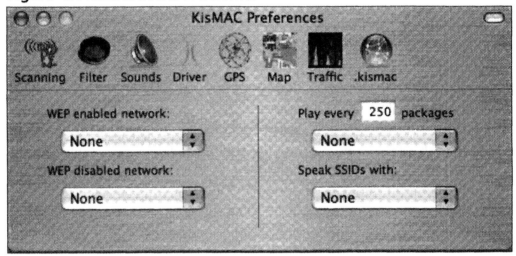

Easy-to-use drop-down menus (Figure 4.5) allow you to assign different sound effects to be played when a Wired Equivalent Privacy (WEP) or WiFi Protected Access (WPA) network is found. Additionally, specific sound effects can be played when a certain number of packets have been captured as well as different voices to speak the network name or SSID as networks are discovered.

**Figure 4.5** Configuring Sound Effects

### Choosing a WLAN Card

KisMAC has built-in support for a wide range of WLAN cards. When choosing a card, you must determine what your goals are. KisMAC has support for both active and passive scanning. Active scanning relies on the use of the broadcast beacon to discover access points (APs). The built-in Airport Extreme card on most iBooks and Powerbooks works in active mode only.

Passive scanning does not rely on the broadcast beacon. In order to passively scan for wireless networks, you must have a card capable of entering monitor mode (rfmon). Once a card has been placed in monitor mode, it can sniff all traffic within range of the card (or its attached antenna) and discover any wireless networks, including those that do not broadcast the beacon.

Kismet supports Airport or Airport Extreme cards in active mode. Passive mode is supported for the Airport and Cisco PCMCIA (Personal Computer Memory Card International Association) cards as well as any PCMCIA card based on the Atheros, Prism2, Hermes, and Prism GT chipsets. Additionally, USB (universal serial bus) devices based on the Prism2 chipset support passive mode.

**Continued**

Figure 4.6 displays the drop-down menu of available chipsets. Table 4.2 indicates some of the common cards and chipsets that will work with KisMAC and the mode they will work in.

**Table 4.2** Examples of Cards That Work with KisMAC

| Manufacturer | Card | Chipset | Mode |
|---|---|---|---|
| Apple | Airport | Hermes | Passive |
| Apple | Airport Express | Broadcom | Active |
| Cisco | Aironet LMC-352 | Cisco | Passive |
| Proxim | Orinoco Gold | Hermes | Passive |
| Engenius | Senao 2511CD Plus EXT2 | Prism 2 | Passive |
| Linksys | WPC11 | Prism 2 | Passive |
| Linksys | WUSB54G | Prism2 | Passive |

If your adapter is not listed in the table above, check out http://linux-wlan.org/docs/wlan_adapters.html.tgz for a more complete list of cards and their respective chipsets.

**NOTE**

12-inch Powerbooks and all iBook models do not have PCMCIA slots and require a USB WiFi Adapter such as the Linksys WUSB54G, or an original Airport to work in passive mode. Unfortunately, there are currently no USB WiFi adapters that have external antenna connectors. Some brave souls have added them, but this should be undertaken, since there is a good chance you will destroy your adapter in the process.

**Figure 4.6** KisMAC Supported Chipsets

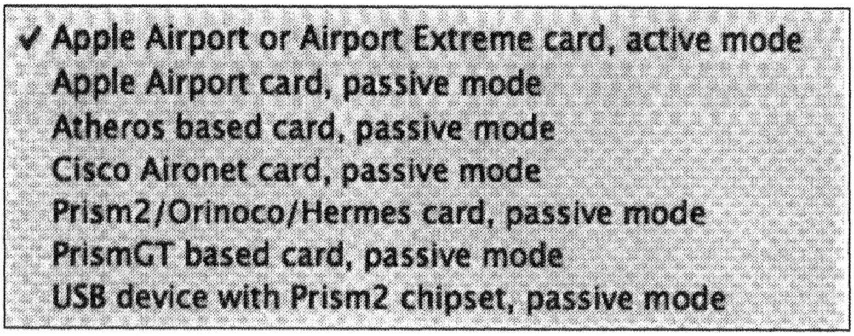

✓ Apple Airport or Airport Extreme card, active mode
Apple Airport card, passive mode
Atheros based card, passive mode
Cisco Aironet card, passive mode
Prism2/Orinoco/Hermes card, passive mode
PrismGT based card, passive mode
USB device with Prism2 chipset, passive mode

# Traffic

KisMAC also affords the WarDriver with the ability to view the signal strength, number pf packets transferred, and number of bytes transferred for the networks that have been detected. Networks can be displayed by the SSID or by the BSSID (basic SSID), also known as the MAC address (see Figure 4.7). The average signal can be calculated based on traffic seen for the last 1-300 seconds and should be adjusted depending on the accuracy you need.

**Figure 4.7** Traffic Preferences

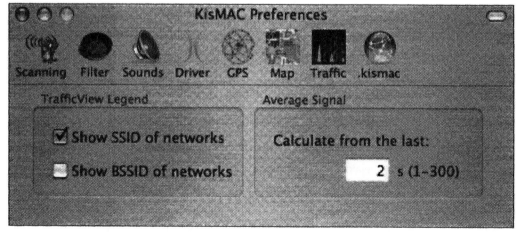

KisMAC Preferences
Scanning
Filter
Sounds
Driver
GPS
Map
Traffic
.kismac
TrafficView Legend
Show SSID of networks
Show BSSID of networks
Average Signal
Calculate from the last:
2
s (1-300)

# .kismac Preferences

*.kismac* is a built-in option that allows you to share your WarDrive data with other KisMAC users very easily. In order to use .kismac you need to have a .kismac account. Luckily, you can create an account in the .kismac preferences window (Figure 4.8).

**Figure 4.8** .kismac Preferences

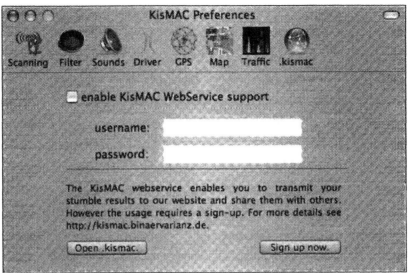

When you click **Sign up now**, your default browser will open the site http://binaervarianz.de/register.php where you can create and register your .kismac account (Figure 4.9).

**Figure 4.9** The .kismac Registration Window

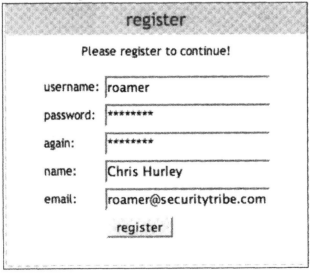

When you have finished your WarDrive, in order to send your data to the .kismac server, simply select the **Export** option from the file menu

(**File | Export | Data to .kismac Server**). In addition to transmitting your results to the .kismac server, an account allows you to search the existing .kismac database. It should be noted that it is a good idea to disable .kismac prior to doing work for a customer, as most would not appreciate their data being sent to a public server.

# Mapping WarDrives with KisMAC

KisMAC, in general, is a very intuitive and easy-to-use tool. The one exception is mapping. Mapping your WarDrives with KisMAC can be a frustrating experience the first few times you try. This section details the steps required to successfully import a map for use with KisMAC.

## Importing a Map

The first step required in mapping your WarDrives with KisMAC is to import a map. This differs from many other WLAN discovery applications (such as Kismet for Linux or NetStumbler for Windows) where maps are often generated at the completion of the WarDrive.

KisMAC requires the latitude and longitude of the center area of your drive in order to import a map. These coordinates can be input manually, but it is usually easier to connect your Global Positioning System (GPS) first and get a signal lock.

### Using a GPS

Most GPS devices that are capable of National Marine Electronics Association (NMEA) output will work with KisMAC. Many of these devices are only available with serial cables to connect to your computer. In most cases you will need to purchase a serial-to-USB adapter (available for around $25) in order to connect your GPS to your Mac. Most of these adapters come with drivers for OS X. Make sure that the one you purchase has these drivers included.

After you have connected your GPS, access the KisMAC Preferences and select the GPS options as shown in Figure 4.10, and select **/dev./ tty.usbserial0** from the drop-down menu if it wasn't automatically selected.

**Figure 4.10** The KisMAC GPS Preferences

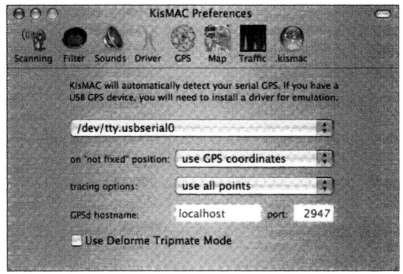

Ensure that the **use GPS coordinates** and **use all points** options are selected and that **GPSd hostname** is listening on **localhost** port **2947**. Your GPS is now configured and ready to go. You must ensure that you have GPSd installed. You can download GPSd for OS X from http://gpsd.berlios.de/. Instructions for compiling and using GPSd can be found on the KisMAC website (http://kismac.binaervarianz.de/wiki/wiki.php/KisMAC/WiFiHacksCompileGPSd).

Another option is to use a Bluetooth GPS. However, according to the KisMAC website there is a problem with the Bluetooth stack in OS X and you must still use GPSd with these devices.

## Ready to Import

Now that your GPS device is connected, you are ready to import a map. You would probably think that this would be accomplished from the **Map** option under KisMAC Preferences, but you would be wrong. To import a map, select **File | Import | Server** (Figure 4.11).

**Figure 4.11** Preparing to Import a Map

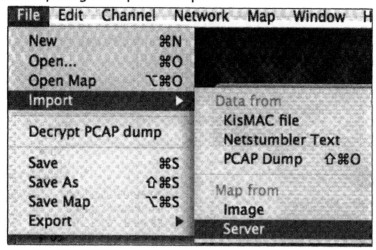

This opens the **Download Map** dialog box (Figure 4.12). Your current GPS coordinates are automatically imported into this box. Choose the server and type of map you want to import.

**Figure 4.12** Choosing the Map Server and Type of Map

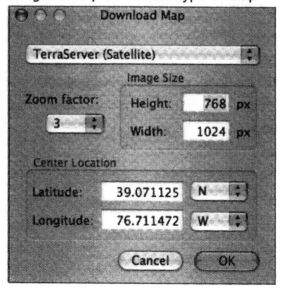

There are several map servers available to you as well as different types of maps (regular map or satellite image), as shown in Figure 4.13.

**Figure 4.13** Available Map Servers and Types of Maps

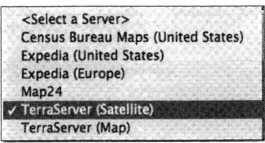

After importing your map, it is a good idea to save it (**File | Save Map**) so that you can use it again later. Also, if KisMAC crashes during your drive, you will have a local copy and won't have to return to your home network with Internet access to download the map again, and this does happen. KisMAC is an outstanding tool, but is prone to crashing occasionally. This can happen when a large number of networks are found simultaneously. Additionally, many of the attacks (discussed later in this chapter) that are included with KisMAC require significant memory and processor power and KisMAC is prone to crashes during their execution. Even more unfortunate is that when KisMAC crashes, the system often stops responding completely, requiring a shutdown and restart of the system to resume operations.

Waypoint 1 is set to your current position. Before beginning your WarDrive, you need to set WayPoint 2. From the OS X Toolbar select **Map | Set Waypoint 2** and place the second WayPoint at your destination, or any other place on the map if you are unsure of your destination.

Next, you should set your map preferences (**KisMAC | Preferences**), shown in Figure 4.14. Here you can set preferences for the color scheme used on your map as well as the display quality and sensitivity levels some colors will denote.

**Figure 4.14** The KisMAC Map Preferences

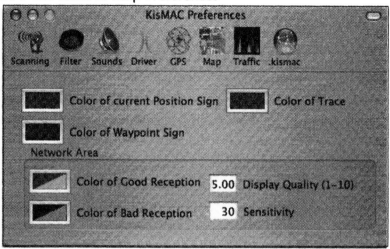

After you have all of your options set, you are ready to WarDrive. As access points are discovered they are plotted on the map. Clicking the **Show Map** button (Figure 4.15) will display your map and you will see access points plotted in real time as you drive. A typical map generated by KisMAC, using a satellite image downloaded form Terraserver is shown in Figure 4.16.

**Figure 4.15** The Show Map Button

**Figure 4.16** A Typical KisMAC Satellite Map

KisMAC includes the ability to manipulate your map as well.

## Notes From the Underground…

### Disabling the Annoying Sleep Function

One of the more irritating features of OS X for WarDrivers is the inability to disable the sleep function in OS X. In many states, driving with your laptop lid up is illegal and since a laptop that is asleep isn't collecting access points, this poses a difficult problem for OS X WarDrivers. Luckily a kernel extension is available that will allow you to temporarily disable the OS X sleep function.

Insomnia (http://binaervarianz.de/projekte/programmieren/meltmac/) is a kernel extension to disable sleep in OS X. After downloading Insomnia, unpack the kernel extension and then issue the following commands:

```
sudo chown -R root:wheel Insomnia.kext
```

**Continued**

This correctly sets the permissions on the kernel extension. This step is only required immediately after download, before the first use of Insomnia. You will need to load the kernel extension each time you want to disable the sleep function:

```
sudo kextload Insomnia.kext
```

Now you can close the lid on your Powerbook or iBook and it will not go to sleep. When you are finished WarDriving and want to re-enable the sleep function the kernel extension must be unloaded.

```
sudo kextunload Insomnia.kext
```

Now your laptop is back to normal operation. It should be pointed out that Apple laptops generate a LOT of heat so it is probably not a good idea to leave this kernel extension loaded all the time, but rather just load it on specific occasions when you need it.

# Practicing WarDriving with KisMAC

Now that you have set your preferences, chosen the correct driver, and imported your map, it is time to go WarDriving. The KisMAC interface is very easy to use and navigate, but it has some advanced functionality that combines the best features from other WarDriving applications, including many commercial applications.

## Using the KisMAC Interface

The KisMAC interface (Figure 4.17) is very straightforward and easy to understand. The main window displays all wireless networks that KisMAC has found, and this list can be sorted by number (in the order it was found), SSID, BSSID (MAC address), the type of encryption used, the current, average, or maximum signal strength, the number of packets transmitted, the size of the data stream (in kilobytes or megabytes), and the time that the access point was last in range (Last Seen).

**Figure 4.17** The KisMAC Graphical User Interface

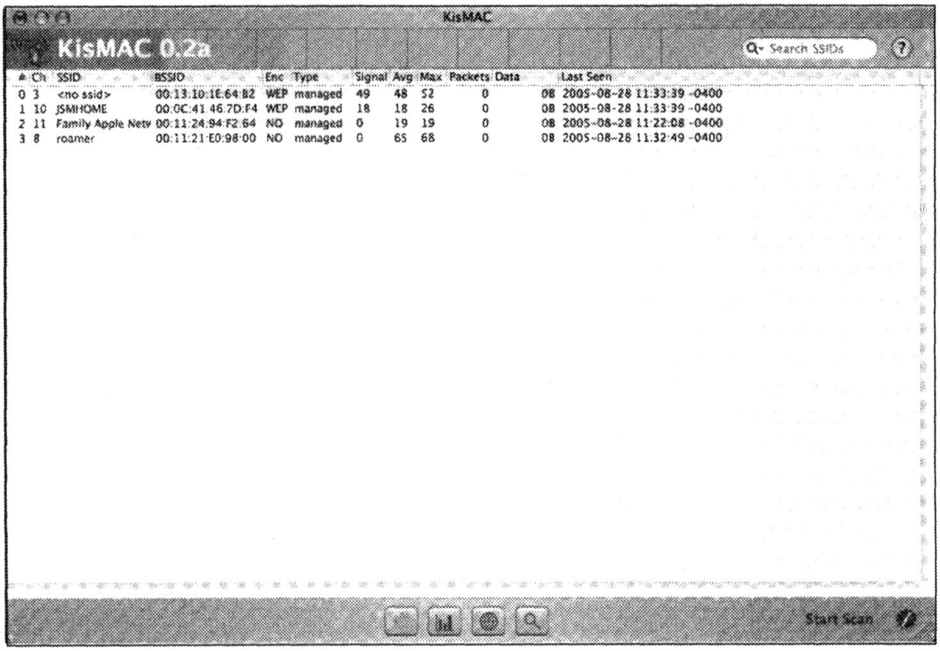

The **Start Scan** button is located in the bottom right corner of the interface. After you have configured the options for your WarDrive, simply click this button to begin locating access points. Additionally, there are four window view buttons across the bottom toolbar that allow you to see specific information about your current drive.

## The KisMAC Window View Buttons

KisMAC allows you to see specific information about your current WarDrive by selecting one of four buttons (Figure 4.18) that are located on the bottom toolbar.

**Figure 4.18** The KisMAC Window View Buttons

The **Show Networks** button on the left is the default view. When you start KisMAC this is the default selection. If you want to return to the default view after selecting the other buttons, simply click this to return and see all of the networks that you have discovered.

To the immediate right of the show networks button is the **Show Traffic** button (which is indicated by a bar graph icon). Selecting this view brings up the signal graph of the networks that have been discovered during your WarDrive. By default, this view shows the signal strength graph, shown in Figure 4.19. Each access point is denoted by a unique color and a key showing which network is assigned to each color is in the upper right corner. Taller lines in the graph indicate a stronger signal.

**Figure 4.19** The Show Traffic View Shows Signal Strength

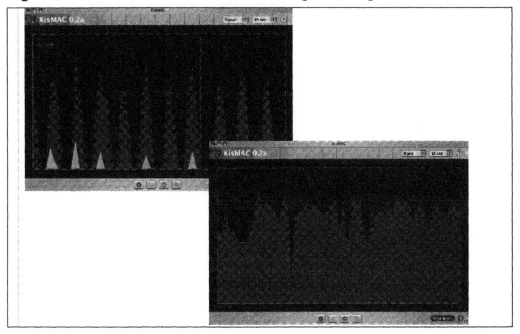

There are two drop-down menus in the upper right corner. One is the display interval (15 seconds by default). To the left of the interval drop-down menu is a menu that allows you to change the type of information that can be viewed. In addition to the signal strength, you can also display the packets per second that are traversing the wireless network or the total number of bytes that have been sent and received by the access points.

The **Show Map** button (with the globe icon) allows you to view a live map of your current WarDrive. For more information on mapping your WarDrive, see the "Mapping Your WarDrive" section earlier in this chapter.

The last view is accessed with the **Show Details** button (indicated by a magnifying glass icon). This view allows you to obtain a significant amount of information about a specific access point, as shown in Figure 4.20.

**Figure 4.20** The Show Details View

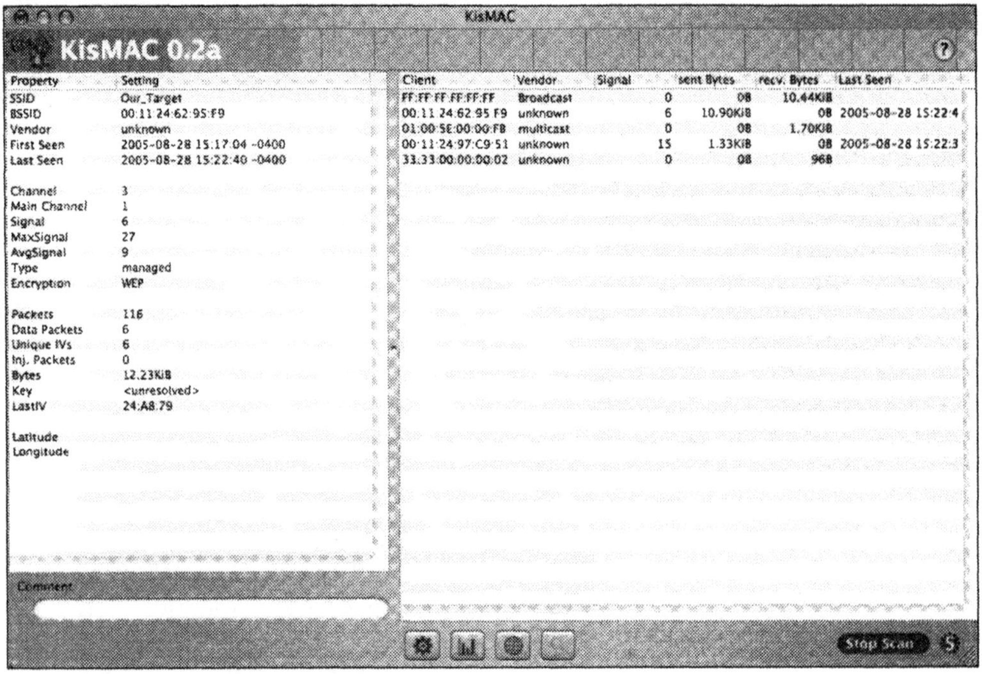

Here we can see the information that is listed in the default view on the left side of the interface. Additionally, we can see information about any clients that are attached to the network in the pane on the right side of the interface. The information available to us in this view is essential to a penetration tester and is discussed in detail in the "Penetration Testing with OS X" section later in this chapter.

## Additional KisMAC View Options

In addition to the Window View buttons, KisMAC provides you with the ability to get additional information about specific networks while staying on

the Show Networks view. Using the OS X menu bar, access **Windows |
Show Hierarchy** (Figure 4.21).

**Figure 4.21** Showing the Hierarchy From the OS X Menu

With the hierarchy pane displayed (Figure 4.22) we can gather more
information about either specific networks or about networks utilizing different types of encryption, or all networks transmitting on a specific channel.
Again, this is information that will be vital to us during our penetration test.

**Figure 4.22** The KisMAC Hierarchy View

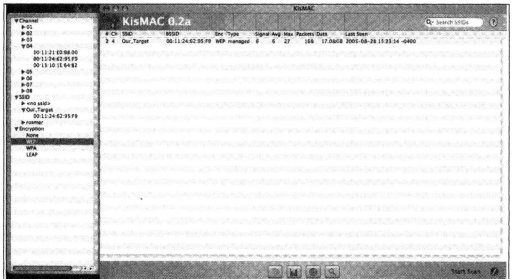

# Penetration Testing with OS X

In addition to its use as a WarDriving application, KisMAC is probably the best tool available for wireless network penetration testing. KisMAC has functionality built in to perform many of the most common WLAN attacks using an easy point and click interface. Additionally, KisMAC can import packet capture dumps from other programs to perform many offline attacks against wireless networks. In this section we'll walk through many of these attacks on our target network.

Here's a testing scenario: Suppose that we are contracted by a company to perform a penetration test. We first have to correctly identify the company's wireless network. Using the information gathered during our WarDrive of the area surrounding the campus of our target, we are able to successfully identify the target network based on the signal strength, map data, and naming convention used on the access point. Lucky for us, our target SSID is called *Our_Target*. In order to successfully penetrate this network, we have to determine what means of encryption is being used.

## Attacking WLAN Encryption with KisMAC

There are several different types of encryption that wireless networks can employ. The most commonly seen encryption schemes are Wired Equivalent Privacy (WEP) and WiFi Protected Access, although there are other, more advanced schemes available, particularly on commercial-grade access points. By looking at the KisMAC display we can see that the access point with the SSID *Our_Target* is a WEP encrypted network.

### Attacking WEP with KisMAC

Since we determined that WEP is being used on our target wireless network, we now have to decide how we want to crack the key. KisMAC has three primary methods of WEP cracking built in:

- Wordlist attacks
- Weak scheduling attacks
- Brute force attacks

In order to use one of these attacks, we have to generate enough initialization vectors for the attack to work. The easiest way to do this is by re-injecting traffic. This is usually accomplished by capturing an Address Resolution Protocol (ARP) packet and spoofing the sender and sending it back to the access point. This will generate a large amount of traffic that can then be captured and decoded. Unfortunately, we can't always capture an ARP packet under normal circumstances. However, when a client authenticates to the access point, an ARP packet is usually generated. Because of this, if we can de-authenticate the clients that are on the network and cause them to re-associate, we may get our ARP packet. .

By looking at the detailed view of Our_Target, we see that there are several clients connected to it. Before continuing with the attack, we need to determine the role that KisMAC will play. Two hosts will be required to successfully crack the WEP key. One host is used to inject traffic and one to capture the traffic, specifically, to capture the initialization vectors (IVs). In this case, we will use KisMAC to inject and will have a second host to capture the traffic. While KisMAC and OS X are very powerful attack tools, the actual cracking is often best performed on a Linux host utilizing tools such as Aircrack (www.cr0.net:8040/code/network). This is because KisMAC does not include support for many of the newer WEP attacks, such as chopping. Hopefully these attacks will be included with future releases of KisMAC.

De-authenticating clients with KisMAC is extremely simple, but before you can begin de-authenticating, you must lock KisMAC to the specific channel that your target network is using. From the top menu, select **KisMAC | Preferences** and select **Driver Preferences**. Highlight the driver you are using and deselect all channels other than the one that the target is using. Also, ensure that the **use as primary device** option is enabled. Close the Preferences window and highlight the access point you want to de-authenticate clients from. From the top menu select **Network | Deauthenticate**. If KisMAC is successful in its attempt to de-authenticate, the dialog box changes to note the BSSID of the access point it is de-authenticating (shown in Figure 4.23). During the time the de-authentication is occurring, clients will not be able to use the wireless network.

**Figure 4.23** De-authentication

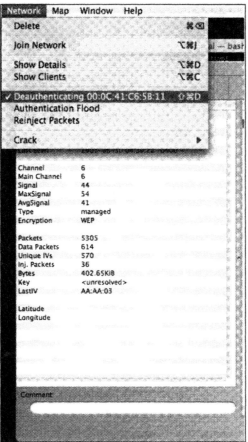

During the de-authentication the number of **Inj. Packets** (injection packets) should increase. After several of these have been captured, the de-authentication should be stopped.

# Re-injection

Once several potentially re-injectable packets have been captured (as indicated in the Show Details view), it is time to attempt re-injection. Select **Network | Reinject Packets** (Figure 4.24).

**Figure 4.24** Preparing to Re-inject Packets

This opens a dialog box (Figure 4.25) indicating that KisMAC is testing each packet to determine if it can be successfully re-injected into the network.

**Figure 4.25** Testing the Packets

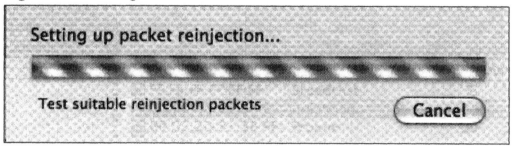

Once KisMAC has found a suitable packet, the dialog box closes and KisMAC begins injection. This can be verified by viewing the Network options again (Figure 4.26).

**Figure 4.26** Re-injection

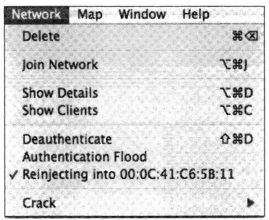

Now the traffic must be captured with a second card (usually on a second machine) in order to capture enough IVs to attempt to crack the key. KisMAC can be used to perform the weak scheduling attacks after enough weak IVs have been captured. However, it is probably more efficient to use KisMAC to inject packets, as demonstrated here, and to use tools such as Aircrack to perform the actual WEP crack, as it needs only unique IVs, which can be collected much faster.

## Attacking WPA with KisMAC

Unlike WEP, which requires a large amount of traffic to be generated in order to crack the key, cracking WPA only requires that you capture the 4-Way EAPOL handshake at authentication. Also, unlike cracking WEP, the WPA attack is an offline dictionary attack. This means that when you use KisMAC to crack a WPA pre-shared key (PSK), or *passphrase*, you only need to capture a small amount of traffic, and the actual attack can be carried out later, even after you are out of range of the access point.

WPA is only vulnerable when a short passphrase is used. Even then, it must be a dictionary word, or one that is in your wordlist. An extensive wordlist with many combinations of letters, numbers, and special characters can help increase the odds of successfully cracking WPA.

To attempt a dictionary attack against KisMAC, you may need to de-authenticate clients, as detailed earlier in this chapter. However, unlike WEP attacks, with dictionary attacks against WPA, you can do everything from one host. This will cause the client to disassociate from the network and force it to reconnect again. This will require that the 4-Way EAPOL handshake be transmitted again.

Once you have captured an association between a client and the WPA network, select **Network | Crack | Wordlist Attack | against WPA Key**. You will be prompted for the location of the wordlist or dictionary file you want to use. After you have selected your dictionary file, KisMAC begins testing each word in that file against the WPA-PSK (Figure 4.27).

**Figure 4.27** WPA Cracking is Underway

When KisMAC has successfully determined the key, it is displayed in the Show Details view.

# Other Attacks

KisMAC offers the ability to perform attacks against other forms of encryption and authentication. Because these other methods have known vulnerabilities, and are rarely seen in use by clients, they are not discussed in detail, but are included here for familiarization.

## Brute Force Attacks Against 40-Bit WEP

KisMAC includes functionality to perform brute force attacks against 40-bit WEP keys. There are four ways KisMAC can accomplish this:

- All possible characters
- Alphanumeric characters only
- Lowercase letters only
- Newshams 21-bit attack

Each of these attacks is very effective, but also very time- and processor-intensive.

## Wordlist Attacks

KisMAC provides the functionality to perform many types of wordlist attacks in addition to the WPA attacks. Cisco developed the Lightweight Extensible Authentication Protocol (LEAP) to help organizations that were concerned about vulnerabilities in WEP. Unfortunately, LEAP is also vulnerable to wordlist attacks. KisMAC includes the functionality to perform wordlist attacks against LEAP. To perform a wordlist attack against LEAP, follow the same procedure as when you are cracking WPA, but choose **against LEAP Key** to start the attack.

Additionally, wordlist attacks can be launched against 40- and 104-bit Apple keys or 104-bit MD5 keys in the same manner. As with any dictionary attack, any of these can only be effective if a comprehensive dictionary file is used when performing the attack. A good dictionary file can be obtained from www.securitytribe.com/~roamer/words.txt.

# Other OS X Tools for WarDriving and WLAN Testing

KisMAC has been the focus of the bulk of this chapter. However, there are several other wireless tools out there that can provide an OS X hacker with hours of fun.

EtherPEG (www.etherpeg.org) is a program that captures and displays all of the JPEG (Joint Photographic Experts Group) and GIF (graphics interchange format) images that are being transferred across the network (to include WLANs). In order to use EtherPEG against a wireless network, encryption must be disabled, or you must be connected to the network.

iStumbler (http://istumbler.net/) is an active WLAN discovery tool for OS X that works with the built-in Airport Express card. In addition to WLAN discovery, iStumbler can also detect Bluetooth devices using the built-in Bluetooth adapter. There is no setup required with iStumbler; simply unpack the archive and click the **iStumbler** icon to begin (Figure 4.28).

**Figure 4.28** iStumbler

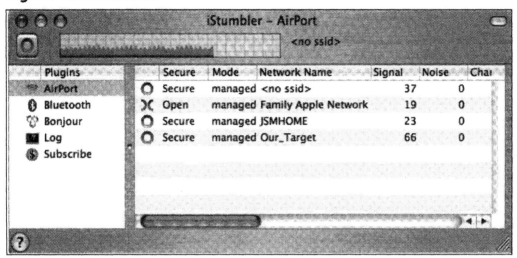

With the release of OS X Tiger, there have been several Dashboard Widgets developed and released that perform active scanning with the Airport and Airport Express cards. Air Traffic Control (Figure 4.29) is one such application.

**Figure 4.29** Air Traffic Control

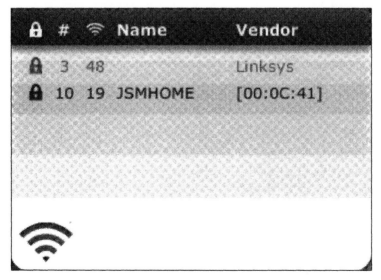

Dashboard widgets are updated regularly and new ones are released nearly every day. You can check out the latest wireless discovery widgets at www.apple.com/downloads/dashboard, and by selecting the **Networking and Security** option from the widget navigation menu.

TcpDump is a network traffic analyzer (sniffer) that ships with OS X. TcpDump can be configured to listen on a wireless interface to capture traffic coming across the WLAN with the following command:

```
crapple:~ roamer$ sudo tcpdump -i en1
```

TcpDump can be used to capture usernames and passwords that are sent in cleartext (e-mail, NetBIOS, etcetera). Another really useful packer sniffer is Ethereal (www.ethereal.org).

# Summary

Often when people think of WarDriving and attacking wireless networks, Linux is the first operating system that comes to mind. While there are fantastic tools available for Linux, there are also several outstanding tools for the wireless hacker available for OS X.

KisMAC is the most popular WarDriving application for OS X. Because it offers the option of both active and passive scanning, as well as a large number of supported chipsets it is perfect for WarDriving. Add to that the ease of setup and configuration and KisMAC stands out as one of, if not the top Wardriving applications available, regardless of operating system.

In addition to its power as a WarDriving application, KisMAC is also a very powerful tool for WLAN penetration testing. It provides many of the most popular attacks (the new chopping attacks against WEP being the only real omission) and offers penetration testers easy, point-and-click options for some attacks that are traditionally more difficult on other operating systems. De-authentication and traffic re-injection are two examples. Tools available for these type of attacks on other operating systems are either very difficult to use, or are so restricted in the cards that they will work with that KisMAC's point-and-click attack method is a welcome change.

While KisMAC is outstanding, it isn't the only WLAN discovery tool available for OS X. iStumbler has a far smaller feature set than KisMAC, but it is extremely easy to use and also includes Bluetooth functionality. There are also several dashboard widgets that can be downloaded from the Apple website that work in conjunction with the Airport and Airport Express cards to perform active WLAN discovery. Wireless hackers are going to be hard pressed to find an operating system that combines power, functionality, and ease of use with a more robust set of available, free tools than OS X.

# Solutions Fast Track

## WarDriving with KisMAC

☑ KismMAC has distinct differences from it's Windows and Linux counterparts

☑ Starting and Configuring KisMAC

☑ Determining a compatible adapter

☑ Using .kismac to share your results

☑ Mapping your WarDrives with KisMAC's built in tools

☑ WarDriving with KisMAC

# Penetration Testing with OS X

☑ Attacking WEP encrypted networks with KisMAC's built in tools

☑ Attacking WPA networks with KisMAC's built in tools

☑ Attacking encrypted networks using KisMAC's Bruteforce capabilities

☑ Attacking encrypted networks using KisMAC's Wordlist attacks

# Other OS X Tools for WarDriving and WLAN Testing

☑ KisMAC is not the only resource available to Mac users for WarDriving and WLAN testing

☑ Other free programs have some of the functionality found in KisMAC

☑ There are many Dashboard Widgets available for OS X Tiger that can identify wireless networks

☑ There are packet sniffers available for use with WLAN cards that can provide a wealth of information to a penetration tester

# Frequently Asked Questions

The following Frequently Asked Questions, answered by the authors of this book, are designed to both measure your understanding of the concepts presented in this chapter and to assist you with real-life implementation of these concepts. To have your questions about this chapter answered by the author, browse to **www.syngress.com/solutions** and click on the **"Ask the Author"** form.

**Q.** Why do some attacks require weak Initialization Vectors (IVs) and some only require unique IVs?

**A.** The traditional attacks against WEP were originally detailed by Scott Fluhrer, Itsik Mantin, and Adi Shamir in their paper "Weaknesses in the Key Scheduling Algorithm of RC4" (www.drizzle.com/~aboba/IEEE/rc4_ksaproc.pdf). These attacks have come to be known as FMS attacks, based on the first initial of the last name of each of the paper's authors. This paper details that a small subset of the total initialization vectors were weak and, if enough were collected, could be used to determine the WEP key. The problem with this method was that it was very time-consuming due to the number of packets required to capture enough weak IVs to crack the key.

In February of 2002, H1kari detailed a new method for attacking WEP (www.dachb0den.com/projects/bsd-airtools/wepexp.txt). With this new method, dubbed *chopping*, weak IVs were no longer required. Instead, approximately 500,000 unique IVs had to be gathered in order to successfully crack the WEP key. This, coupled with the ability to re-inject ARP packets into the network greatly reduced the amount of time required to crack WEP. Using the FMS method of WEP cracking could take weeks or even months to successfully crack the WEP key. The chopping method has reduced this to a matter of hours (and sometimes less). This attack took a theoretical threat and turned it into a significant vulnerability for wireless networks utilizing WEP.

More information on WEP cracking and the tools available for cracking can be found in Chris Hurley's paper "Aircrack and WEPlab: Should You Believe the Hype" available for download at www.securityhorizon.com/journal/fall2004.pdf

**Q.** I remember a tool call MacStumbler. Why isn't it mentioned in this chapter?

**A.** MacStumbler (www.macstumbler.com) was one of the first WLAN discovery tools available for OS X. Unfortunately, it only operated in active mode, and development and maintenance ceased in July of 2003. Many tools, such as KisMAC, have taken WLAN discovery for OS X to the next level and essentially rendered MacStumbler obsolete. It is, however, still available for download and is compatible with both Airport Express cards and OS X Tiger.

**Q.** Can KisMAC logs be imported into other applications?

**A.** Yes. You can export KisMAC to NetStumbler and MacStumbler readable formats.

**Q.** Why in the world would I want to export to NetStumbler format?

**A.** There are a couple of good reasons to export to NetStumbler format. First, it allows you to map your drives after completion using the assorted mapping tools available for NetStumbler. Second, NetStumbler has excellent support for exporting WarDrive data to different formats. Once you have imported your KisMAC data into NetStumbler, you have the ability to export to any of these formats.

# Mac OS X
# for Pen Testers

## Solutions in this chapter:

- The OS X Command Shell

- Compiling and Porting Open Source Software

- Using the "Top 75 Security Tools" List

- Installing and Using the "Big" Tools

- Other OS X "Must Haves"

☑ Summary

☑ Solutions Fast Track

☑ Frequently Asked Questions

# Introduction

A *penetration test* (often abbreviated as *pen test*) is a client-authorized simulation of an attack on a computer system or network. The purpose is to determine network vulnerabilities and repair them before a compromise occurs. Upon completion of this test, the tester produces a report outlining discovered weaknesses and provides detailed repair procedures. In some cases, a pen testing team will also assist in the *defensive* repair work, but most often this type of team focuses on *offensive* procedures. Once the network is repaired (or *patched*) the test is repeated at regular intervals, ensuring that the network remains secure. Penetration testing is a lucrative, honorable, and highly technical profession. By contrast, *malicious hackers* perform *unauthorized* attacks against computer systems and networks. There is no report produced. There is no defensive patching performed unless the objective is to lock out *other* attackers. Although malicious hacking is highly technical and may be fairly lucrative, it is also highly illegal.

Malicious hackers and skilled pen testers have a great deal in common, however. While their *motives* differ, their *actions* are nearly identical. After all, the point of a pen test is to secure a network by properly emulating all permutations of a real attack. A home alarm system is ineffective if it fails to protect against every tactic of a burglar, and this holds true for network security as well. Because of this, malicious hackers and pen testers share a symbiotic relationship. The two are so closely related that they are often distinguished by only the color of their "hats"; pen testers are referred to as *white hats* and malicious hackers are referred to as *black hats*. In order to maintain their skills, black hats and white hats attend the same conferences, frequent the same digital hangouts, and practice the same digital hijinks. They congregate in person and online, speak the same lingo rife with acronyms and tech jargon, and trade *code* (computer programs) like little kids trade Pokemon cards. And although Hollywood has painted a specific picture of what a hacker looks like, those outside the industry would be hard-pressed to distinguish between the good guys and the bad guys at a large security conference. Many of the best and brightest hackers in the world are really quite normal-looking people IRL (in real life).

White hats and black hats alike take great pride in their skills and abilities, and in the content and capabilities of their software toolkits. These toolkits contain very specific programs, which, when run properly, produce effective results. This may seem fairly straightforward, but there is a great deal of debate (and personal preference) about which tool is the best tool for the job. In this industry, however, there's hardly ever a *best* tool for any job. There are usually many tools that can perform a port scan, for example, but *nmap* is regarded as one of the best. It's entirely possible to pull off a perfectly good pen test without nmap, and most automated tools do just that. The point is that there are different strokes for different folks, and this is certainly true of the operating system you decide to use. While there is great debate amongst the hacker community as to which operating system is the best, the simple truth is that there really is no best OS, but rather preferred operating systems for specific tasks. An adept pen tester or hacker can operate in just about any environment, regardless of operating system. The best pen testing platform simply becomes a matter of personal preference. Mac OS X is an excellent choice due mainly to its robust, industry-accepted use of an underlying BSD-based (UNIX) operating system. Although many pen testers use Windows-based systems, the standard tools available with most UNIX operating systems (like *sed*, *awk*, *grep*, *PERL*, etcetera) have become "must haves" in the industry, forcing Windows users to find (or code) replacements for nearly all of these tools. Beyond the utilities included with the operating system, the Linux community in particular has worked feverishly to create an absolutely stunning amount of UNIX-based software for just about any purpose imaginable. Most of this software is accessible to OS X users, although some of that software requires *porting*, or conversion, to OS X.

The purpose of this chapter is to reveal ways that OS X can be used as a platform for penetration testing. This discussion will primarily focus on installing many of the popular pen testing tools, rather than the actual *techniques* and *processes* used to *operate* these tools. We will begin this chapter by discussing the Mac's BSD subsystem and set the stage for installation of open source tools on Mac OS X. We will discuss the Mac OS X command shell and Terminal applications, the Apple Developer Tools, and the X Windows environment. We will take a look at methods of running software *on*, or porting software *to* the OS X platform, namely the use of direct compilation, DarwinPorts, and Fink. We will also take a look at the "Top 75 Security Tools," available from www.insecure.org/tools.html. This list has become an industry standard list of must-have security tools, many of which will run on or have been ported to Mac OS X. Next, we will discuss a few must haves, namely Ethereal and Nessus, describing the process for installing each natively, as well as Virtual PC, which makes the complete library of Windows and Linux software available for the Mac.

# The OS X Command Shell

We'll start discussing more juicy Mac hacking tools in short order, but it's important to discuss the Mac command shell interface, and install the baseline utilities required to compile non-native programs on OS X. If you've never had any exposure to this side of Mac OS X, be warned. You won't be seeing much of the sweet graphics you've grown accustomed to with OS X, but the path to true Mac enlightenment lies in letting go of the mouse every now and then. As shown in Figure 5.1, the command shell is entirely text-based. This interface may seem foreign to many "point-and-clickers", but it enables access to the powerful heart and soul of the Mac OS X operating system: the BSD (Berkeley Software Distribution) subsystem.

**Figure 5.1** Welcome to the Mac Terminal

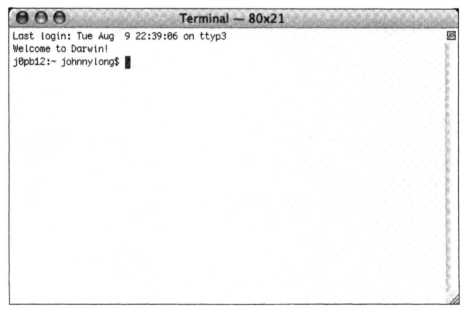

The BSD subsystem is installed by default during a standard OS X install. After installation of the subsystem, you should have a file called BSD.pkg in the /Library/Receipts directory of your hard drive. If you have performed a custom installation that bypassed the installation of the BSD subsystem, or the Receipts directory is missing the receipt for BSD, you will need to install it from the OS X install disc before working with the command shell interface. Follow these steps to install the BSD subsystem:

1. Insert the Mac OS X CD or DVD.

2. Double-click the **Install Mac OS X** icon located in the root of the installation disk.

3. Click **Restart** to continue the installation.

4. After the system has rebooted, follow the prompts to the Installation Type phase of the installer.

5. Click **Customize**.

6. Select the **BSD** subsystem option.

7. Finish the installation by following the prompts.

## Notes From the Underground...

### Mac OS X Family Tree

Historically, the Mac's OS X operating system was based on Berkeley Software Distributions UNIX of the early seventies. Some design considerations were implemented from Carnegie Mellon University's MACH operating system as well, but the core of Mac OS X is most often referred to as *Darwin*. Darwin can function as a standalone (text-based) operating system, but OS X adds many advanced capabilities such as Quartz Extreme (for 2D graphics rendering), OpenGL (for 3D graphics rendering), and the QuickTime multimedia architecture, to create a truly capable, unique, and powerful operating system.

Although the BSD subsystem consists of hundreds of programs and services, one of the most commonly used programs is Terminal, which can be found in the Finder's **Applications | Utilities** folder. Double-clicking this icon will launch the Terminal program shown in Figure 5.1. When launched, the Terminal program displays the last login date, time, and terminal location, the message of the day, the hostname of the system, the current working directory, and a $ prompt. Running inside Terminal's window is a UNIX command-line or *shell*, specifically (under OS X 10.4) the *bash* shell. Although OS X ships with a wide variety of shell interfaces including the C shell (csh), the Z shell (zsh), and the ever-popular GNU Bourne-Again SHell (bash), each of these shells operates in a similar fashion; they each accept typed commands, and display the results of those commands back to the user.

Although the Terminal window may appear to be quite foreign, it is really nothing more than a standard UNIX interface to OS X commands. For example, running **open/Applications/TextEdit.app/** from the Terminal will launch the TextEdit program. Although the command is run from inside the Terminal window, TextEdit runs exactly as if it were launched from the dock or the Finder.

## Notes From the Underground...

### Bash Auto Complete

The bash shell has many handy features, but the *auto complete* feature may be one of the most popular. Auto complete is triggered with the **Tab** key. After pressing Tab, auto complete will attempt to finish the text you started typing. If the letters you typed were specific enough, auto complete will finish typing the command for you. Otherwise, if the letters you typed were not specific enough, auto complete will offer suggestions for that command each time you press Tab. For example, to fly through the command **open /Applications/TextEdit.app/**, simply type **open /App**, then press **Tab** to complete the name of the /Applications directory. Since this was the name of a directory, auto complete will finish typing the name of the directory and place a slash after the name. Next, type **Tex** and press **Tab** to auto complete the name of the TextEdit.app directory. Simply press **Enter** to execute the command. In this example, less than half the keystrokes are required to execute the command.

Most UNIX users recognize the familiar $ prompt, which is an indicator that the shell is logged in as a standard user. By default, the shell is logged with the permissions of the user that launched the Terminal program, in this case, the *johnnylong* user. The vast majority of commands can be run as a standard user, but some commands, especially system administration commands, require a higher level of access. This is handled through the use of a *root*, or superuser account. Like most versions of UNIX, Mac OS X has a built-in root user that can be accessed in a number of ways. Typically, the **su** command is used to invoke a root-level shell, and it's not uncommon for first-time Mac users to attempt to su to the root user, but OS X does not ship with an *enabled* root user.

While it is possible to enable the root user and set a root password with the **sudo passwd root** command, this is generally frowned upon, and is unnecessary. Most system administration functions on OS X can be performed via the **sudo** command (or by visiting the built-in OS X configuration programs like System Preferences), and a root shell can be spawned with the **sudo su** or **sudo bash** command without actually enabling the root user account. It's generally accepted security practice to have as few enabled accounts as possible, and despite OS X's very solid security posture, it's best not to tempt fate. Leave the root user disabled, and get accustomed to using **sudo** whenever possible!

Once the Terminal program has launched, take a moment to relish in your geekness! You're now sitting in the *real* Mac OS X driver's seat, interfacing with the Mac's BSD UNIX-styled shell. Even mundane tasks like manipulating text files take on a whole new edge when performed from the shell. Any decent Mac OS X hacker has shell skills, and this is where the magic happens. Time spent learning your way around the shell will ultimately pay off in increased productivity, and an appreciation for what all the grizzled UNIX vets have been raving about for years. We'll talk more about the *bash* shell in Chapter 2, *Automation*. Mac OS X's help system includes some basic information about the BSD subsystem (try searching for "BSD" or "UNIX" in Mac help), but OS X also includes standardized UNIX manuals via the **man** (manual) command-line program. The "M" in the term RTFM ("Read The Friggin' Manual") most likely refers to the UNIX manual program, and RTFM is very good advice for the novice UNIX user. If you're unfamiliar with the UNIX bash shell, for example, look at its man page by issuing the **man bash** command. The man program itself even has it's own man page, which can be accessed via the **man man** command. Either way, take some time to learn your way around the Mac's command shell before jumping into more advanced topics.

# Compiling and Porting Open Source Software

Many veteran Mac users relish the look and feel of the very slick OS X interface. The interface is intuitive, uncluttered, and when mastered, makes life so much easier. However, despite what the zealots may tell you, the world does not revolve around Apple. Not every software developer writes Apple-specific software, but a large majority of developers these days write freely distributable *open source* software under the GNU General Public License. Much of this software is written for the UNIX platform, and in most cases, this software can be installed and run under Mac OS X thanks to its UNIX BSD roots. In most cases, this software will not have the slick look and feel of native OS X software, but there are hundreds of specific tasks that many technical users perform that are just not possible without the use of open source tools.

Before reaping the benefits of any piece of software, you'll first need to get that software installed. If you're lucky, the developer has taken the time to code the software specifically for the Mac. In this case, the developer often makes a *disk image* (.dmg) file available, which can be simply downloaded and executed. This type of installation is a very simple point-and-click affair. Unfortunately, most open source tools are not distributed this way. If no disk image file is available, there are two other options for getting the software up and running. The first option is to compile the software from *source code*, or human-readable format into a format the computer can understand and execute. This requires the use of a compiler, and is often prone to error, as many programs of this type are designed to work on fairly specific platforms, like Linux. A third option involves installing preconfigured *ported* (modified) software from either source or binary (ready to run) packages. We'll take a look at the latter two options in fair detail, but we must first install some software to facilitate the porting of software to OS X..

# OS X Developer Tools

Although OS X ships with a ton of UNIX tools (around a thousand tools between the /bin, /sbin, /usr/bin and /usr/sbin directories according to the ls and wc -l commands) the open source library brings many more tools to the Mac. As we'll see in the next few sections, the open source tools available are indispensable, including vulnerability scanners like *Nessus*, network protocol analyzers like *Ethereal*, intrusion detection systems like *Snort*, and even attack toolkits like *Metasploit*. The open source software library is virtually limitless, so hang in there. The results of all this setup will soon be very apparent, and you'll soon be running these tools on your Mac!

Many open source tools are distributed as source code. Although source code can be somewhat difficult to get running, standardized source code is often fairly portable, meaning that it can be installed on a variety of different operating systems, assuming that system has a compiler and the libraries that are required by that source code. This may seem confusing to most novices, but programs written in the popular *C* language can be compiled very easily on most operating systems, OS X included, thanks to compilers such as gcc, the GNU C and C++ Complier.

Modern versions of OS X ship with the gcc compiler, as part of the Apple Development Tools package, but this package is not installed by default during a standard installation of the OS X operating system. In most cases, the Apple Development Tools package is included on the OS X installation CD or DVD, but it can also be downloaded for free from http://developer.apple.com/tools. Be warned that the developer tools require a fairly significant amount of disk space, so be sure to pay attention to the disk requirements as you proceed through the installer. If installing from the OS X DVD, the installation package (XcodeTools.mpkg) can be found in the Xcode Tools directory. Launching this package begins a typical Apple installer wizard, allowing you to set various options for the installation of the various tools. As shown in Figure 5.2, there are many different tools, documents and software development kits that can be installed, but the default options will be sufficient for most users. The gcc packages (gcc 4.0 and gcc 3.3 under OS X 10.4) are required to install software written in C and C++.

**Figure 5.2** Apple Developer Tools Options

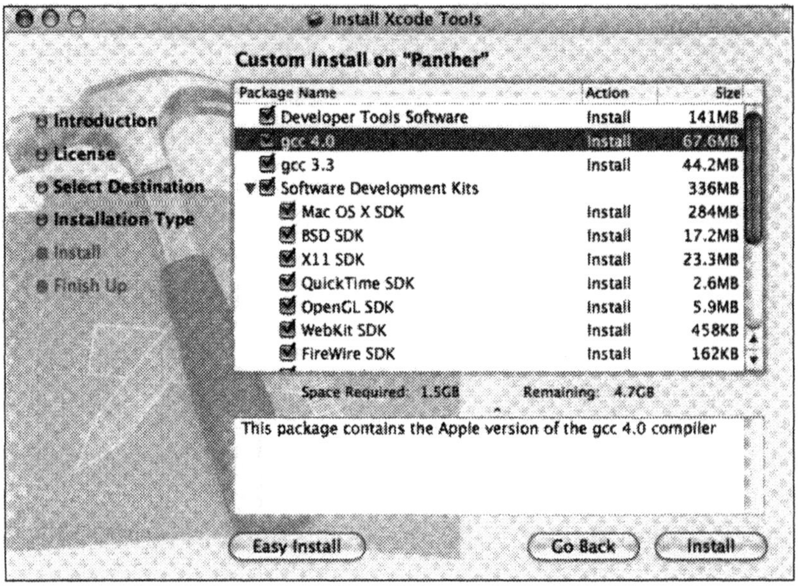

Once the installation has completed, several tools will be available in various directories:

- The /Developer/Tools directory contains many OS X specific command-line tools such as MvMac (a Mac file mover that preserves metadata and resource forks) and documentation available via the **man** command.

- The /Developer/Applications directory contains many graphical tools for program development, performance monitoring, and more.

- The /usr/bin and /usr/sbin directories contain many additional programs that were not included as part of the BSD subsystem install, including the gcc compiler we'll use to compile C programs. After installation of the Developer Tools, you should be able to test the *gcc* compiler by running *gcc* from the Terminal shell.

# Perl

Although C is a very popular language for open source software, PERL certainly runs a close second, thanks to its geek-friendly syntax and portability. Unlike C, which is strictly a compiled language, PERL requires not a com-

piler, but an interpreter (the PERL executable program itself) to convert the
PERL source code into executable instructions. There is some debate as to
whether PERL is compiled or interpreted or both, but this author will
humbly avoid jumping into that fray, offering only "it's a bit of both". PERL
is popular, powerful, and portable, and is *included with the OS X installation*,
allowing access to another large library of open-source software. A basic
PERL script can be launched by simply running *perl* followed by the name of
the script at a terminal prompt.

## Notes From the Underground…

### Geek Alert!!!

Non-technical users are bound to be confused by certain prompts or messages
received when using compilers, configure scripts, and programs like *cpan*. Don't
worry thought, the correct choice for most confusing prompts is most often the
default one. Simply pressing **Enter** when prompted with an odd prompt will
select the default choice. It's always a good idea to actually *read* the question
first though. You would feel rather silly answering **yes** to a question like, "Do you
want to delete all the songs in your iTunes library now?"

## Configuring CPAN

In some cases, extra *modules*, or software components, may be required for
certain scripts to run properly. PERL modules are available through the
Comprehensive PERL Archive Network (CPAN) which can be interfaced via
the `/usr/bin/cpan` program, installed along with the OS X PERL distribution. To avoid confusion, we'll refer to the online archive of PERL modules as
CPAN, and the *program* used to download and install modules from CPAN
as *cpan*.

The *cpan* program automatically installs PERL modules, and resolves all
the dependencies of those modules as needed. This means that if a PERL
script requires module *foo*, and module *foo* requires module *bar*, *cpan* will
download, install and configure both *foo* and *bar* automatically. In order to get
to this state of dependency-resolving bliss, however, we'll need to configure

the *cpan* script itself. Although this is a bit tricky for beginners, the process need only be run once. Once *cpan* is configured, you'll be able to run even the most complex PERL scripts with relative ease.

To begin configuring cpan, simply run **sudo cpan** from the Terminal. The program will begin to ask various questions, such as, "Are you ready for manual configuration?" followed by a default selection, for example **[yes]**. Simply pressing **Enter** will accept the default selection. You'll find yourself pressing **Enter** quite a few times before you come to a series of questions which, if answered properly, will help speed up all CPAN downloads. This series of questions refers to your geographical location. The first question will begin with, "First, pick a nearby continent and country" and will proceed to present a list of continents. Select your continent, or the one closest to you, and press **Enter**. You will next be prompted to select your country. Again, select your country or the country closest to you. Next, cpan will prompt you to enter a list of download mirrors. This selection is a bit awkward, and depending on the continent and country you selected, may look something like the output shown below.

```
(1)  ftp://archive.progeny.com/CPAN/
(2)  ftp://carroll.cac.psu.edu/pub/CPAN/
(3)  ftp://cpan-du.viaverio.com/pub/CPAN/
(4)  ftp://cpan-sj.viaverio.com/pub/CPAN/
(5)  ftp://cpan.calvin.edu/pub/CPAN
(6)  ftp://cpan.cs.utah.edu/pub/CPAN/
(7)  ftp://cpan.cse.msu.edu/
(8)  ftp://cpan.erlbaum.net/
(9)  ftp://cpan.llarian.net/pub/CPAN/
(10) ftp://cpan.mirrors.redwire.net/pub/CPAN/
(11) ftp://cpan.mirrors.tds.net/pub/CPAN
(12) ftp://cpan.netnitco.net/pub/mirrors/CPAN/
(13) ftp://cpan.pair.com/pub/CPAN/
(14) ftp://cpan.teleglobe.net/pub/CPAN
(15) ftp://cpan.thepirtgroup.com/
(16) ftp://csociety-ftp.ecn.purdue.edu/pub/CPAN
42 more items, hit SPACE RETURN to show them
Select as many URLs as you like (by number),
put them on one line, separated by blanks, e.g. '1 4 5' [] 1 2 3 4 5 6
: []
```

Ultimately, CPAN will prompt you to *enter another URL or press Return* (Enter) to quit, at which point you will be expected to enter several numbers separated by spaces. Each number will represent a specific site cpan will use (when requested) to attempt to download software. In the example above, all of the first six sites were selected, and the **Enter** key was pressed. Pressing **Enter** a second time (on a blank line this time) will end the selection process, save your changes, and end cpan's configuration process. This configuration process is awkward, but remember, it only has to be performed once. Once cpan is up and running, you can use larger and more complex Perl scripts with relative ease, and there's a virtual *ton* of free Perl software available!

## Notes From the Underground…

### Blasted Control Keys!!!

When using cpan, one of the first things you may notice is that control keys such as the arrows and **Backspace** just don't work. This is easily remedied with the installation of the TERM::ReadLine module. This and other modules can be easily installed by running **install Bundle::CPAN** from within cpan. This quick and easy install will give you the ability to backspace and access command history through the use of the up and down arrow keys.

## Using CPAN's Interactive Mode

There are times when PERL runs into a dependency problem. Similar to a *human* dependency problem, this means that the script desperately *needs something* in order to properly function. Thankfully, a Perl dependency can be resolved (without rehab) thanks to CPAN. In most cases, the problem lies in a missing module. For example, the *dns-mine.pl* script written by SensePost, allows for some pretty cool Google digging, but launching the script produces the error message shown in Figure 5.3.

**Figure 5.3** Confusing Perl Errors

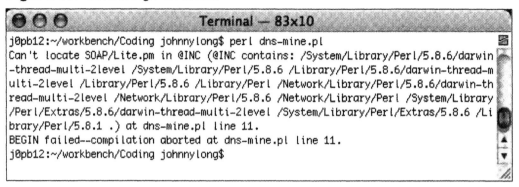

```
j0pb12:~/workbench/Coding johnnylong$ perl dns-mine.pl
Can't locate SOAP/Lite.pm in @INC (@INC contains: /System/Library/Perl/5.8.6/darwin
-thread-multi-2level /System/Library/Perl/5.8.6 /Library/Perl/5.8.6/darwin-thread-m
ulti-2level /Library/Perl/5.8.6 /Library/Perl /Network/Library/Perl/5.8.6/darwin-th
read-multi-2level /Network/Library/Perl/5.8.6 /Network/Library/Perl /System/Library
/Perl/Extras/5.8.6/darwin-thread-multi-2level /System/Library/Perl/Extras/5.8.6 /Li
brary/Perl/5.8.1 .) at dns-mine.pl line 11.
BEGIN failed--compilation aborted at dns-mine.pl line 11.
j0pb12:~/workbench/Coding johnnylong$
```

This is a typical dependency error, and the first line of the error message indicates that the script can't locate something it needs. Specifically, Perl "can't locate SOAP/Lite.pm," which is a specific module. Now in some cases, simply installing a specific module is the easiest way to resolve this problem, but in other cases, the module will depend on other modules, making for a Linux-esque headache that makes most Mac users want to mercilessly mangle the nearest penguin. Fortunately, CPAN is keenly aware of inter-module dependencies, and automatically resolves the dependencies for you, serving up groups of dependency-fulfilling modules in a sort of recipe known as a *bundle*. For the most part, downloading and installing a bundle is just as easy as installing a single module. The *libwww* bundle, for example, lets you do all sorts of Web mangling from Perl with a few lines of code. Most often, however, you'll be dealing with Perl modules, and not bundles or *distributions*, which are very specific releases of modules used primarily by those users wanting only the latest, greatest, and often untested code.

Let's take a look at the dependency problem in the *dns-mine.pl* script, and see how it would be resolved with cpan. First, we'll need to search within CPAN to figure out what name this SOAP/Lite.pm file goes by. To search for a specific string, first launch cpan from Terminal with **sudo cpan**. You'll be shuttled to a cpan> prompt, as shown in Figure 5.4.

**Figure 5.4** The CPAN Shell

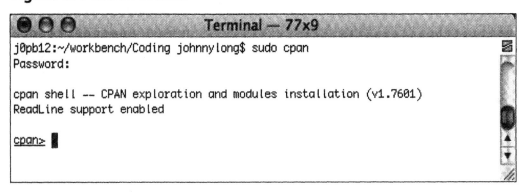

From this point, you can enter commands that will be interpreted by the program. The most commonly used functions, some of which can be listed by entering **help** at the prompt, are listed in Table 5.1.

**Table 5.1** Common CPAN Commands

| Command | Parameter(s) | Description |
|---|---|---|
| help | | Display the help menu |
| install | Distribution or bundle | Install a distribution or bundle |
| force install | Distribution or bundle | Force installation of a distribution or bundle |
| a, b, d, m | | List *all* authors, bundles, distributions, or modules |
| a, b, d, m | WORD or expression | Search within authors, bundles, distributions, *or* modules |
| i | | List *all* authors, bundles, distributions, *and* modules |
| i | WORD or expression | Search within authors, bundles, distributions, *and* modules |

Perl has patiently explained that the script we're running has a dependency on SOAP, or specifically *SOAP/Lite.pm*, so we'll need to search through CPAN. One of the easiest way to accomplish this is with the **i** command, which searches CPAN authors, bundles, distributions or modules for a specific string. For example, the command **i SOAP** will return the following:

```
cpan> i SOAP
Strange distribution name [SOAP]
Module id = SOAP
    DESCRIPTION   SOAP/Perl language mapping
    CPAN_USERID   KBROWN (Keith Brown <kbrown@develop.com>)
    CPAN_VERSION  0.28
    CPAN_FILE     K/KB/KBROWN/SOAP-0.28.tar.gz
    DSLI_STATUS   cmpO (pre-alpha,mailing-list,perl,object-oriented)
    INST_FILE     (not installed)
```

This indicates that a module with the id of **SOAP** does indeed exist, but the error message from our Perl script was a bit more specific. That script is in need of SOAP *Lite*. CPAN allows us to expand our search by way of regular expressions, which means our search must be enclosed in forward slashes. Changing our command to **i /SOAP/** will search all records for the existence of the word "SOAP", providing a glance of each record so we can decide if it's the record we're looking for. Although over a hundred records are returned, they are listed in alphabetical order, and one entry beginning with "Module SOAP::Lite" describes by name the exact module we're looking for. In order to properly subdivide modules in a unique and specific way, CPAN refers to specific modules using a specific hierarchy, and that the hierarchy involves the use of *double colons* (::). For example, SOAP is a large library of modules. While you could install each and every module within the SOAP library, this is not necessary, and it would needlessly burn way too many bits. Instead, install the specific modules you'll need, in this case *SOAP::Lite*. To install the SOAP::Lite module, simply type **install SOAP::Lite** at the cpan prompt, taking care to honor the case sensitivity of the command. In most cases, after accepting the default selection for each prompt, you'll be rewarded with an error-free install. In some cases, however, the installation may fail with errors (especially during the testing phase) and you'll need to force the installation of the module. This isn't nearly as bad as it sounds, as most modules will work just fine if you need to install them forcibly. To force an installation of SOAP::Lite, simply enter **force install SOAP::Lite** at the cpan prompt. Once the install is completed, running **install SOAP::Lite** a second time will check to see if updates for the module are available and, if not, will inform you of that. This highlights another important capability of the cpan script: the ability to update to the latest modules very easily. Once SOAP::Lite is installed, the dns-mine.pl script runs flawlessly, despite the fact that the modules required a *forced* installation.

## Using CPAN in Command-Line Mode

Once you get the hang of the interactive mode of the *cpan* program, you'll probably want to get CPAN working for you even faster, and this is easily accomplished with the command-line interface to CPAN. Instead of launching the cpan program, you'll instead run *perl* with various parameters describing what, exactly, you want the cpan program to do for you. Perl's **-M** and **-e** parameters allow you do specify which *module* and *command* you wish to execute. For example, to launch cpan's interactive mode, you would run **perl -MCPAN -e shell** from a root shell, or **sudo perl -MCPAN -e shell** from a user shell. This command specifies that you want to interact with the CPAN module, and you want that module to run the **shell** command from within CPAN. This can be extended to install modules or bundles with a command like **perl -MCPAN -e 'install Bundle::CPAN'**, which would install the CPAN bundle. This, of course, also works if you want to force an install with **perl -MCPAN -e 'force install Bundle::CPAN'**.

Perl is an amazingly flexible language, and many programs have been written using the language. Thanks to Mac OS X's built-in implementation of the Perl interpreter and the CPAN archive and program, you can run the vast majority of Perl programs directly on the Mac with little or no fuss.

## Installing XWindows

XWindows (www.x.org) is a standard toolkit and protocol used for graphical interfaces. XWindows is currently very popular on Linux systems, and window managers such as KDE and GNOME have become a standard user interface for Linux users. Installing XWindows on OS X allows many of these types of graphical programs to run under OS X. XWindows can be installed in a variety of ways, but one of the most straightforward methods involves installing an

Apple-supplied version of XWindows. XWindows X11 (the current protocol version) is included on the current Mac OS X installation media, but is not installed as part of the standard OS X install. Launching the **Optional Installers** installer disk image on the OS X CD produces a list of optional applications that can be installed, including X11, as shown in Figure 5.5.

**Figure 5.5** Apple's X11 Installation

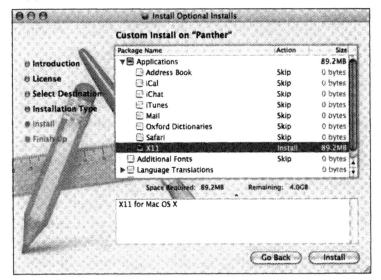

Once X11 is installed, an X11 icon is placed in the /**Applications** /**Utilities** folder, and several applications are installed, including many common XWindows applications in /usr/X11R6/bin. When the X11 program is run, an *xterm* is presented, and XWindows programs (such as xclock) can be run from the xterm window, as shown in Figure 5.6.

**Figure 5.6** XWindows and xclock Running on Mac OS X

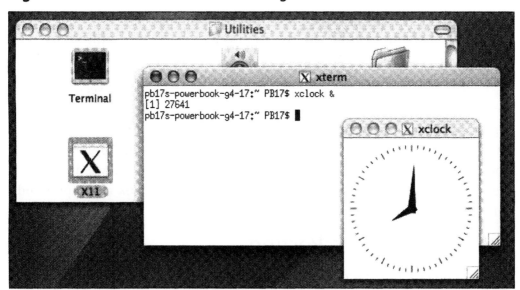

XWindows programs are most often run from the xterm window, not from the OS X Terminal window. As we will see later in this chapter, even complex XWindows programs such as Ethereal can be run from the xterm window.

# Compiling Programs on Mac OS X

Although there are many different programming languages to consider, the vast majority of open source applications are written in either C or C++. It is often preferable to acquire a ported source or binary as we'll discuss in the next section, but most standardized source code may install and run quite well on OS X. Although we can't possibly cover all the nuances of compiling programs on Mac OS X, most "friendlier" applications require a very simple procedure:

1. Download the source code.

2. Decompress the source code (if required) using Stuffit or similar programs.

3. Change into the directory created by the decompression process.

4. Run the **configure** script from the command line.

5. Run **make** from the command line (assuming the *configure* script ran properly).

6. Run **make install** from the command line (assuming the **make** command executed properly).

In many cases, this process will result in the creation of an executable binary file, as well as supporting documentation (usually in the form of man pages) and various support and configuration files. However, life isn't always this simple, and some software requires porting (specific program modification) before it can be installed on a particular platform. Before we dive into the process of installing ported software, let's take a brief look at the pros and cons of both compiling and installing ported software.

# Compiling Versus Porting

A programmer has many options for distributing open source software code. He or she can opt to distribute the source code as is without any installation files, distribute the source along with a *Makefile* to aid in compilation of complex code, or distribute the source along with a *configure* script which the user runs to create a Makefile. The first option is extremely rudimentary, and with the exception of very simple software, may cause unforeseen compatibility issues on the end user's system. If these issues arise, the user may not be able to compile or run the software. Distributing source code with a Makefile (read by the *make* program, which is executed from the software's root directory) will certainly help the end user compile especially large or complex programs, but depending on the configuration of the user's system, incompatibilities may still arise. The current best way for a programmer to distribute open source software that is widely compatible with many operating environments is through the use of the *automake* program. This program creates *configure* scripts which, when executed on the user's system, will automatically detect the operating environment and attempt to create a custom-tailored Makefile for the installation of that software. If a program ships with a configure script, there's a fair chance that the software will ultimately compile and run on Mac OS X. However, your mileage may vary.

Porting is the process of tweaking and modifying software to run on a specific platform. This process often results in a clean installation of a program, since in most cases experienced programmers have examined, modified, and tested the code on the specific platform before distributing it as a package. Ported software is available in either *source* or *binary* format. Source packages have been modified to compile cleanly and binary packages are ready to run. Source packages are often the most recent. Regardless of which format you select, the software may require additional software to fulfill certain dependencies. Package managers do a decent job of automating this process for you (as we'll see in the next chapter), but using multiple package managers can become a bit confusing, especially when you install more than one version of a specific program using different package managers. In the next section we'll begin looking at two popular package managers and discuss how they streamline the process of installing ported software.

# Installing Ported Software on Mac OS X

Before we get into the details of *how* to download and install ported code, let's take a look at a source code installation gone bad. Understanding how difficult it can be to install programs from source will help you understand why porting can be a much preferred approach.

## Why Port: A Source Install Gone Bad!

For this example, we'll attempt to install Fyodor's excellent *nmap* port scanner. This program is an absolute necessity, but in some cases the source distribution can be difficult to install.

First, we would download the distribution file in either .tar.gz or .tgz (tar gzip) or .bz (bzip) format from www.insecure.org. For example, the gzip file for version 3.75 of nmap would be nmap-3.75.tgz. The file would then have to be uncompressed and untarred with the command **tar −zxvf nmap-3.75.tar**. This would create a subdirectory named *nmap-3.75*, which could be entered with the command **cd nmap-3.75**. The README for this version of nmap notes that CPP=/usr/bin/cpp must be added to the end of the ./configure command on Mac OS X, so the command **./configure CPP=/usr/bin/cpp** would be run in order to create the Makefile, which is required for the next step. Once the configure command eventually completed, the **make** command would be run followed by make install. However, an ugly error message would be produced a few minutes into the make process:

```
g++ -Lnbase -Lnsock/src/  -o nmap main.o nmap.o targets.o tcpip.o
nmap_error.o utils.o idle_scan.o osscan.o output.o scan_engine.o timing.o
charpool.o services.o protocols.o nmap_rpc.o portlist.o NmapOps.o
TargetGroup.o Target.o FingerPrintResults.o service_scan.o NmapOutputTable.o
MACLookup.o  -lnbase -lnsock libpcre/libpcre.a -lpcap -lssl -lcrypto
/usr/bin/ld: can't locate file for: -lstdc++
collect2: ld returned 1 exit status
make: *** [nmap] Error 1
j0pb12:~/Desktop/nmap-3.75 johnnylong$
```

Any decent Google user would fire off a few queries to locate the source
of the problem, and after much frustration would realize that there was no
readily obvious solution for resolving the problem. This experience is reminiscent of what many UNIX and Linux users face when installing software and
is not at all what Mac users expect of their systems. In fact, this type of digital
bumbling to get a piece of software running is what *drives* many people to use
a Mac in the first place. Software porting takes the guesswork out of this process, and gets the nasty technical details far, far away from the user.

In the following section, we will begin to discuss package managers. These
programs take much of the guesswork out of installing open source software,
and as shown in Figure 5.7, a package manager is capable of installing nmap
3.75 with one simple command. This is obviously much preferred to the process of downloading, compiling, and troubleshooting source code, especially if
you don't mind not having the absolute latest software version.

**Figure 5.7** A Painless Install of nmap

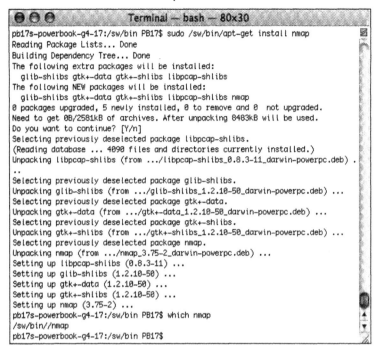

```
pb17s-powerbook-g4-17:/sw/bin PB17$ sudo /sw/bin/apt-get install nmap
Reading Package Lists... Done
Building Dependency Tree... Done
The following extra packages will be installed:
  glib-shlibs gtk+-data gtk+-shlibs libpcap-shlibs
The following NEW packages will be installed:
  glib-shlibs gtk+-data gtk+-shlibs libpcap-shlibs nmap
0 packages upgraded, 5 newly installed, 0 to remove and 0  not upgraded.
Need to get 0B/2581kB of archives. After unpacking 8483kB will be used.
Do you want to continue? [Y/n]
Selecting previously deselected package libpcap-shlibs.
(Reading database ... 4090 files and directories currently installed.)
Unpacking libpcap-shlibs (from .../libpcap-shlibs_0.8.3-11_darwin-powerpc.deb) .
..
Selecting previously deselected package glib-shlibs.
Unpacking glib-shlibs (from .../glib-shlibs_1.2.10-50_darwin-powerpc.deb) ...
Selecting previously deselected package gtk+-data.
Unpacking gtk+-data (from .../gtk+-data_1.2.10-50_darwin-powerpc.deb) ...
Selecting previously deselected package gtk+-shlibs.
Unpacking gtk+-shlibs (from .../gtk+-shlibs_1.2.10-50_darwin-powerpc.deb) ...
Selecting previously deselected package nmap.
Unpacking nmap (from .../nmap_3.75-2_darwin-powerpc.deb) ...
Setting up libpcap-shlibs (0.8.3-11) ...
Setting up glib-shlibs (1.2.10-50) ...
Setting up gtk+-data (1.2.10-50) ...
Setting up gtk+-shlibs (1.2.10-50) ...
Setting up nmap (3.75-2) ...
pb17s-powerbook-g4-17:/sw/bin PB17$ which nmap
/sw/bin//nmap
pb17s-powerbook-g4-17:/sw/bin PB17$
```

In order to get to this point of open source software installation nirvana, we need to take a closer look at package managers. In the next section, we'll look at *apt-get*, *Fink*, and *DarwinPorts*.

# DarwinPorts

DarwinPorts (http://darwinports.opendarwin.org) is "a software build, install and packaging infrastructure" whose project goal is "to provide an easy way to install various open-source software products on the Darwin OS family", including Mac OS X. In short, DarwinPorts allows you to easily obtain, install, upgrade and remove ported software from source code. The project uses the term "port" to describe a ported software package, and at the time of this writing there are over 2500 ports available for OS X. DarwinPorts is a great package manager, although most novices will be put off by either the installation and configuration process or the somewhat confusing process used to install ports. If ease of use if paramount to you, consider using Fink and Fink Commander, discussed in the next section. It's not a bad idea, however, to use both Fink and DarwinPorts to take advantage of the large combined software library.

In order to use DarwinPorts, the  you must first install the DarwinPorts software, or *base*. This process relies on the Concurrent Versioning System (CVS). First, change to a directory that will house the downloaded software:

```
$ cd ~/Documents
```

It is not necessary to create a subdirectory, as a darwinports directory will automatically be created by the CVS transfer. A single CVS command will log in to the DarwinPorts CVS server. No password is required to access the server, so when prompted, simply press **Enter** to continue.

```
$ cvs -d :pserver:anonymous@anoncvs.opendarwin.org:/Volumes/src/cvs/od login
```

Once logged into the CVS server, this command will begin the download of DarwinPorts:

```
$ cvs -d :pserver:anonymous@anoncvs.opendarwin.org:/Volumes/src/cvs/od co -P
darwinports
```

If all goes well, the download will begin, and over 80MB of programs and software ports will be downloaded. After the file transfer completes, the DarwinPorts software will have to be built. These commands follow the fairly standard procedure discussed earlier for installing most open source software:

```
$ cd darwinports
$ cd base
$ ./configure
$ make
$ sudo make install
```

The final command will actually install the DarwinPorts program (*port*) into the /opt/local/bin directory, which should be added to your path (via export PATH=$PATH:/opt/local/bin in bash or setenv PATH ${PATH}:/opt/local/bin in tcsh). Once the installation is complete, DarwinPorts will have to know where the ports are that you just downloaded. Remember that both the DarwinPorts program and the open source packages (or ports) were both downloaded as part of the DarwinPorts CVS install. In order to make DarwinPorts aware of the location of these port files, the /opt/local/etc/ports/sources.conf file must be updated to point to the local copy of the ports, which are stored in the ~/Documents/darwinports/dports directory, following our example above. By adding a single line to the end of the sources.conf file with a URL pointing to this subdirectory, DarwinPorts will know where to look. Following our example installation, the line *file:///Users/johnnylong/Documents/darwinports/dports* should be appended to the /opt/local/etc/ports/sources.conf file. Naturally, you should change the username to your own username, unless of course you happen to be Johnny Long! Instead of manually updating this file, consider a shell shortcut involving a single line of shell, and creative use of the back tick character (the one under the tilde key in the upper left corner of the keyboard). First, change to your home directory with **cd ~/Documents**, and execute this single line of shell:

```
echo `pwd` >> /opt/local/etc/ports/sources.conf
```

Once this file has been modified, DarwinPorts can be tested with a command like **/opt/local/bin/port list**, which will list the available ports. If an error message is produced, be sure to check the /opt/local/etc/ports/sources.conf file for the proper syntax of the file line. While you're at it, you may as well add /opt/local/man to your MANPATH variable with export **MANPATH=$MANPATH:/opt/local/man** in bash or **setenv MANPATH ${MANPATH}:/opt/local/man** in tcsh so that the man program knows about DarwinPorts. Once this is set up, you'll be able to read more about DarwinPorts with the man program via **man port**. Although this all seems a bit unwieldy, DarwinPorts only has to be set up and configured once before the easy (and fun) part begins!

### Notes From the Underground...

## Making Environment Changes Stick

By this point, you're beginning to see more command-line instructions, some of which don't stick between shell sessions. For example, the *PATH* variable, which describes the location of programs, has to be updated after the installation of DarwinPorts. Instead of setting this each time, you could update your *~/.bash_profile* file with an appropriate *PATH* line. Any commands in this file are executed every time a login shell is launched. If you're not comfortable with built-in editors like *vi*, consider using the TextEditor to edit the file with **open ~/.bash_profile**.

The primary tool used with the DarwinPorts package is *port*, which accepts multiple options:

- **list** This option will list the available ports that can be installed via DarwinPorts.

- **search** This will search for a port using the string provided.

- **install** This option will install a port, which is specified by name. DarwinPorts will check for and install any dependencies for each application installed.

- **clean** This option will delete all the files used during the build process, although this can be done automatically by adding the **–c** option to a port command.

- **uninstall** This option will uninstall a port by name.

- **upgrade** This will upgrade a port, if an upgrade is available.

Installing software with the *port* program is fairly straightforward. First, ensure that you have downloaded the latest and greatest port collection from the OpenDarwin servers:

```
$ sudo port selfupdate
```

The *list* option will show you a list of ports that can be installed, but if you already know the name of the port you wish to install, you can simply install it with the *install* option. For example, to install the Ruby object-oriented programming language, simply run:

```
$ sudo port install ruby
```

Keeping current with the latest available releases of installed software is easy as well. You can either update *all* your ports with a command like:

```
$ sudo port -a upgrade
```

or, you can update an individual package (like Ruby) with a command like:

```
$ sudo port upgrade ruby
```

Installing software via DarwinPorts is so much easier than installing from source, despite the somewhat cumbersome initial installation and configuration. However, as with most things in life, it's great to have choices. The primary alternative to DarwinPorts is Fink. Let's take a look at Fink.

# Fink

The Fink project (http://fink.sourceforge.net) also aims to bring the wealth of open source software to the Mac OS X platform using a method similar to the DarwinPorts project: porting. Fink uses the Debian tools (such as aptget and dpkg) behind the scenes and allows for the downloading of binary software distributions, which means no build or compile is necessary to run the software. Most often, binary distributions are older than source distributions, but remember that binary distributions are easier and faster to install, and generally suffer fewer technical problems than source packages. Either way, Fink makes open source software installation on OS X a snap. As with most package managers, Fink offers the ability to install, upgrade, and remove packages, and through a graphical user interface, the Fink Commander software adds point-and-click ease of use.

In order to begin using Fink, the software must be first downloaded and installed. The installation is quite simple. First, download the installer disk image from http://fink.sourceforge.net/download. Double-click the icon to mount the disk image and then double-click the package inside. Following the installation, Fink will run the *pathsetup* utility, and you will be prompted for your login password. Once pathsetup has completed, Fink is installed, as indicated by the existence of the /sw/bin directory. For most Mac users, this installation process is much preferred to DarwinPorts's.

## Notes From the Underground…

### Kill Them All!

Package managers are great and all, but eventually you'll need to troubleshoot the installation of a bit of software. The first thing you'll need to determine is whether the software was installed with a package manager. One of the handiest commands for this purpose is the **which** command. Run from the terminal, **which man** will report the directory name that contains the man program. If your buggy program is installed in /sw/bin, it was installed with fink or apt-get. If you want to back up (or destroy) everything you've installed with Fink, look no further than the /sw directory. Fink installs nothing outside of this directory. DarwinPorts operates in a similar fashion, placing all files in a quarantined /opt/local directory.

# Installing Binary Packages Using apt-get

Included with the Fink installation are two programs, specifically *apt-get,* and *fink,* which we'll use to download and install ported software. While apt-get can be used to install both source and binary ports, it is most often used to install binary ports since the fink program is used to install source ports. The apt-get program should be run as the root user via the **sudo** command. There are many options available for using apt-get, but the most common functions are listed below:

- **install** When run with the name of a package, apt-get will download and install the package. For example, running **sudo apt-get install ircii** will install the ircII program, as shown in Figure 5.8. In some cases, apt-get may complain about various things, but in most cases, apt-get will suggest a workaround or fix. For example, one encountered error message might indicate that the user should run **apt-get –f install**. Running this command via sudo clears the error and allows the install to be rerun, without further issue.

- **upgrade** This option will upgrade any installed packages, if new versions are available. This option is invoked with **sudo apt-get upgrade**.

- **remove** This option will remove the selected package, and requires the name of that package as an argument. For example, running **sudo apt-get remove ircii** will remove ircII from your system.

## Notes From the Underground…

### Where's My Stuff?

One problem that many users run into with automated package management tools is actually locating their packages after installation. Fink and it's support tools (like apt-get) install software in the /sw/bin directory, which is often not a part of the default path. This makes the binaries somewhat difficult to find and run. After installing Fink, be sure to run the **pathsetup.sh** command, or add /sw/bin and /sw/sbin to the default path.

**Figure 5.8** Apt-get in Action: Binary Package Install

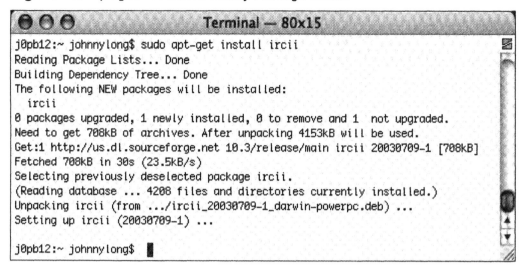

```
j0pb12:~ johnnylong$ sudo apt-get install ircii
Reading Package Lists... Done
Building Dependency Tree... Done
The following NEW packages will be installed:
  ircii
0 packages upgraded, 1 newly installed, 0 to remove and 1  not upgraded.
Need to get 708kB of archives. After unpacking 4153kB will be used.
Get:1 http://us.dl.sourceforge.net 10.3/release/main ircii 20030709-1 [708kB]
Fetched 708kB in 30s (23.5kB/s)
Selecting previously deselected package ircii.
(Reading database ... 4208 files and directories currently installed.)
Unpacking ircii (from .../ircii_20030709-1_darwin-powerpc.deb) ...
Setting up ircii (20030709-1) ...

j0pb12:~ johnnylong$ 
```

## Installing Source Packages using fink

In addition to enabling the installation of binary packages (as we've already seen with apt-get) the *fink* tool allows for the installation of source packages as well. In most cases, the source install of a package is much more up to date than a binary installation, and the process is nearly as simple. Source installation requires the use of a compiler (usually gcc), which is installed along with the rest of the development tools during the Apple Developer Tools installation. Even though *manual* installation of source-based packages is generally somewhat difficult, Fink does most of the heavy lifting behind the scenes, sparing the user most of the pain of a manual install. The **fink** tool has several options, including:

- **list** This option will list the packages that are available for source installation. Run as **fink list**, this will produce a list of packages, versions and a description as well as the installation state of each package, shown in the first column of output. The installation state will show as not installed (blank), installed (indicated by an i), or installed but not current (indicated by i in parentheses). This provides a simple, quick look at the packages available and the state of each package on your system.

- **describe**  This produces a much more detailed look at an individual package. Invoked with the name of a package (for example **fink describe 3dpong**), fink will display a long description, a version number, the website, and the name and address of the tool's maintainer.

- **apropos**  This option will scan for a list of packages that contain a specific supplied search string. For example, **fink apropos calc** will list all packages that contain the string *calc* in the name or description of the package.

- **install**  This option requires the name of a package and will install that package after first checking for (and satisfying) any dependencies the tool may have on other software packages and libraries. Fink will ask for verification before downloading external dependencies, and proceed to download, compile, install, and configure each of them, very often resulting in a smooth installation of the tool. In some cases, error messages may be produced, but most often the installation proceeds without a hitch, dumping the compiled tool into the /sw/bin directory. In order to install the *wcalc* package, for example, simply **run fink install wcalc**. This requires root privileges, although Fink will automatically run the command through sudo, often generating a root password prompt before proceeding with the installation.

- **remove**  This will delete the named packages. For example, when run as **fink remove 3dpong**, Fink will delete the 3dpong program. This does not delete configuration files.

- **purge**  This will delete the named packages, *and* any associated configuration files.

- **update**  This will update the named packages. Multiple packages can be supplied on the command line. For example, **fink update 3dpong xmms** will update both the 3dpong package and the xmms package.

## Installing Source or Binary Packages using Fink Commander

Fink commander is a nice graphical front-end for apt-get and Fink. Available either with the binary distribution of Fink (in the FinkCommander folder) or as a separate download from http://finkcommander.sourceforge.net, Fink Commander is perhaps the easiest way to install, update and remove software packages thanks to the point-and-click interface, as shown in Figure 5.9.

**Figure 5.9** Fink Commander

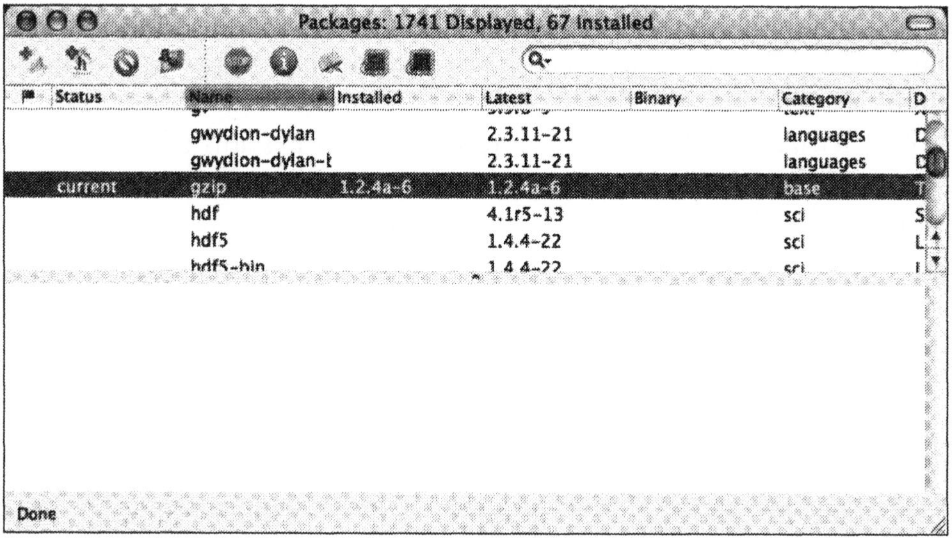

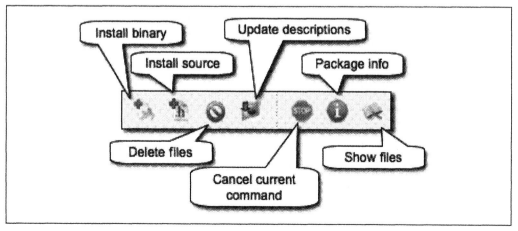

The Fink Commander interface is fairly intuitive, listing each package on a separate line. When a package is highlighted, the buttons at the top of the interface become active, allowing various actions. The major package actions are shown in Figure 5.10.

**Figure 5.10** Fink Commander's Action Buttons

From left to right, the buttons allow for installation of binary or source package, deletion of packages, package description updates, canceling of current action, display of package info, and listing of files contained inside a package, respectively. The process of installing a binary package is as simple as highlighting the package name, and clicking the first button on the left, or selecting **Binary | Install** from the Fink Commander menu. Fink Commander can be used interchangeably with the *fink* and *apt-get* commands without any conflicts. All of these tools read from and write to the same internal package list. This keeps each tool aware of the status of each package.

In summary, each package management system has its own benefits and drawbacks, and it's not uncommon for users to rely on DarwinPorts, Fink, *and* apt-get to install ported software. In most cases, it's simply a question of whatever works to get the software installed. Although Mac OS X veterans will undoubtedly miss the slick look and feel of native Mac software, ported open source software can greatly expand the toolkit of the true Mac OS X hacker.

Now that we've made it through the somewhat sketchy process of configuring the development environment and various package managers, it's time to have some fun! In the next section, we'll explore some amazing tools that will now run wonderfully on the Mac!

# Using The "Top 75 Security Tools" List

Created and maintained by Fyodor, and available from www.insecure.org/tools.html, the "Top 75 Security Tools" list has become the industry standard list of must-have tools. Although nearly 20 of the tools only run on the Windows platform (and by extension will run fine under programs like Virtual PC, discussed later in this chapter), 70% of the remaining tools run, or have been ported to Mac OS X, and that number is still increasing as more and more tools are tweaked to run seamlessly on the Mac.

This section will list the tools from the "Top 75" list that currently run on, or have been ported to OS X. The majority of this information has been listed verbatim from the list itself, and the tools' authors or development teams have provided most descriptions. In addition to the information provided by Fyodor, each tool has been assigned a classification describing the approximate function of each tool, and information about how to get the tool running on OS X has been listed as well. Each tool in this list is either *native* to OS X (meaning that it is included as part of the operating system, or runs without modification), or has been *ported* to OS X via the DarwinPorts or Fink projects. If a tool has been ported, the current latest available version of each tool (at time of printing) is listed.

## Category: Attack (Network)

Name: *dsniff*
Rank: 7
URL: http://naughty.monkey.org/~dugsong/dsniff/
Mac availability: DarwinPorts as version 2.3, 2.4b1 Fink as version 2.3
Description: A suite of powerful network auditing and penetration-testing tools.

This popular and well-engineered suite by Dug Song includes many tools. Dsniff, filesnarf, mailsnarf, msgsnarf, urlsnarf, and webspy passively monitor a network for interesting data (passwords, e-mail, files, etcetera). arpspoof, dnsspoof, and macof facilitate the interception of network traffic normally unavailable to an attacker (for example, due to Layer 2 switching). sshmitm and webmitm implement active *monkey in the middle* attacks against redirected SSH (Secure Shell) and HTTPS (Hypertext Transfer Protocol over Secure Sockets Layer) sessions by exploiting weak bindings in ad-hoc PKI.

Name: *ettercap*
Rank: 9
URL: http://ettercap.sourceforge.net/
Mac availability: DarwinPorts as version 0.6.b, 0.7.1, Fink as version 0.7.3
Description: Ettercap is a terminal-based network sniffer/interceptor/logger for Ethernet LANs.

In case you still thought switched LANs (local area networks) provide much extra security, Ettercap is a terminal-based network sniffer/interceptor/logger for Ethernet LANs. It supports active and passive dissection of many protocols (even ciphered ones, like SSH and HTTPS). Data injection in an established connection and filtering on the fly is also possible, keeping the connection synchronized. Many sniffing modes were implemented to give you a powerful and complete sniffing suite. Plug-ins are supported. It has the ability to check whether you are in a switched LAN or not, and to use OS fingerprints (active or passive) to let you know the geometry of the LAN.

> Name: *nemesis*
> Rank: 40
> URL: http://www.packetfactory.net/projects/nemesis/
> Mac availability: DarwinPorts as version 1.4beta3, Fink as version 1.4
> Description: Packet injection simplified.

The Nemesis Project is designed to be a command line based, portable human IP (Internet Protocol) stack for UNIX/Linux (and now Windows). The suite is broken down by protocol, and should allow for useful scripting of injected packet streams from simple shell scripts. If you enjoy Nemesis, you might also want to look at hping2. They complement each other well.

## Category: Attack (Scanner)

> Name: *nessus*
> Rank: 1
> URL: http://www.nessus.org
> Mac availability: DarwinPorts as version 2.0.12, Fink as version 2.2.4
> Description: The premier open source vulnerability assessment tool.

Nessus is a remote security scanner for Linux, BSD, Solaris, and other Unices. It is plug-in-based, has a GTK interface, and performs over 1200 remote security checks. It allows for reports to be generated in HTML (Hypertext Markup Language), XML (Extensible Markup Language), LaTeX, and ASCII text, and suggests solutions for security problems.

## Category: Attack (Web)

> Name: *whisker*
> Rank: 10
> URL: http://www.wiretrip.net/rfp/p/doc.asp?id=21&iface=2
> Mac availability: Native (Perl)
> Description: Rain.Forest.Puppy's CGI vulnerability scanner and library.

Whisker is a scanner that allows you to test HTTP (Hypertext Transfer Protocol) servers for many known security holes, particularly the presence of dangerous CGIs (common gateway interfaces). Libwhisker is a Perl library (used by Whisker) that allows for the creation of custom HTTP scanners. If you wish to audit more than just Web servers, have a look at Nessus.

Name: *nikto*
Rank: 16
URL: http://www.cirt.net/code/nikto.shtml
Mac availability: Native (Perl)
Description: A more comprehensive Web scanner.
Nikto is a Web server scanner that looks for over 2000 potentially dangerous files/CGIs and problems on over 200 servers. It uses LibWhisker, but is generally updated more frequently than Whisker itself.

# Category: Crypto

Name: *ssh*
Rank: 12
URL: http://www.openssh.com/
Mac availability: native, DarwinPorts as version 3.8.1p1, Fink as version 4.0p1
Description: A secure way to access remote computers.
SSH is a program for logging into or executing commands on a remote machine. It provides secure encrypted communications between two untrusted hosts over an insecure network. X11 connections and arbitrary TCP/IP (Transmission Control Protocol/Internet Protocol) ports can also be forwarded over the secure channel. It is intended as a replacement for rlogin, rsh, and rcp, and can be used to provide rdist and rsync with a secure communication channel. OpenSSH is affiliated with the OpenBSD project, though a portable version runs on most UNIX systems.

Name: *gnupg*
Rank: 30
URL: http://www.gnupg.org/
Mac availability: DarwinPorts as version 1.4.0, Fink as version 1.4.0
Description: Secure your files and communication w/advanced encryption.
PGP is the famous encryption program by Phil Zimmerman which helps secure your data from eavesdroppers and other risks. GnuPG is a very well regarded open source implementation of the PGP standard (the actual exe-

cutable is named gpg). While GnuPG is always free, PGP costs money for some uses.

Name: *openssl*
Rank: 38
URL: http://www.openssl.org
Mac availability: DarwinPorts as version 0.9.7e, Fink as version 0.9.6m
Description: The premier SSL/TLS encryption library.

The OpenSSL Project is a collaborative effort to develop a robust, commercial-grade, full-featured, and open source toolkit implementing the SSL v2/v3 and Transport Layer Security (TLS v1) protocols as well as a full-strength general-purpose cryptography library. The project is managed by a worldwide community of volunteers who use the Internet to communicate, plan, and develop the OpenSSL toolkit and its related documentation.

Name: *stunnel*
Rank: 46
URL: http://www.stunnel.org/
Mac availability: DarwinPorts as version 4.0.5, Fink as version 4.10
Description: A general-purpose SSL cryptographic wrapper.

The stunnel program is designed to work as an SSL encryption wrapper between remote client and local (inetd-startable) or remote server. It can be used to add SSL functionality to commonly used inetd daemons like POP2 (Post Office Protocol v2), POP3 (Post Office Protocol v3), and IMAP (Internet Message Access Protocol) servers without any changes in the programs' code. It will negotiate an SSL connection using the OpenSSL or SSLeay libraries.

# Category: Defense

Name: *snort*
Rank: 3
URL: http://www.snort.org
Mac availability: DarwinPorts as version 2.2.0, Fink as version 2.3.3
Description: A free intrusion detection system (IDS) for the masses.

Snort is a lightweight network intrusion detection system capable of performing real-time traffic analysis and packet logging on IP networks. It can perform protocol analysis, content searching/matching, and can be used to detect a variety of attacks and probes, such as buffer overflows, stealth port scans, CGI attacks, SMB probes, OS fingerprinting attempts, and much more. Snort uses a flexible rule-based language to describe traffic that it should collect or pass, and a modular detection engine. Many people also suggested that the Analysis Console for Intrusion Databases (ACID) be used with Snort.

Name: *honeyd*
Rank: 43
URL: http://www.citi.umich.edu/u/provos/honeyd/
Mac availability: DarwinPorts as version 0.4
Description: Your own personal honeynet.

Honeyd is a small daemon that creates virtual hosts on a network. The hosts can be configured to run arbitrary services, and their TCP personality can be adapted so that they appear to be running certain versions of operating systems. Honeyd enables a single host to claim multiple addresses on a LAN for network simulation. It is possible to ping the virtual machines, or to *tracerute* them. Any type of service on the virtual machine can be simulated according to a simple configuration file. It is also possible to proxy services to another machine rather than simulating them. The Web page is currently down for legal reasons, but the version 0.5 tarball is still available at www.citi.umich.edu/u/provos/honeyd/honeyd-0.5.tar.gz.

Name: *tcpwrappers*
Rank: 52
URL: ftp://ftp.porcupine.org/pub/security/index.html
Mac availability: DarwinPorts as version 7.6
Description: A classic IP-based access control and logging mechanism.

Name: *bastille*
Rank: 57
URL: http://www.bastille-linux.org/
Mac availability: Native
Description: Security hardening script for Linux, Mac OS X, and HP-UX.

# Category: Defense / Forensics

Name: *lsof*
Rank: 41
URL: ftp://vic.cc.purdue.edu/pub/tools/unix/lsof/
Mac availability: DarwinPorts as version 4.70
Description: LiSt Open Files.

This Unix-specific diagnostic and forensics tool lists information about any files that are open by processes currently running on the system. It can also list communications sockets opened by each process.

# Category: Evasion

Name: *fragroute*
Rank: 48
URL: http://www.monkey.org/~dugsong/fragroute/
Mac availability: DarwinPorts as version 1.2
Description: IDS systems' worst nightmare.

Fragroute intercepts, modifies, and rewrites egress traffic, implementing most of the attacks described in the Secure Networks IDS Evasion paper (www.insecure.org/stf/secnet_ids/secnet_ids.html). It features a simple rule set language to delay, duplicate, drop, fragment, overlap, print, reorder, segment, source-route, or otherwise monkey with all outbound packets destined for a target host, with minimal support for randomized or probabilistic behavior. This tool was written in good faith to aid in the testing of intrusion detection systems, firewalls, and basic TCP/IP stack behaviour. Like Dsniff and Libdnet, this excellent tool was written by Dug Song.

# Category: Footprinting

Name: *stdtools*
Rank: 22
URL: N/A
Mac availability: Native
Description: (traceroute/ping/telnet/whois)

While there are many whiz-bang high-tech tools out there to assist in security auditing, but don't forget about the basics! Everyone should be very familiar with these tools as they come with most operating systems (except that Windows omits *whois* and uses the name *tracert*). They can be very handy in a pinch, although for more advanced usage you may be better off with Hping2 and Netcat.

Name: *xprobe2*
Rank: 33
URL: http://www.sys-security.com/html/projects/X.html
Mac availability: DarwinPorts as version 0.3
Description: Active OS fingerprinting tool.
XProbe is a tool for determining the operating system of a remote host. They do this using some of the same techniques (www.insecure.org/nmap/nmap-fingerprinting-article.html) as Nmap, as well as many different ideas. Xprobe has always emphasized ICMP (Internet Control Message Protocol) in their fingerprinting approach.

Name: *dig*
Rank: 65
URL: http://www.isc.org/products/BIND/
Mac availability: Native
Description: A handy DNS (Domain Name System) query tool that comes free with Bind.

Name: *visualroute*
Rank: 69
URL: http://www.visualware.com/visualroute/index.html
Mac availability: Native
Description: Obtains traceroute/whois data and plots it on a world map.

# Category: Monitor (Sniffing)

Name: *ethereal*
Rank: 2
URL: http://www.ethereal.com
Mac availability: DarwinPorts as version 0.10.8, Fink as version 0.10.12
Description: Sniffing the glue that holds the Internet together.
Ethereal is a free network protocol analyzer for UNIX and Windows. It allows you to examine data from a live network or from a capture file on

disk. You can interactively browse the capture data, viewing summary and detail information for each packet. Ethereal has several powerful features, including a rich display filter language and the ability to view the reconstructed stream of a TCP session. A text-based version called tethereal is included.

Name: *tcpdump*
Rank: 5
URL: http://www.tcpdump.org
Mac availability: Native
Description: The classic sniffer for network monitoring and data acquisition.

is a well-known and well-loved text-based network packet analyzer (sniffer). It can be used to print out the headers of packets on a network interface that matches a given expression. You can use this tool to track down network problems or to monitor network activities. TCPdump is also the source of the Libpcap (www.tcpdump.org) / WinPcap (http://winpcap.polito.it) packet capture library, which is used by Nmap among many other utilities. Note that many users prefer the newer Ethereal sniffer.

Name: *kismet*
Rank: 17
URL: http://www.kismetwireless.net/
Mac availability: Fink as version 3.0.1
Description: A powerful wireless sniffer.

Kismet is an 802.11b network sniffer and network dissector. It is capable of sniffing using most wireless cards, automatic network IP block detection via UDP (User Datagram Protocol), ARP (Address Resolution Protocol), and DHCP (Dynamic Host Control Protocol) packets, Cisco equipment lists via Cisco Discovery Protocol, weak cryptographic packet logging, and Ethereal- and TCPdump-compatible packet dump files. It also includes the ability to plot detected networks and estimated network ranges on downloaded maps or user supplied image files.

Name: *ngrep*
Rank: 35
URL: http://www.packetfactory.net/projects/ngrep/
Mac availability: DarwinPorts as version 1.4.2, Fink as version 1.4.0
Description: Convenient packet matching & display.

ngrep strives to provide most of GNU grep's common features, applying them to the network layer. ngrep is a pcap-aware tool that will allow you to specify extended regular or hexadecimal expressions to match against data payloads of packets. It currently recognizes TCP, UDP and ICMP across Ethernet, PPP (Point to Point Protocol), SLIP (Serial Line Internet Protocol), FDDI (Fiber Distributed Data Interface), Token Ring and null interfaces, and understands bpf filter logic in the same fashion as more common packet sniffing tools, such as TCPdump and snoop.

Name: *ntop*
Rank: 39
URL: http://www.ntop.org/
Mac availability: DarwinPorts as version 3.0, Fink as version 1.1
Description: A network traffic usage monitor.

Ntop shows network usage in a way similar to what top does for processes. In interactive mode, it displays the network status on the user's terminal. In Web mode, it acts as a Web server, creating an HTML dump of the network status. It sports a NetFlow/sFlow emitter/collector, an HTTP-based client interface for creating ntop-centric monitoring applications, and RRD for persistently storing traffic statistics.

Name: *etherape*
Rank: 64
URL: http://etherape.sourceforge.net/
Mac availability: Darwin 0.9.0
Description: A graphical network monitor for UNIX modeled after etherman.

Name: *arpwatch*
Rank: 75
URL: http://www-nrg.ee.lbl.gov/
Mac availability: DarwinPorts as version 2.1a11, Fink as version 2.1a11
Description: Keeps track of Ethernet/IP address pairings and can detect certain monkey business (such as dsniff).

Name: *tcpreplay*
Rank: 71
URL: http://tcpreplay.sourceforge.net/
Mac availability: Fink as version 2.3.5
Description: a tool to replay saved tcpdump or snoop files at arbitrary speeds

# Category: Multipurpose

Name: *netcat*
Rank: 4
URL: http://www.atstake.com/research/tools/network_utilities/
Mac availability: Native
Description: The network Swiss army knife.
A simple UNIX utility that reads and writes data across network connections using TCP or UDP. It is designed to be a reliable back-end tool that can be used directly or easily driven by other programs and scripts. At the same time, it is a feature-rich network debugging and exploration tool, since it can create almost any kind of connection you would need and has several interesting built-in capabilities.

# Category: Password Cracking

Name: *john*
Rank: 11
URL: http://www.openwall.com/john/
Mac availability: DarwinPorts as version 1.6
Description: An extraordinarily powerful, flexible, and fast multi-platform password hash cracker.

John the Ripper is a fast password cracker, currently available for many flavors of UNIX (11 are officially supported, not counting different architectures), DOS, Win32, BeOS, and OpenVMS. Its primary purpose is to detect weak UNIX passwords. It supports several crypt(3) password hash types which are most commonly found on various UNIX flavors, as well as Kerberos AFS and Windows NT/2000/XP LM hashes. Several other hash types are added with contributed patches.

Name: *l0phtcrack*
Rank: 19
URL: http://www.atstake.com/research/lc/
Mac availability: DarwinPorts as version (l0phtcrack) 1.5
Description: Windows password auditing and recovery application L0phtCrack attempts to crack Windows passwords from hashes that it can obtain (given proper access) from standalone Windows NT/2000 workstations, networked servers, primary domain controllers, or Active Directory. In some cases it can sniff the hashes off the wire. It also has numerous methods of generating password guesses (dictionary, brute force, etcetera).

Name: *crack*
Rank: 66
URL: http://www.users.dircon.co.uk/~crypto/
Mac availability: DarwinPorts as version (cracklib) 2.7
Description: Alec Muffett's classic local password cracker.

# Category: Password Cracking (Remote)

Name: *hydra*
Rank: 50
URL: http://www.thc.org/releases.php
Mac availability: DarwinPorts as version 4.4
Description: Parallelized network authentication cracker.
This tool allows for rapid dictionary attacks against network login systems, including FTP (File Transfer Protocol), POP3, IMAP, Netbios, Telnet, HTTP

Auth, LDAP (Lightweight Directory Access Protocol), NNTP (Network News Transport Protocol), VNC, ICQ, Socks5, PCNFS, and more. It includes SSL support and is apparently now part of Nessus. Like Amap, this release is from the fine folks at THC (www.thc.org).

# Category: Programming

Name: *PERL, Python*
Rank: 36
URL: http://www.perl.org
Mac availability: Native (PERL)
Description: Portable, general-purpose scripting language.

While many canned security tools are available on this page for handling common tasks, it is important to have the ability to write your own (or modify the existing ones) when you need something more custom. Perl and Python make it very easy to write quick, portable scripts to test, exploit, or even fix systems! Archives like CPAN (www.cpan.org) are filled with modules such as Net::RawIP (www.ic.al.lg.ua/~ksv) and protocol implementations to make your tasks even easier.

Name: *libnet*
Rank: 54
URL: http://www.packetfactory.net/libnet/
Mac availability: DarwinPorts as version 1.0.2a, 1.1.2.1, Fink as version 1.0.2a, 1.1.2.1
Description: A high-level API (Application Program Interface) allowing the application programmer to construct and inject network packets.

# Category: Scanning

Name: *hping2*
Rank: 6
URL: http://www.hping.org/
Mac availability: DarwinPorts as version hping2 (rc3), hping3 alpha-2
Description: A network probing utility like ping on steroids.

hping2 assembles and sends custom ICMP/UDP/TCP packets and displays any replies. It was inspired by the *ping* command, but offers far more control over the probes sent. It also has a handy traceroute mode and supports IP fragmentation. This tool is particularly useful when trying to traceroute/ping/probe hosts behind a firewall that blocks attempts using the standard utilities.

Name: *fping*
Rank: 56
URL: http://www.fping.com/
Mac availability: DarwinPorts as version 2.4b2_to, Fink as version 2.4b2
Description: A parallel ping scanning program.

Name: *tcptraceroute*
Rank: 59
URL: http://michael.toren.net/code/tcptraceroute/
Mac availability: DarwinPorts as version 1.5beta4, Fink as version 1.5beta5
Description: A traceroute implementation using TCP packets.

# Installing and Using The "Big" Tools

There are only a handful of "big tools" in the security arena, and we'll look at installing two of them: the Ethereal network analyzer and the Nessus security scanner. A large portion of this chapter has been dedicated to developer tools and package management utilities and shells, and all sorts of things that don't really have too much to do with security. However, now that these mechanisms are in place, you'll get to finally enjoy the fruits of your labors by installing some of these big tools without so much as breaking a sweat. Let's tackle Ethereal first.

## Ethereal

*Ethereal* (www.ethereal.com) is a powerful network analyzer (presented in a very nice graphical interface) that has become practically a standard tool for anyone involved in network security. Ethereal has become so popular, in fact, that it's not uncommon to see Ethereal's text-based twin, *tethereal*, being used in place of old standbys like *tcpdump* and *snoop*. Unfortunately, Ethereal can be somewhat temperamental to install, and even the Windows version (despite a nice graphical installer) requires the installation of the WinPcap libraries before it will work. Fortunately for us, installation of Ethereal on our prepped and ready OS X machine takes two steps:

```
$ fink install gtk+2
$ fink install ethereal
```

The first step installs the GTK libraries (which may not be required depending on various factors) and the second step installs Ethereal. That's all there is to it! When Ethereal is run from an *xterm* (not Terminal) window with **sudo /sw/bin/ethereal**, Ethereal is launched. After selecting the proper interface and sniffing network traffic for a few moments, it's obvious that Ethereal works like a champ, as shown in Figure 5.11.

**Figure 5.11** Ethereal Running on Mac OS X

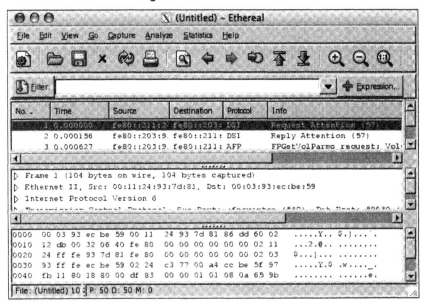

Although the Fink-installed version of Ethereal is not the most bleeding edge version, a newer version can be downloaded and installed from source fairly easily. Although this may take a bit more work, the point is that depending on the amount of effort you wish to exert, there's an Ethereal version that's right for your needs. For more information about Ethereal, be sure to check out *Ethereal Packet Sniffing* by Angela Orebaugh.

# Nessus

Nessus (www.nessus.org) has become the de facto standard for open source vulnerability scanning. With a decent enough interface, and a wide range of community-contributed vulnerability checks, even pen testers with a big budget run Nessus right alongside their most expensive network icebreakers. Nessus has two major components: a *server* program, or *daemon*, which performs the actual scan, and a *client* program that you, the user, will interface with. In most cases, the server and client are run on the same machine, in which case the server *listens* on the *loopback address* (127.0.0.1) and the client connects to that address and a specific port. The client and server can also run on separate machines, in which case the server must listen on a remotely accessible port and remote clients connect to that address and port. Either way, Nessus requires clients to authenticate to the server, helping to prevent unauthorized access. Keep the Nessus authentication information close so an attacker cannot perform unauthorized scans from your server, an act that is certainly considered offensive by most server administrators.

Thanks to Fink, Nessus is a snap to install on Mac OS X. Nessus also requires a bit of configuration after it is installed.

## Notes From the Underground…

### Penetration Testing and Vulnerability Scanning

*Penetration testing* and *vulnerability scanning* are oft-confused terms. Vulnerability scanning is a phase of a penetration test in which the engineer attempts to determine vulnerabilities on a system. A *vulnerability scanner* is a tool that automates a vulnerability scan. Although a vulnerability scan is a critical phase of a penetration test, they are not the same thing.

First, run **/sw/bin/fink install nessus**. As shown in following script, you will be prompted about X11 support and whether or not to use an SSL-enabled version of lynx. Since X11 was already installed in the previous section, simply press **Enter** at the first prompt, and select either **lynx** or **lynx-ssl** for the second prompt. Simply press **Enter** for the third prompt to install Nessus.

```
$ /sw/bin/fink install nessus
Password:
Information about 1766 packages read in 2 seconds.

fink needs help picking an alternative to satisfy a virtual dependency. The
candidates:

(1)      nessus-common: Core package for Nessus
(2)      nessus-common-nox: Core package for Nessus (No X11)


Pick one: [1]


fink needs help picking an alternative to satisfy a virtual dependency. The
candidates:

(1)      lynx: Console based web browser
(2)      lynx-ssl: Console based web browser (SSL-enabled)


Pick one: [1]
The following package will be installed or updated:
 nessus
The following 9 additional packages will be installed:
 daemonic libdnet-shlibs libnasl-shlibs libnessus-shlibs libxml2-bin
 libxml2-shlibs lynx nessus-common nessus-plugins
Do you want to continue? [Y/n]
```

Once Nessus is installed, simply run **sudo /sw/sbin/nessus-adduser** to add a Nessus user account. Enter your system password at the sudo prompt, followed by the name you wish to use to log into the Nessus server. Selecting **pass** for the authentication method is the easiest and most straightforward option. Enter a password at the Login Password prompt, and simply press **Ctrl + D** at the rules prompt for the most basic user creation. At the OK prompt, simply press **Enter** to create the user. The following code shows what this session might look like.

```
$ sudo /sw/sbin/nessus-adduser
Password:
Using /var/tmp as a temporary file holder
```

```
Add a new nessusd user
----------------------


Login : j0hnny
Authentication (pass/cert) [pass] :
Login password : m@xr0xmYp@ntx0rz

User rules
----------
nessusd has a rules system which allows you to restrict the hosts
that j0hnny has the right to test. For instance, you may want
him to be able to scan his own host only.

Please see the nessus-adduser(8) man page for the rules syntax

Enter the rules for this user, and hit ctrl-D once you are done :
(the user can have an empty rules set)
^D


Login           : j0hnny
Password        : m@xr0xmYp@ntx0rz
DN              :
Rules           :


Is that ok ? (y/n) [y] y
user added.
$
```

Next, simply run **sudo /sw/sbin/nessusd −D &** to launch the Nessus daemon. In order to launch the client, simply run **/sw/bin/nessus &** from an *xterm* window (not from Terminal) and the Nessus client screen will be displayed, as shown in Figure 5.12. Log into the Nessus server, and you're ready to go.

**Figure 5.12** The Nessus Client Screen

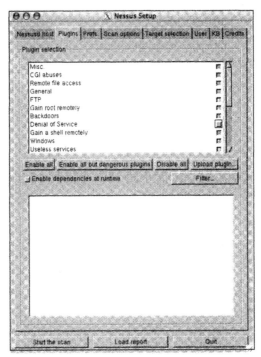

Nessus has a ton of features and functionality, and although we can't fit much detail in this chapter, be sure to check out *Nessus Network Auditing* from Syngress publishing for more details about this excellent tool.

# Other OS X "Must Haves"

Microsoft VirtualPC (originally written by Connectix) is a program that allows the creation of virtual machines. A virtual machine is an operating system that runs as guest inside a host operating system. This essentially allows the user to run more than one operating system at the same time. The Mac version of Virtual PC is also technically an emulator, as it allows for the installation of guest operating systems like Windows that would not normally run on a Mac at all! While this may not seem entirely useful, this allows the Mac user to run other operating systems such as Windows or Linux from within Mac OS X. Figure 5.13 shows a Virtual PC session running Windows XP under Mac OS X. The Finder window floating in front of a Windows XP desktop may look odd, but it demonstrates the concept very well – Mac OS X and Windows can co-exist on the same Mac platform.

**Figure 5.13** Windows XP Running on a Mac

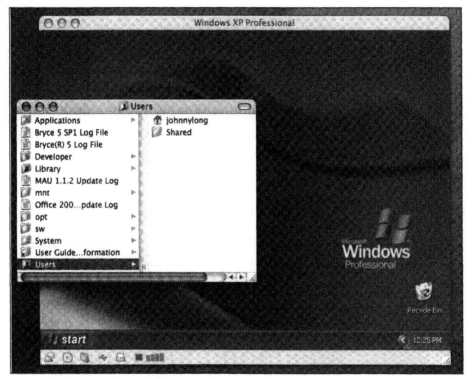

When Virtual PC is running a guest operating system, that operating system is blissfully unaware that it is a virtual machine. The guest operating system thinks it's running on native hardware, and that it has that hardware all to itself. The virtual instance of Windows XP can be configured to share the network connections of Mac OS X, or it can be configured to have its own distinct IP address, via the **Virtual Switch** feature. Virtual machine sessions can be paused, or *hibernated*, allowing fast restarts, and documents can be shared between the Mac and Windows environments with drag-and-drop ease.

Virtual PC is inexpensive (around $225 or $125 without Windows XP) and relatively small, although guest operating systems may consume a decent amount of the host's disk and memory resources. A *basic* Linux install may consume a few hundred megabytes of disk space, while a *typical* Linux or Windows install will consume several gigabytes of space. Most of this disk

space is consumed *as it is used*. You needn't worry about pre-allocating space if
you plan on storing tens of gigs of files on the guest machine; you simply set
the size of the drive during the guest installation and the virtual hard drive
will expand to that size as you use it. As far as memory requirements, guest
systems share your Mac's memory. A virtual installation of Windows XP will
run much better with 512 MB than it will with 256 MB, but more memory
allocated to the guest system means less memory for your Mac. If you're not
interested in clogging up your Mac with tens and tens of gigs worth of operating systems, you may want to consider running a CD-based Linux distribution under Virtual PC. These lightweight distributions strike a good balance
between performance and functionality, while leaving you plenty of room on
your Mac for more interesting things. Let's take a look at how CD-based distributions run under Virtual PC.

# Running CD-based Linux Distributions

Although porting and compiling tools to run on Mac OS X is an option,
there are many CD-based Linux distributions that incorporate tons of tools
and features well suited for pen testing. You could conceivably port or compile each of these tools to the Mac OS X platform, but this simply isn't necessary, thanks to the *capture CD image* feature of Virtual PC. This feature allows
you to download a CD-based distribution, and run it as a virtual machine,
allowing access to the many tools available on the distribution.

The Auditor security collection, available from http://new.remote-
exploit.org/index.php/Auditor_main, and the WHAX (formerly Whoppix)
distribution available from http://iwhax.net are excellent Linux distributions
which provide a staggering number of well-organized tools perfectly suited
for pen testers. In order to run these distributions under Mac OS X, simply
download the ISO images from the respective website, saving it as a file under
OS X. From within VirtualPC 7, create a new machine. Select **Install your
own operating system** as a setup method, and click **Begin**. Continue to
the **hard disk format** screen, and select **Linux** as the operating system. This
will automatically select **Unformatted** as the hard disk format type.
Continue to the **Create PC** screen, and enter a name for your virtual
machine. Select a location on your hard disk for the VirtualPC file. The location is simply a matter of preference, since CD-based Linux distributions
require little (or no) actual space on the hard disk other than the ISO image

itself. Select **create** to create the virtual machine, remove any bootable media from your Mac OS X machine, and select **Start PC** to boot the virtual machine. With no bootable media inserted into the Mac, the virtual machine will begin booting, but will present an error message, requesting that you insert some type of boot media in order to continue the installation of the machine. Click **Drives | Capture CD image...** and select the ISO image (.iso file) of the distribution you downloaded as shown in Figure 5.14.

**Figure 5.14** Booting from an ISO Image

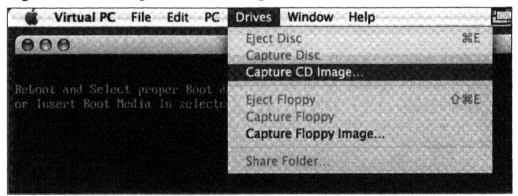

Once the image is mounted, select **PC | Reset** to reboot the virtual machine and click **Reset** to reboot. VirtualPC will boot fro the ISO image, just as if it was a CD, and the virtual machine will boot into the CD–based Linux distribution. Figure 5.14 shows VirtualPC running the WHAX Linux distribution.

## Notes From the Underground…

### Virtual Switching

By default, VirtualPC will set the networking option to **Shared Networking**, meaning that the virtual machine will share the Mac's network connection. This uses network address translation (NAT) and your virtual machine will not have a distinct IP address. If you need to assign a separate IP address for the virtual machine, change this setting to **Virtual Switch**, but make sure you've installed the latest patch to VirtualPC (currently 7.0.2), which enables virtual switching under Mac OS X Tiger.

**Figure 5.15** Mac OS X Running WHAX (Whitehat Knoppix) Linux

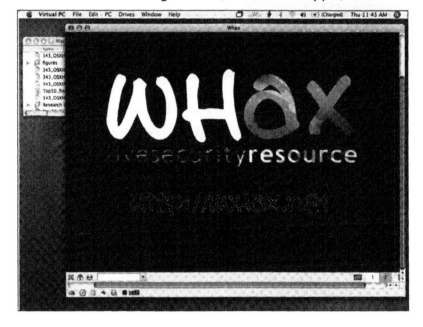

Since CD-based Linux distributions don't normally write to the hard drive of the host machine, changes to the system (created files, modified settings, etcetera) are lost between reboots. In order to address this issue, most Knoppix and many other portable Linux distributions support the *persistent home* concept which, enables the saving of various system settings and files to a removable media device such as a USB *thumb drive* or similar device. This means that you can very easily insert a USB drive into the Mac (which will normally be auto-recognized by Virtual PC), save your configuration data, reboot the system, and the system will (in most cases automatically) detect and restore your files and settings. Knoppix distributions in particular ship with the *saveconfig* utility, which facilitates this process. As shown in Figure 5.16, the Auditor distribution's version of *saveconfig* presents a fairly standard wizard-style interface, which outlines the various settings that can be saved.

**Figure 5.16** The saveconfig Command's Options

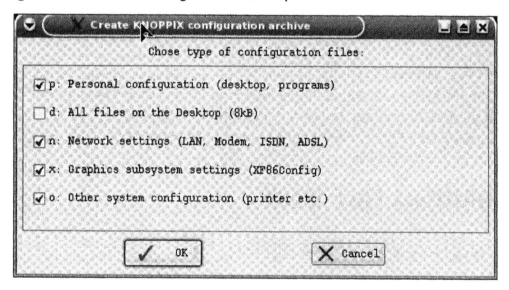

# Summary

With its BSD roots, super-slick graphical interface and near-bulletproof reliability, Apple's Mac OS X operating system provides a great platform for penetration testing. Although many excellent tools have been written specifically for OS X, many open source tools can be compiled directly on OS X using mainstream compilers and interpreters included in the free Apple Developer's Kit. A great deal of code has also been ported to Mac OS X, and thanks to package managers like DarwinPorts and Fink, these can be installed with relative ease. Many "big tools" like Ethereal and Nessus can be installed with a few simple package manager commands. In some cases, however, it's nice to have access to other operating systems like Windows and Linux, and Microsoft's VirtualPC brings the functionality of these operating systems to the OS X platform, making it possible to run non-native code and even CD-based distributions. Slogging through the setup of the Apple Development Kit and the various package managers is well worth it; this provides you with a dizzying array of tools running under a nearly bulletproof OS on the sexiest hardware on the market.

# Solutions Fast Track

## The OS X Command Shell

☑ The OS X command shell provides command-line access to the Mac via well-known shells like *tcsh* and *bash*.

☑ Many must-have utilities, such as *awk*, *sed*, and *Perl* are included as part standard BSD subsystem of the Mac OS X base install.

## Compiling and Porting Open Source Software

☑ The Apple Developer Tools are freely available from Apple, and provide access to many development utilities including the GNU C and C++ compiler.

☑ The XWindows toolkit and protocol can be installed on Mac OS X, allowing graphical programs using that interface to run on the Mac.

☑ Porting, or modifying, software requires subtle changes to the code to allow it to run on various platforms. Porting code can be difficult, but tools such as *dselect* and *apt-get* and projects such as DarwinPorts and Fink make installing software ports as simple as running a few commands.

# Using the "Top 75 Security Tools" List

☑ This list, from Fyodor at www.insecure.org, lists the most popular security tools according to the nmap-hackers list and is considered by many to be the de facto standard in must-have tools. Most of the tools on the list will compile on the Mac, or have been ported to it, and this section discussed each of those tools, describing the process for installing each on Mac OS X.

# Other OS X "Must Haves"

☑ Virtual PC (www.microsoft.com/windows/virtualpc) allows OS X users to run Intel-based software as a *guest* operating system, concurrent with OS X. This brings a whole host of software to the Mac platform, including Windows and Linux applications.

# Links to Sites

- http://developer.apple.com/unix/index.html: UNIX Development on Mac OS X

- http://darwinports.opendarwin.org/: DarwinPorts

- http://fink.sourceforge.net/: Fink

- http://finkcommander.sourceforge.net/: Fink commander

- www.microsoft.com/windows/virtualpc/default.mspx: Microsoft Virtual PC

- www.insecure.org/tools.html: Top 75 Security Tools List

- http://slagheap.net/darwin: Peter Bartoli's Useful Darwin Ports

- http://slagheap.net/etherspoof: Peter Bartoli's Mac Address Spoofing Page

- http://new.remote-exploit.org/index.php/Auditor_main: The Auditor Linux distribution

- http://iwhax.net: The WHAX Linux distribution

# Frequently Asked Questions

The following Frequently Asked Questions, answered by the authors of this book, are designed to both measure your understanding of the concepts presented in this chapter and to assist you with real-life implementation of these concepts. To have your questions about this chapter answered by the author, browse to **www.syngress.com/solutions** and click on the **"Ask the Author"** form.

**Q:** I'm getting 403 forbidden messages or other such strangeness when using fink or apt-get. What should I do?

**A:** This is a fairly common problem that's easy to fix. Either run **fink reinstall fink** or **fink selfupdate** to try to get the latest and greatest Fink package, or manually modify your /sw/etc/apt/sources.list file, changing the last two *deb* lines to read *deb http://bindist.finkmirrors.net/bindist 10.3/release main crypto* and *deb http://bindist.finkmirrors.net/bindist 10.3/current main crypto*, respectively. For general help with Fink, refer to the Fink FAQ at http://fink.source-forge.net/faq.

**Q:** If portable Linux distributions can be run from Mac OS X under VirtualPC, why should I bother with porting and compiling tools natively?

**A:** Guest operating systems run well enough under VirtualPC, but running tools natively on the Mac is significantly faster. VirtualPC uses a significant amount of system resources, and most users will find it slow for long-term use.

# Mac Tricks (Stupid Powerbook Stunts That Make You Look Like a God)

## Solutions in this chapter:

- Desktop Console
- Screensavers
- Widgets
- Apple Motion Sensor
- VNC with Apple Remote Desktop
- Gestures
- Sogudi
- GUI Scripts

☑ Summary
☑ Solutions Fast Track
☑ Frequently Asked Questions

# Introduction

This chapter is a lighter read than the rest of the book, but nonetheless contains a lot of useful and fun tips for getting the most out of Mac OS X. If you've ever wondered how to use a screensaver as a desktop picture or integrate GUI (graphical user interface) elements into your shell scripts, you'll find the answer here. You'll even get some practice in talking like Yoda.

# Desktop Console

Apple's Console application provides a slick interface for accessing the system's logfiles. These logs, and in particular the CrashReporter files, are indispensable when troubleshooting problems with Mac OS X. In addition to the Mac OS X logfiles, which are stored in either /Library/Logs or ~/Library/Logs, all the standard UNIX /var/log files are also present. The most interesting of these logs is system.log, which describes network changes, system wake and sleep, crashes, obsolete function calls, and a plethora of other information.

Reading system.log is great for troubleshooting, but it's difficult to spot abnormalities if you're not familiar with standard operation. You could force yourself to regularly read the logfile, but this turns the task into a chore. MkConsole, by Mulle kybernetiK, places system.log right on the desktop. The logfile text appears above the desktop picture, but below icons and windows (Figure 6.1). The text cannot be selected and for all purposes is part of the desktop picture. The text updates whenever an event is added to the log, scrolling the screen upward.

**Figure 6.1** MkConsole Output

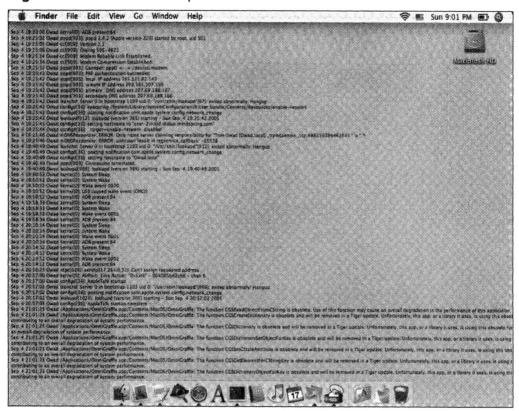

With these instantaneous updates, you get a real feel for how system behavior is reflected in the log. MkConsole can be automatically launched at startup by adding it to the Login Items in **System Preferences | Accounts** (Figure 6.2).

**Figure 6.2** Configuring Login Items

MkConsole was written with logfiles in mind, but it actually allows for any text file to be displayed on the desktop, in any font, size, and color. RSS feeds, Applescript output, shell script output, or even just personal notes... if it can be saved to a text file, it can be displayed on the desktop.

MkConsole can be found at www.mulle-kybernetik.com/software/ MkConsole/.

# Screen Savers

Years ago, screensavers were essential for preventing screen burn-in on CRT (cathode ray tube) monitors. On modern LCDs (liquid crystal displays), screensavers are useless, and even detrimental. An LCD is far better preserved by dimming the backlight or turning off the display with Mac OS X's Energy Saver function than by displaying random screensaver patterns. Apple didn't included a screensaver with the Mac OS, back when it was actually needed, but now that they're useless, these screen gimmicks are built right into the operating system.

Adding new screensavers to Mac OS X is easy, if not intuitive. System-wide screensavers are stored in /Library/Screen Savers. User-specific screensavers are in ~/Library/Screen Savers. If you haven't already added any of your own screensavers, this latter directory won't exist and you'll have to create it yourself. I store my custom screensavers in ~/Library/Screen Savers so that they get backed up with my home directory.

A simple Google search will find countless screensavers, but few are as fascinating as the breveWalker. breve is a, "3d Simulation Environment for Multi-Agent Simulations and Artificial Life." It allows programmers to develop creatures in a simulated world and then observe their behaviors. One such creature, breveWalker, has been adapted as a screensaver. breveWalker (Figure 6.3) learns to walk using a genetic algorithm that starts with random movements and eventually develops into walking motions. The state is saved after each run, so whenever you turn the screensaver on, it picks up where it left off.

**Figure 6.3** breveWalker Screen Saver

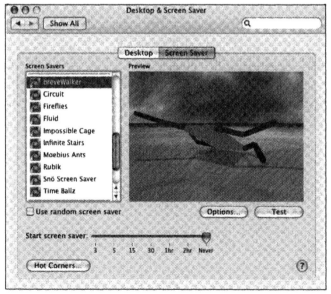

Of course, the fact remains that there's no good reason a screensaver should ever be running. As a much more novel alternative, BackLight 2 allows screensavers to be run as desktop pictures. With this tool (if you can even call it a tool) you can have breveWalker constantly evolving on your desktop, or the birds of breveSwarm constantly flocking and landing. Pretty pictures are one thing, but with breve you have actual simulated environments, transforming on the desktop while you work.

Another favorite screensaver, when used in conjunction with BackLight 2, is Fluid. Fluid begins with a screenshot of the desktop and then distorts it with flowing liquid, in a manner almost reminiscent of a cracked LCD. The icons in the screenshot slowly begin to sway and shimmer, revealing themselves beneath the actual icons on the desktop. The effect is that of the desktop icons and dock, reflected in a stream over which they are suspended.

There are countless other screensavers that take on new life when used on the desktop. Desktop Aquarium will place a scenic aquatic scene beneath the folders of your desktop, Time Ballz provides a full screen clock, and there are many others. Like MkConsole, BackLight 2 can be added to the Startup Items so that the effects automatically begin on startup.

# Widgets

Apple introduced the DashBoard with Mac OS X Tiger. With it came over a dozen widgets that could now be placed only an F key away. Within weeks of Tiger's introduction, hundreds of third-party widgets were written. These are a few of the most useful, most creative—and most fun. All of these widgets are free and can be found at www.apple.com/downloads/dashboard/?r=dbw.

## System

Of foremost interest to any hacker is the status of his computer. The SysStat widget (Figure 6.4) provides instantaneous access to your system's CPU, memory, network, and hard disk statistics, as well as the top processes, load average, and system uptime. There are also widgets that perform each of these functions individually, namely HardStat, miniBattery, miniCpuHeat, miniFreeRAM, miniFreeStorage, miniUptime, NetworkStat, and Traffic Meter. If you use Airport, Wireless Grapher (Figure 6.5) is another useful utility that will graph the strength of your wireless connection.

**Figure 6.4** SysStat Widget

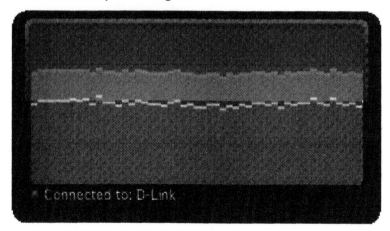

**Figure 6.5** Wireless Grapher Widget

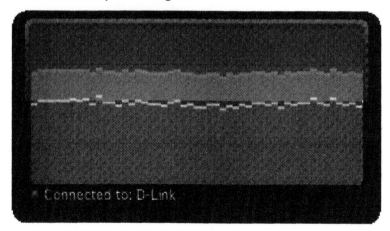

# Internet

Internet tools have become essential to any geek and there are countless widgets that provide access to Internet databases or RSS feeds. One of my favorites is Whoisdget, which provides fast access to an enhanced whois database. With IP Locator (Figure 6.6), you can type in a server name or IP (Internet Protocol) address and quickly get the location of the server. Another excellent widget is Google Maps (Figure 6.7), which provides Dashboard access to Google's maps, satellites, and directions. The Wikipedia widget (Figure 6.8) delivers thousands of community-written encyclopedia articles right to the Dashboard. TinyURL uses the tinyurl service to quickly generate a... tiny URL (Uniform Resource Locator).

**Figure 6.6** IP Locator Widget

**Figure 6.7** Google Maps Widget

**Figure 6.8** Wikipedia Widget

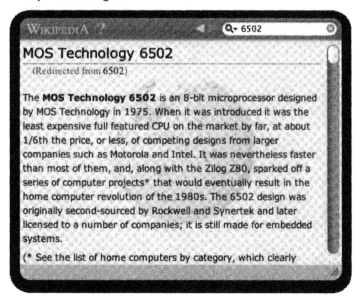

# Calculators and Converters

Network and system tools are OK, but the softest place in my heart as always been reserved for calculators. There are a couple of RPN (reverse polish notation) calculators for Dashboard. My favorite is rpnCalc (Figure 6.9), which provides an easy interface and a variable stack size. For number base conversions and binary operations there is HexCalculator (Figure 6.10). EnDecoder makes it easy to encode and decode text in Base64, Hex, Rot13, and other formats. LockSmith encrypts a string of text using the md5 or crypt functions.

**Figure 6.9** rpnCalc Widget

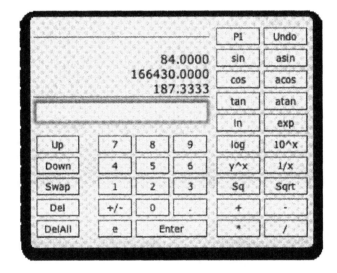

**Figure 6.10** HexCalculator Widget

# Fun

RPN calculators and wireless graphs are great, but sometimes what you really need is a talking Yoda. The Yoda widget (Figure 6.11) takes a string of text, rearranges it in Yoda fashion, and then speaks it in a surprisingly accurate synthetic voice. A lot of fun, this widget can be.

If the wisdom of Yoda isn't enough… there's the Einstein widget, which offers a collection of rotating quotes from the scientist. More practically, level-widget (Figure 6.12) uses the sudden motion sensors in Apple's latest PowerBooks to produce a working level. It's a tremendous boon for folks who can't afford a real one. Finally, there are the peeps. The *marshmallow* peeps. They look innocent enough, but they attack in groups, taking over the dashboard of an unsuspecting colleague.

**Figure 6.11** Yoda Widget

**Figure 6.12** levelwidget

# Apple Motion Sensor

Throw your PowerBook off a cliff. As it tumbles, sensors will detect changes in orientation and gravitational force. With this data, your PowerBook will wisely ascertain that all is not well. Faster than you can knock a laptop off a desk, it will swing the hard drive's head away from the platter and park it, preventing a deadly collision with your data.

The *Sudden Motion Sensor* in Apple's latest PowerBooks implements this technology. The sensors are not built into the hard drive – they're an integral part of the system, compatible with any drive you install. It's even possible to read the sensor output yourself. Amit Singh has written several programs that do just that (available at www.kernelthread.com/software/ams/).

This is where the fun starts. Amstracker is a simple command-line utility that returns the values for the sensors' x-, y-, and z-axes. X is left/right tilt, y is forward/back, and z is the change in G-force. Amit's utility can output these values and then exit or can be configured to provide a continuous stream of data.

The trick with a cool utility like this is coming up with a practical application. One possibility is to keep a motion log. Here's a sample in which data was collected every tenth of a second. To produce these values, I let my PowerBook drop about eight inches and then gently caught it. The X, Y, and Z columns in Table 6.1 contain the values output by each sensor. Each line represents one tenth of a second.

**Table 6.1** Values Output by Sensor

| X | Y | Z |
|---|---|---|
| 3 | 27 | 49 |
| 1 | 26 | 51 |
| 2 | 24 | 53 |
| 4 | 28 | 49 |
| 2 | 31 | 49 |
| 2 | 27 | 53 |
| 9 | 8 | 16 |
| -6 | 8 | 16 |
| 9 | 47 | 821 |
| 1 | 28 | 46 |
| 5 | 18 | 67 |
| -1 | 22 | 55 |
| -2 | 24 | 51 |
| 1 | 23 | 49 |
| -1 | 23 | 51 |

The first indication that something has gone wrong is a major the change in G-force from 53 to 16. At the same time, the y-axis shifts from 27 to 8, indicating a sudden backwards tilt, caused by the weight of the display. A tenth of a second later, the logs indicate a rightward tilt as the x-axis changes from 9 to -6. Another tenth of a second – and impact. The G-force leaps from 16 to 82 as the PowerBook collides with my hands.

If you often lend your computer out, this data could make for some very interesting conversations. "Larry, why did my PowerBook experience a sudden spike in gravitational force at 6:43 P.M.?"

The numbers are fun, but a visual makes for a more interesting demo. Amit has done just this with AMSVisualizer (Figure 6.13), which displays a PowerBook on screen and tilts it in sync with the computer's actual movements. This is great for demoing the PowerBook to potential customers.

**Figure 6.13** AMSVisualizer

Amit has written one more entertaining demo: StableWindow. You can tilt your PowerBook any way you like, but this window refuses to tilt with it. Those interested in reading more about these programs and the technology behind them should visit Amit Singh's website.

Of course, we haven't even addressed one of the most obvious uses for motion sensors: games. It took Peter Berglund just four days after reading Amit's article to have a simple game working based on the motion sensors. Berglund's BubbleGym (Figure 6.14) gives the player a marble on a board. Tilting the computer tilts the board and causes the marble to roll. The objective is to roll the ball into the cloud. With each success, a new cloud appears and the allotted time grows shorter. The player has four balls (lives) and each one exhibits different physical characteristics. Graphics and gameplay are rudimentary, but as a technology demonstration, the game is excellent. BubbleGym is mildly fun to play and a lot of fun to share with others.

**Figure 6.14** BubbleGym, using the Apple Motion Sensors

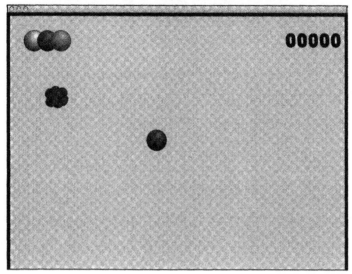

# VNC with Apple Remote Desktop

Apple Remote Desktop (ARD) is Apple's VNC (virtual network computing), enhanced with the sorts of features useful to a teacher administering a school lab. For the low price of $299, you get a copy of it for yourself and can administer up to 10 computers ($499 for unlimited). With Mac OS X 10.4, however, the Apple Remote Desktop server comes standard. Enable **Apple Remote Desktop** in the **Sharing** preference pane (Figure 6.15), and it's up and running. Administrator software to connect to this ARD server would cost $299, but ARD is really just glorified VNC, and any VNC client can be used to connect. After enabling ARD in **Sharing**, click **Access Privileges...** Enable **VNC viewer can control screen with password:** and provide a password (Figure 6.16).

## Tools and Traps…

### About VNC

Virtual Networking Computing is a protocol for controlling computers remotely. A VNC server runs on the remote system and awaits connections. The VNC client is run on the local machine. (that is, the one you're sitting at). The client, once provided with the VNC server's IP address, establishes a connection with the server. The server generally requires authentication from the client in the form of a password. Once authenticated, the client loads a window that contains the entire screen of the server, which the client now has complete access to. From the client, it is possible for the user to remotely control both the cursor and keyboard input of the server, and generally operate the server as if he was sitting right in front of it. Apple Remote Desktop is based on VNC, but also includes features useful to lab administrators, such as the ability to simultaneously monitor or install software on all systems.

**Figure 6.15** Turning on VNC

**Figure 6.16** Configuring the VNC Server

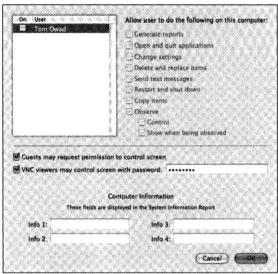

*Chicken of the VNC* is my favorite VNC client and I've had a lot of success using it with ARD server. Launch Chicken of the VNC and enter the IP address of the server for host (Figure 6.17). ARD always uses port 5900, so enter that as the port. If the server is behind a router, ensure you have forwarding turned on for port 5900. Enter the password you set on the ARD server. Click **Connect**, and you're in.

**Figure 6.17** Logging in with Chicken of the VNC

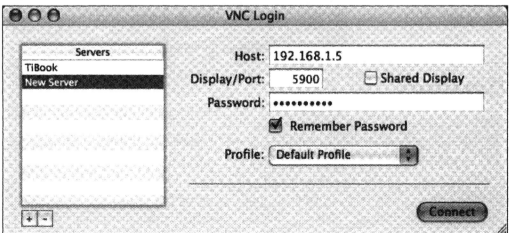

This setup provides you with VNC access, but only if you know the IP address. As most home machines have dynamic IP addresses, this can be very difficult. With Loopware's free IPMenu, keeping track of your IP address becomes trivial. Launch the app and an **IP** menu appears on the left side of the menu bar (Figure 6.18). Select this menu, choose **Preferences**, and enable the **When external IP changes, email:** option. Provide your email address, set up a filter in your e-mail client to corral these e-mails, and you'll always know where to find your server. The **external IP** is the address of your DSL or cable router, which is visible to the outside world.

**Figure 6.18** IP Menu

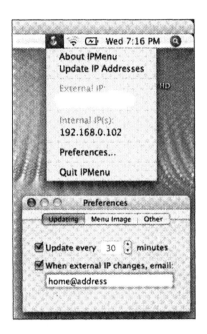

# Gestures

Apple has always focused on the mouse as the primary input device for Mac OS. The original Mac's keyboard even lacked arrow keys, to force the user toward the mouse. The mouse was great for beginners, but advanced users loathed having to take their hands off the keyboard. Now with Apple's Mighty Mouse and software such as bitart's CocoaGestures and CocoaSuite, it's the *mouse* you'll rarely have to take your hands off of.

CocoaGestures is a freeware application that integrates gesture recognition into and Cocoa application for Mac OS X. CocoaSuite ($30) goes beyond this by also providing mnemonics and scripting. The screenshots in this section are of CocoaSuite, as it offers better graphical feedback.

## Notes From the Underground...

### Cocoa and Carbon

The move from Mac OS 9 to X created a lot of work for Mac OS developers. To ease in the transition, Apple created the Carbon API (application program interface), which allowed developers to make their classic apps Mac OS X-compatible, with a minimum of effort. Cocoa, by contrast, is an application framework derived from NeXT's OPENSTEP programming environment. Cocoa applications are not compatible with Mac OS 9 and offer a much higher level of integration with Mac OS X than is possible in Carbon applications.

CocoaGestures and CocaSuite are input managers, so once installed, you'll find them in ~/Library/Input Managers. Their preferences appear in the application menu of any Cocoa application. Carbon apps, such as the Finder and Microsoft Office, are not supported.

Gestures can be either application-specific or universal and can be assigned to any menu item. In Safari (Figure 6.19), I created a gesture that loads my homepage (applefritter.com) whenever I draw an 'h' with the cursor. To configure this yourself, first install **CocoaSuite**, then launch **Safari**. Navigate to the menu **Safari | Cocoa Suite | Manage Gestures**. This will bring up the Define Gestures dialog box (Figure 6.20), where you can add a new gesture. Select **History/Home** from the list of options in the popup menu, then double click on the in the gesture field to the right of the popup menu. In the window that appears, draw your gesture (in this case the letter 'h'). Click **OK** to exit.

Gestures can be extremely complex. I created and successfully used one consisting of 25 motions. Since gestures can be used not only for the selection of menu items, but also for the insertion of blocks of text and the activation of scripts, this opens up an immense array gestures and actions. The greatest limitation is that they're not compatible with the Finder, but that can be replaced with Cocoatech's Path Finder.

**Figure 6.19** Gesturing with the Mouse

**Figure 6.20** Defining Gestures

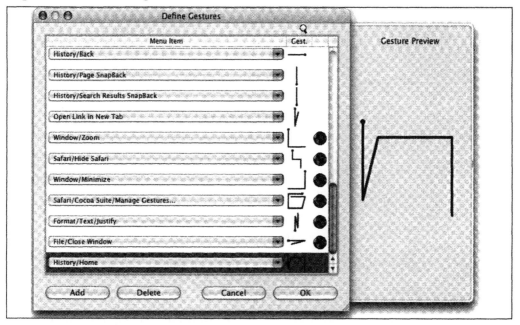

# Sogudi

The Google search bar was a great time-saver when it was added to Safari. With Sogudi, a free add-on to Safari, you can extend this feature to any website you visit regularly, to perform a search of that site. Type a predefined shortcut and your search term into the address bar, press **Enter**, and the desired website with the requested search results will load.

For example, to search Amazon for the title, "Apple I Replica Creation", you would type **amazon Apple I Replica Creation**. Shortcuts for Version Tracker (shortcut: **vt**), the Internet Movie Database (**mov**), Wikipedia (**wikip**), Yahoo (**yoo**), and many others are already built in. Additional shortcuts are on the Sogudi site and you can also add your own using a simple formula where you replace the search string with *@@@* (Figure 6.21).

**Figure 6.21** Configuring Sogudi Shortcuts

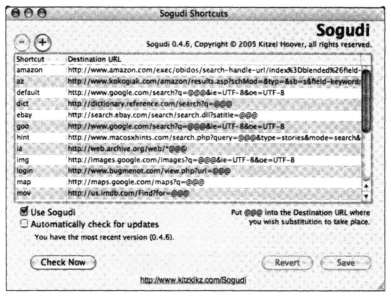

Sogudi also provides a fast and convenient interface for viewing man pages. In the URl field, type **man:page** where **page** is the name of the page you want to view. For example, **man:grep** would load the page shown in Figure 6.22. The man pages in Sogudi are the actual pages on your system, translated with man2html. Sogudi is available at www.kitzkikz.com/Sogudi.

**Figure 6.22** Man Pages in Sogudi

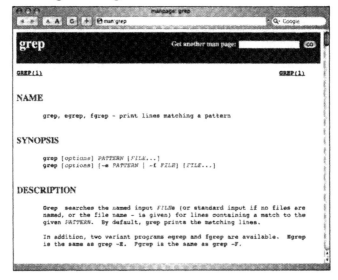

# GUI Scripts

With the move to Mac OS X, Mac users obtained not just the most intuitive graphical interface, but also the most powerful command line. The command line stands apart in Mac OS X, however, relegated to the Terminal app that few users ever touch, but tools such as CocoaDialog and Platypus make it possible to integrate shell scripts with the graphical user interface. With these tools, it is possible to quickly develop custom shell scripts that anybody can use.

Platypus is a script wrapper that allows you to make a script double-clickable and to view it's output in the GUI. Suppose, for example, you wanted a simple application that displayed the free space on all mounted volumes. A simple script that performs this action is:

```
#!/bin/sh
```

```
df -h
```

Save that script as dfh.sh and launch Platypus. Drag dfh.sh to the **Script Path** field and choose an **App Name** (Figure 6.23). Select **Text Window** for **Output** and enable **Remain running after completion**. With this configuration, standard out will be directed the text window, which will be left open until the user clicks **Quit**.

**Figure 6.23** Creating an Application with Platypus

Click **Create** and save your application. Double-click the new app and you'll be presented with the output window shown in Figure 6.24. The interface is simple, but it's an easy way to give ordinary users access to your shell scripts.

**Figure 6.24** DiskSpace, Created with Platypus

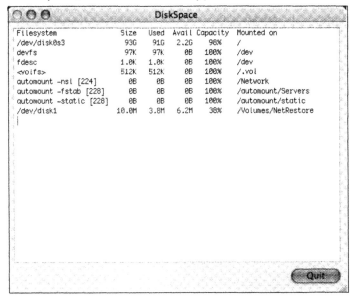

By adding CocoaDialog to the mix, it becomes possible to make these scripts interactive. Below is a simple program called *Access Tracker*, which is useful for tracking which files a program creates and which files a program accesses. To use it, first launch AccessTracker. A dialog box with a timestamp, as in Figure 6.25, will appear. Next, run the application or installer you want to watch. When the watch process is completed, go back to AccessTracker and select **Accessed**, **Changed**, or **Both**. You'll be presented with the Platypus text window (Figure 6.26), which will eventually fill with file paths.

**Figure 6.25** A CocoaDialog in AccessTracker

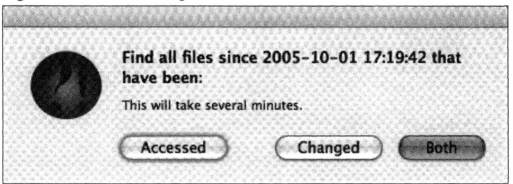

**Figure 6.26** AccessTracker Output with Platypus

```
○ ○ ○                    accesstracker3
All files modified since 2005-10-01 17:21:58:

/dev/fd/2
/dev/console
/Library/Logs/Console/501/console.log
/private/var/log/asl.log
/private/var/log/secure.log
/private/var/tmp/folders.501/TemporaryItems
/private/var/tmp/folders.501/TemporaryItems/dftmpPKGBGFPLlokkkkkk---------
/private/var/tmp/folders.501/TemporaryItems/mso01298FF6
/private/var/tmp/folders.501/TemporaryItems/Word Work File D_1726
/private/var/tmp/folders.501/TemporaryItems/Word Work File S_1
/Users/owad/Desktop
/Users/owad/Desktop/.DS_Store
/Users/owad/Desktop/ipodlinux
/Users/owad/Desktop/test
/Users/owad/Desktop/tricks
/Users/owad/Desktop/tricks/tricks.doc
/Users/owad/Library/Application Support/AddressBook/.database.lockN
/Users/owad/Library/Mail
/Users/owad/Library/Mail/Envelope Index
/Users/owad/Library/Mail/Envelope Index-journal
/Users/owad/Library/Mail/Mailboxes/ClassicCmp.mbox/Messages

                                                      Quit
```

The code behind this program is very simple:

```
#!/bin/bash

# Locate CocoaDialog.
dir=`echo $0 | sed 's|^\(.*\)/[^/]*|\1|'`
cocoa_dialog=$dir/CocoaDialog.app/Contents/MacOS/CocoaDialog

# Mark the current time, for later use.
start_time=`date "+%C%y-%m-%d %H:%M:%S"`
```

```
# Get response from dialog box (button clicked).
rv=`$cocoa_dialog msgbox --no-newline \
    --text "Find all files since $start_time that have been:" \
    --informative-text "This will take several minutes." \
    --button1 "Both" --button2 "Changed" --button3 "Accessed"`

# Find and print the files specified by the dialog selection.
if [ "$rv" == "1" ]; then
    echo -e "All files accessed since $start_time:\n"
    find / -newerat "$start_time"
    echo -e "\n\n\nAll files modified since $start_time:\n"
    find / -newermt "$start_time"
elif [ "$rv" == "2" ]; then
    echo -e "All files modified since $start_time:\n"
    find / -newermt "$start_time"
elif [ "$rv" == "3" ]; then
    echo -e "All files accessed since $start_time:\n"
    find / -newerat "$start_time"
fi
```

First, the shell script determines the location of CocoaDialog. Next, it grabs the date and time to search from. The next line launches CocoaDialog and sets the labels. At this point, the script waits for the output of CocoaDialog, which comes in the form of an integer (0, 1, or 3, depending on the button selected). The *if* statement uses this integer to determine whether to display accessed files, modified files, or both. **Echo** prints an explanatory line, then **find** finds all the desired accessed or modified since the start time. The interface isn't perfect, but by combining these two programs, Platypus and CocoaDialog, it's possible to quickly add a GUI interface for any shell script you write.

Platypus is available at http://sveinbjorn.sytes.net/platypus and CocoaDialog at http://cocoadialog.sourceforge.net/. Both are licensed under the GNU GPL.

# Summary

Whether your interests are in rapidly developing GUI applications or in talking like Yoda, I hope you found something in this chapter that, if not useful, was at least a bit of fun. For an extended project, try making a graphical shell script that uses the output from amstracker and uses the orientation of the PowerBook to perform a seemingly rand operation. Yoda can commentate (hint: look up **man:say** with Sogudi).

# Solutions Fast Track

## Desktop Console

- ☑ MkConsole makes it possible to place console output right on the desktop.
- ☑ Any log, or even any text file, can be displayed with MkConsole.
- ☑ MkConsole can be automatically launched at login by adding it to Login Items.

## Screensavers

- ☑ Though they serve no real purpose, screensavers can still be a lot of fun.
- ☑ BreveWalker uses a genetic algorithm to develop the ability to walk.
- ☑ Backlight 2 makes it possible to use screensavers as desktop pictures.

## Widgets

- ☑ Widgets, introduced in Mac OS X 10.4, are the modern equivalent of System 6's desktop accessories.
- ☑ Apple's website contains a large database of free third-part widgets, available for download.

# Apple Motion Sensor

☑ Apple's new PowerBooks have built in motion sensors to protect against hard drive damage.

☑ amstracker is a command-line utility that makes it possible to read this sensor output.

☑ Numerous games and utilities are available that take advantage of this feature.

# VNC with Apple Remote Desktop

☑ VNC is a protocol for connecting to remote computers.

☑ Mac OS X 10.4 has a VNC server-included standard, but it is hidden within the Apple Remote Desktop software.

☑ IPMenu is a simple tool that will e-mail you a machine's IP address whenever it changes.

# Gestures

☑ CocoaGestures makes it possible to assign mouse gestures to any menu operation in a Cocoa-based Mac OS X program.

☑ Cocoa is an application framework, specific to Mac OS X, that is used for most modern Mac apps.

# Sogudi

☑ Sogundi makes it possible to develop search shortcuts for Safari.

☑ UNIX man pages can be quickly accessed by typing **man:page** into Safari's URL bar.

## GUI Scripts

- ☑ Platypus allows users to quickly put a graphical front end on their shell scripts.

- ☑ CocoaDialog makes it possible to integrate Cocoa GUI elements into shell scripts.

# Frequently Asked Questions

The following Frequently Asked Questions, answered by the authors of this book, are designed to both measure your understanding of the concepts presented in this chapter and to assist you with real-life implementation of these concepts. To have your questions about this chapter answered by the author, browse to **www.syngress.com/solutions** and click on the **"Ask the Author"** form.

**Q:** How can I access logfiles without using MkConsole or the terminal?

**A:** Apple's "Console" app, in /Applications/Utilities provides access to console.log, system.log, and all logs in ~/Library/Logs, /Library/ Logs, and /var/log.

**Q:** Are screen savers necessary on LCDs?

**A:** Nope. You're bettor off just dimming the screen to preserve the backlight.

**Q:** What are Widgets?

**A:** Widgets are the modern equivalent of the "Desk Accessories" found in System 6. They are small programs that run inside Apple's Dashboard application and provide a wide array of useful information.

**Q:** What does the Apple Motion Sensor do?

**A:** The Apple Motion Sensor contains tilt and G force sensors that detect when your PowerBook is in motion and then park the hard drive heads to prevent damage upon impact.

# OS X For
# the Road Warrior

## Solutions in this chapter:

- Safe and Secure E-mail
- Connecting from Anywhere (Almost)
- Battery Management

☑ Summary

☑ Solutions Fast Track

☑ Frequently Asked Questions

# Introduction

The term "road warrior" can bring to mind an image of a high powered executive flying around the country, pockets full of gadgets that make his life easier and a mass of IT professionals helping him get his job don. In reality, road warriors are often mobile geeks who want to use their computers where they want, and on their terms. Be it at home, at a coffee shop, stuck in the car, or even at the office, having secure and consistent connectivity is critical to getting the job done.

It should come as no surprise that many of mobile professionals choose to use OS X as their operating system of choice. Not only is the operating system geared towards mobile users, the hardware is also well suited for the task. Powerbooks have a long battery life, integrated wireless networking, and are relatively light for their size. A potential unintended design feature of the 12-inch Powerbook is that it is small enough to avoid being crushed by the reclining seat in front of you in coach class. I've personally had several bad incidents with larger PC laptops on airplanes, but my 12-inch Powerbook always comes out unscathed.

The purpose of this chapter is to discuss tips and tricks that make a Mac even easier to use on the road. From battery management to Internet connectivity to secure e-mail, there are a wide variety of techniques that can make your life easier as a road warrior. So while you may not be a high-powered exec with a massive IT support staff, you can at least look (and work) like you are.

# Safe and Secure E-mail

E-mail is a critically important part of the road warrior's life. E-mail is a constant line of communication to the office, to home, and to customers. In some cases, you will be able to build a VPN (virtual private network) connection between your laptop and a trusted network in order to securely access your e-mail and other services. However there may be times when a VPN connection cannot be setup, such as when a network's firewall blocks IKE traffic or when a wireless access point doesn't understand IPSec (Internet Protocol Security) data. Even in these circumstances, there are secure e-mail solutions.

*Mail.app* is the mail reader bundled with OS X, and the reader we will use for the examples in this chapter. There are other mail readers available for OS X, including Microsoft's Entourage and Mozilla's Thunderbird and there are pros and cons to each mail program. However, Mail.app is included in the operating system, has support for a number of security features and is integrated with Apple's Spotlight technology. Spotlight is to Mac's what Google Desktop is to PC's; a quick-response search engine for data that lives locally on your laptop. Spotlight understands individual E-mail messages in Mail.app and allows you to index and search them. If you're like me, you'll find this to be a great feature, since Spotlight allows you to be messy but still find your stuff, as shown in Figure 7.1.

**Figure 7.1** Spotlight Can Find Individual E-mail Messages in Mail.app

Thankfully, we live in a time when most mail readers actually understand security and provide users with a variety of security options. The technologies presented in this section are available with most mail readers although the steps required to implement these security protections can vary.

# IMAP SSL

There are three basic parts to e-mail: sending e-mail, receiving e-mail, and storing e-mail. It is important to make this distinction as the protection technologies for each part are dramatically different. This is particularly apparent in the sending and receiving of e-mail, as these are areas where the average user may not fully understand what's going on.

When you are receiving e-mail, you want to only receive *your* e-mail, not someone else's. Further, you don't want someone else getting your messages. Therefore, when you receive e-mail, you must first authenticate yourself to the mail server on the far end so that the server knows who you are and what mail to give to you.

There are a variety of protocols that can be used for retrieving e-mail. Post Office Protocol (POP) and Internet Message Access Protocol (IMAP) are two of the most common. There are differences between these two protocols, but IMAP is conducive to having multiple computers access a single account and multiple mailboxes per user. POP has been designed for offline mail reading, in which messages are retrieved from the server and deleted from the server immediately. IMAP allows for a number of different ways of handling messages, including just downloading the headers and assuming that network connectivity will always be there. IMAP is generally more flexible than POP and is widely supported by mail servers including Microsoft's Exchange server and Netscape's Enterprise server. Mail.app also natively supports IMAP.

When connecting to an IMAP-enabled mail server, your username and password are sent to the remote mail server to authenticate your identity. The password is hashed to prevent eavesdropping, however there are still security issues.

First, an attacker may still be able to brute force guess your password given enough time to analyze the hash that is sent across the network. For weak passwords, this process may only take seconds. Also, there's no obvious way to determine if you're talking to the intended mail server. An attacker on the network may still intercept your session and act as a man-in-the-middle or simply pretend to be your mail server and send you malicious e-mail. Finally, your mail is delivered in clear text over the network allowing anyone to see the contents of your messages.

These threats are particularly dangerous in public networks like WiFi hotspots in coffee shops or at conferences. Some security conferences, like the DefCon hacker conference in Las Vegas are war zones, and any data sent across the wireless network is likely to be inspected by someone you would rather not have reading your e-mail.

So what can be done to address these threats? Well, thankfully a standard has been developed which uses SSL (Secure Sockets Layer) to protect an IMAP connection. Using SSL will protect your hashed password when it is sent and your mail when it is received. And, honestly, it couldn't be easier to use. In the Mail.app **Preferences** pane, there's an **Accounts** tab. Click on the account you want to enable SSL for, click **Advanced**, and click **Use SSL,** as shown in Figure 7.3

**Figure 7.2** Enabling IMAP Over SSL

When clicking *Use SSL,* the IAMP port number changes from 443 to 993. If you are using a host-based firewall, be sure to update your rules. That's all there is to it. If it doesn't work, make sure that your mail server supports IMAP SSL. If it does not, go harass your mail server administrator. If you are like me, your are your own administrator, so go Google your way to a secure IMAP server.

# STARTTLS

So now that you can retrieve your e-mail safely from your WiFi hot spot, what about sending mail? Sending mail is an entirely different animal than receiving it. Historically, anyone on the Internet could send E-mail to anyone through any mail server that used Simple Mail Transport Protocol (SMTP). However, the invention of spam closed that little loophole and forced mail servers to become more restrictive.

In many enterprises, mail servers restrict who can send outbound mail based on IP address or hostname. This is not a strong form of authentication, but it is generally sufficient to keep spammers at bay. When trying to send mail from your WiFi hotspot, these anti-spam rules unfortunately keep you from using just any mail server.

Just like IMAP, some SMTP servers such as *Sendmail* have the ability to use SSL to provide a secure connection between the mail server and your laptop. The protocol for SMTP over SSL is called *STARTTLS*. Beyond SSL, many mail servers also support additional types of security including username and password authentication. SSL authentication assures your *outbound* mail connection, providing protection similar to that applied to your *inbound* IMAP mail.

Configuring STARTTLS in Mail.app is as easy as configuring IMAP SSL. The first order of business is to make sure your mail server supports STARTTLS and *per-user authentication*. If it doesn't, you should once again go harass your mail server administrator. Under the account you want to enable STARTTLS for, click on **server settings**, select **Use SSL,** and supply a user name/password combination as shown in Figure 7.3. Click **OK**.

**Figure 7.3** A Checkbox, Username, and Password is All it Takes for Secure Outbound Mail

By default, STARTTLS runs on port 25, so you should not need to update any host-based firewall rules you have running. Now, when you send mail, it will be encrypted on its connection to the mail server.

# GnuPG

Keeping mail safe and secure on the network may not be enough for you. Once mail leaves your mail server it is sent unencrypted across the Internet, and depending on the type of data you're sending (or your level of paranoia) this may not be good enough. You may also wish to consider ways to keep mail secure while it's stored on other people's disks and when it is in transit around the Internet.

*GnuPG* (Gnu Privacy Guard) is an open source implementation of the famous mail security program Pretty Good Privacy (PGP). GnuPG implements the same type of encryption as PGP and is interoperable with most mail clients using PGP. In a nutshell, PGP works via a web of trust between you and other PGP users. In PGP, you create a public and private key that uniquely identifies you and your data to those you exchange mail with. The public key is used by others to validate that mail really came from you and to encrypt mail they are sending to you. The private key is your secret key that you use to sign e-mail with so others know the mail was really from you.

MacGPG (http://macgpg.sourceforge.net) is an implementation of GnuPG that runs on OS X. It contains several utilities that help manage keys and perform file-level encryption. While this is interesting, MacGPG does not by itself provide you the ability to send secure e-mail. However it is required by other programs, including GPGMail, so you need to download it and install it per the instructions on the Web page.

GPGMail is an application that hooks into Mail.app that allows you to send and receive GPG encrypted and signed E-mail from directly in Mail.app. GPG Mail is available from www.sente.ch/software/GPGMail/ English.lproj/GPGMail.html and requires MacGPG to be configured before being installed. Although GPGMail and MacGPG are complicated, the installation procedures are well-documented. Check the product websites for installation details, especially since they are likely to change (GPGMail in particular uses undocumented hooks in Mail.app).

Now, armed with IMAP-SSL, STARTTLS, and GPGMail, you can safely send e-mail from your home, your work, and your coffee shop even if your VPN is not running. Once you get used to using these protocols, you'll wonder what to do with the time you once spent constantly  troubleshooting your VPN connection.

# Connecting From Anywhere (Almost)

We live in a connected world. No surprise there. The Internet has been around for several decades, residential broadband is now affordable in the US (and has been elsewhere for a while), and even Paris Hilton can read her E-mail on her phone. We have become accustomed to having access to the Internet on our terms.

Almost. When we are away from our networks of choice, things get a bit more difficult. Apple laptops have shipped with built-in WiFi for some time now. Wireless networking has been a key capability for Apple devices and users have generally accepted WiFi networking. Unfortunately WiFi networks are not (yet) ubiquitous in our lives. Some cities such as Portland, Oregon have large-scale municipal networks and companies like Starbucks have become renowned for having wireless access in most of their stores. However, even with WiFi networks like these, WiFi is not as available as cellular networks.

So why not use your cellular phone to connect to the Internet? All the major cell providers have a packet-based data service that allows users to access the Internet wherever they have cellular connectivity. And by connecting your laptop through your phone, you can use your phone to access the Internet from your Powerbook or iBook.

The costs and speeds of these connections vary from provider to provider. At the time of this writing, T-Mobile offered unlimited Global Packet Radio Service (GPRS) Internet access for $20/month. GPRS is widely supported, but is only capable of 56kbps. Enhanced GPRS (EGPRS or EDGE) is offered by Cingular and provides data rates of up to 300kbps. Unfortunately, with enhanced speed comes enhanced price (up to $80/month for unlimited access). EGPRS is not available everywhere that Cingular is, however EGPRS will scale back to standard GRPS connectivity which is nearly ubiquitous. Stand-alone phones or PC Card radios from both of these providers can be used within OS X with little difficulty.

On the Verizon side of the house, there is much faster bandwidth to be had. EVDO is a data service that allows for Internet connections of greater than 1Mbps, and while it's not available everywhere in the US, it tends to be very fast. EVDO is available for only $70/month for unlimited access. That's better than many are currently paying for DSL.

OS X supports connecting with all these different types of packet radio services, however the support is not seamless. Quite the contrary; it can take a bit of hand standing to make everything work the way you want it. But once it works the end result is quite nice… Internet access anywhere you have cellular access. Even if it is slow, it is a non-zero amount of connectivity, which can make all the difference in the world.

# GPRS Example

For our example, we will use the Motorola A610 cellular phone with T-Mobile's GPRS service. The A610 is a Bluetooth capable phone that can provide an Internet connection via the Bluetooth link. To use the Bluetooth connection, your laptop must have either the integrated Apple Bluetooth radio or have an external Bluetooth radio (but what's the point in that?).

When a laptop is connected to the Internet through a GPRS phone, the phone is basically treated as a modem. In order to work properly, OS X requires a modem script that properly configures and accesses the phone.

Ross Barkman maintains a list of modem scripts with GPRS-specific configurations on his homepage at http://www.taniwha.org.uk/. Download his zip file and copy the scripts that correspond to your phone into */Library/Modem Scripts/*. It may not be obvious which script is going to work with your phone, but don't worry! Just copy any you think you might need and experiment with them once your phone is set up.

Next you will need to get your phone paired with your laptop. Bluetooth pairing is the process by which two devices set up a secure relationship between each other. When devices are paired, they exchange cryptographic keys that can be used to setup secure connections. By pairing your phone with your laptop you provide security for the link between your laptop and phone when you connect to the Internet.

You must put your phone into discoverable mode in order for OS X to find it for pairing. That process will vary depending on the make and model of your phone, so consult your phone's documentation. Once your phone is in discoverable mode, open up the Bluetooth **System Preferences** pane. Click on the **Devices** tab to see any existing known Bluetooth devices, as shown in Figure 7.4.

**Figure 7.4** Any Devices You Have Already Connected to Will be Listed in this Pane

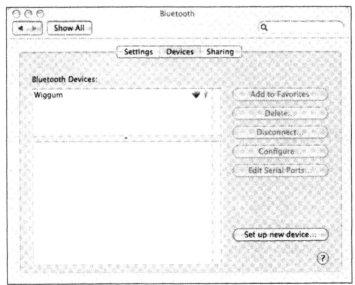

Select **Set up new device…** to start the pairing process. You will be prompted to select the type of device you want to pair with. Select **Mobile Phone**. Once your device has been discovered, it will show up in the Bluetooth Setup Assistant, as shown in Figure 7.5.

**Figure 7.5** Any Discoverable Bluetooth Devices Are Listed in the Setup Assistant

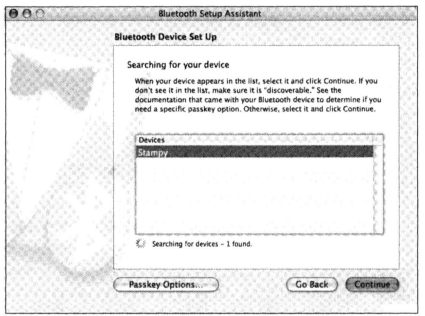

Click **Continue** once your device has been discovered. Enter the PIN provided by the Setup Assistant into your mobile phone. After a few seconds, the pairing process will complete. The Bluetooth Setup Assistant should recognize that your phone has the ability to connect to the Internet by displaying the dialog shown in Figure 7.6.

**Figure 7.6** The Setup Assistant Will Prompt on How to Connect to the Internet

Make sure **Use a direct, higher speed connection** option is selected and click **Continue**. Next, fill in the proper values for your Internet service and phone as shown in Figure 7.7. For T-Mobile, the GPRS CID String is **internet2.voicestream.net**. Selecting the proper modem script can be a bit tricky. Googling for your phone is generally helpful, but experimenting with different options may be quicker for you. For the Motorola A610, the **Motorola GPRS CID157k +CGQREQ** script should do the trick.

**Figure 7.7** This is the Setup for a Motorola A610 on T-Mobile

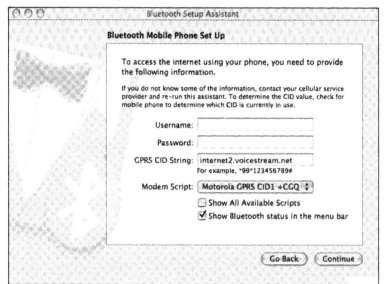

Click **Continue** to finish up the Assistant and you should be all set. Now, open **Internet Connect** in your Applications folder, click on the Bluetooth tab, select your connection and click **Connect**. After a few seconds, you should get notification that your connection is successful. If there is an error, you might change the connection script you are using via **Internet Connect.**

That's all there is to it. Now wherever you have T-Mobile voice service, your OS X laptop can get on the Internet. Each phone is a bit different and has its own set of interesting oddities. My A610, for example, needs to be rebooted after it connects via GPRS otherwise it will not connect to any other Bluetooth device (such as my Bluetooth ear bud). However, in general, phones have become more reliable over the years on their packet connections and should provide you reasonable service

# Firewalling Your Mac

OS X has a built in firewall, but unlike Windows XP, the firewall in OS X is not turned on by default. When connecting to a hostile environment such as a coffee shop WiFi network or your cellular provider's GPRS network, it is important that you have your firewall turned on.

Like most things on OS X, turning on your firewall is pretty simple. Open up the **Sharing Systems Preferences** Pane as shown in Figure 7.8, and click the **Firewall** tab. By default the firewall will allow inbound connections for any sharing services you have running. If you want to prevent access to anything you are sharing, simply uncheck the box before you start the firewall. Click **Start** to enable the firewall and inbound connections are instantly prevented from reaching your computer.

**Figure 7.8** Your Firewall can be Enabled with One Button Click

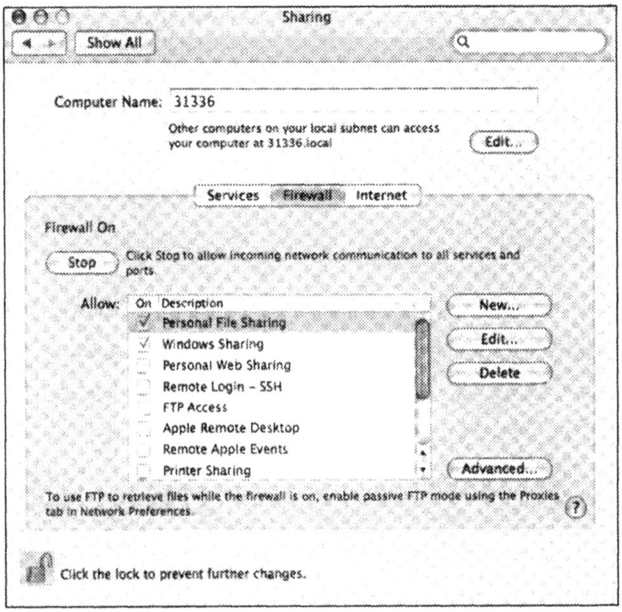

If you click on the **Advanced** tab as shown in Figure 7.9, there are a few options you may want to enable for your firewall. If are not sharing any services, you can put the computer in "stealth" mode. When in stealth mode, the computer will not respond to any inbound requests, even if the port is otherwise closed. This may confuse attackers and divert them away from your laptop. This is basically a "security through obscurity" feature that may not be that useful. What *is* useful, however, is the logging capability. By turning on firewall logging you can see what packets are bouncing off your firewall. If nothing else, it is a source of entertainment while you are drinking your latte at the local coffee shop.

**Figure 7.9** Enabling the Firewall's Logging Feature Can Be Useful for Troubleshooting

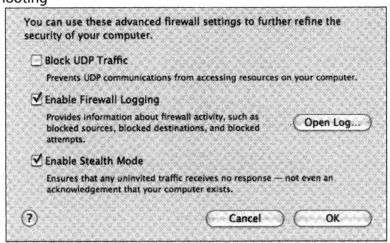

# Battery Management

It's a fact; laptops rely on batteries. Apple's mobile computers (the Powerbooks and iBooks) have gone through a number of different types of batteries over the years, but in general the batteries today have higher capacity and longer life than those of the previous generation. However that doesn't mean batteries are infinite buckets of power. They still hold a finite amount of energy, and once a battery has run dry your laptop is only a fashion statement, not a mobile computing device. There are a variety of ways to help get the most of your battery and your productive time on your laptop. Some of these techniques are intuitive…others may surprise you.

## Conservation Tips

First and foremost in getting the most out of your laptop's battery is understanding the power saving options that come in OS X. The **Energy Saver Preferences** pane (shown in Figure 7.10) has a wide variety of options you can set including:

- Sleep time for disk
- Sleep time for display
- Processor optimization for speed or power conservation
- Display brightness

**Figure 7.10** The Energy Saver System Preference Pane Has a Number of Tunable Power Options

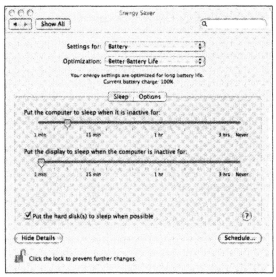

Obviously, putting parts of the system to sleep quickly, running with reduced processor performance, and keeping the display dimmed will all help conserve your battery life. If you find you want to temporarily save some power, you can dim your screen on demand using the F1 key. Hit F1 enough, and your screen will go completely blank. It is amazing how long your battery will power a laptop with the screen off. So even dimming it completely for a few minutes of non-use can make a big difference.

To help further conserve battery life, be sure to shutdown resources you aren't using. Bluetooth and WiFi networking can take a great deal of power from the laptop, and in situations where they aren't needed, they should be turned off. Having a CD in the drive can also waste power. The CD may be spun up at times for no reason, sucking power out of the battery. And unneeded programs can be a huge drain, especially long running programs like Web browsers. Web browsers and similar software have a nasty habit of growing in memory footprint and CPU needs the longer they run. By closing these programs when they are not needed, it will help keep your battery charged longer.

These tips may seem well into the "no duh" category of things to be on the lookout for. However, it's easy to forget about battery life until it's too late. For instance, before getting on a plane, I make sure my battery is fully charged. I also make sure I've recently rebooted the laptop, have all spinning media removed, all network interfaces shut down, and all unnecessary programs terminated. This saves me several minutes of grief when I get on the plane but probably also saves 10-15 minutes of battery life... critically important time when I'm 2 hours into a 2.5 hour long movie and my battery dies somewhere over Kansas.

# Calibration and Total Discharge

Batteries of old tended to be either Nickel-Cadmium (NiCad) or Nickel Metal Hydride (NiMH). NiCad and NiMH batteries had this nasty feature called *memory*. A battery's "memory" keeps it from holding a full charge when it is not fully (and regularly) discharged. So if your battery is only unplugged from its charger for short periods of time and is then recharged again, it will get used to the short discharge cycle and only power the device for a limited amount of time. In the newer generation Powerbooks and iBooks, the older style batteries were replaced by Lithium Ion batteries that have  much less of a memory problem. Also, Lithium Ion battery technology can store more energy by size and weight than other battery types.

The drawback of Lithium Ion batteries is that they're much more complicated to charge. Therefore Lithium Ion batteries usually have an onboard power manager that helps them regulate their charge and discharge to ensure a safe and long life. The batteries in modern Powerbooks and iBooks are no exception. These batteries are expensive but are well engineered, just like nearly everything Apple produces.

The power manager helps maintain the battery's health, however it still can't totally win the war over physics. Over time, even Lithium Ion batteries lose their ability to hold a charge. After 300 full charge and discharge cycles, even a properly maintained battery will only have the ability to reach 80% of it's original charge. However, a poorly maintained battery can die well before 300 full charge/discharge cycles.

First, when you get a new laptop (or a new battery for that matter) the internal battery power manager needs to be calibrated. The calibration process helps the power manager determine the characteristics of the battery and how best to maintain it. So you should install the battery and charge it to full capacity. Then unplug the charger from the laptop and let it completely discharge. Eventually, your laptop will go to sleep and not allow itself to be woken up. Then, plug in the charger and let the battery come to full charge again. Voila, your battery power manager is calibrated.

Calibration is only the first step however. Even a properly calibrated battery can lose its effectiveness if not taken care of. At least once a month you should try and fully run down the battery in your laptop. This helps the battery avoid memory problems. Also, it is important to not have your laptop plugged in all the time. By allowing the laptop battery to do some work once in a while, you will prevent it from becoming stagnant and losing its charge.

By following these few simple rules you should be able to extend the life of your battery and hopefully see 80% of its original charge after 300 cycles. If not, be prepared to buy a new battery. If you're like me, you will keep your Mac laptop long after your first battery kicks the bucket.

## Resetting the Power Manager

The intelligence of the new Lithium Ion batteries comes at a cost. The power manager is a small computer inside of the battery, and like any computer it can get a bit out of sorts. Sometimes, in fact, the power manager can cause the laptop to become completely inoperable by not allowing the system to boot or awake from sleep.

The power manager can be reset to factory settings if it seems to have freaked out. Resetting the power manager should not be taken lightly, however. A power manager reset will:

- Reset the date to January 1, 1970

- Kill any RAMdisks that may be been created

- Set all power settings including display brightness and trackpad control back to factory defaults

In the process of troubleshooting your power or battery problems, it may be worth it to reset the power manager. Each Powerbook and iBook has its own procedure for resetting the power manager. See http://docs.info. apple.com/article.html?artnum=14449 for complete directions for your computer.

# Summary

OS X is a capable operating system for users of many types, but it is well suited for those always on the go. With built in security, OS X helps keep you and your mail safe when in hostile environments. When paired with a good cellular phone, you can access the Internet from all over the country and not have to spend time looking for the nearest Starbucks. And with a bit of attention, the battery in your Powerbook or iBook can provide satisfactory results for years. Regardless of your reason for choosing OS X, you'll find it to be a good traveling companion.

# Solutions Fast Track

## Safe and Secure E-mail

☑ Even without a VPN, you can securely send E-mail from WiFi hotspots

☑ IMAP-SSL is supported natively in Mail.app and can be used to secure your *inbound* e-mail

☑ STARTTLS is supported natively in Mail.app and can be used to secure your *outbound* e-mail

## Connecting from Anywhere (Almost)

☑ All the major US cellular providers offer some kind of packet data service that can be used to connect to the Internet

☑ Using your phone as a Bluetooth-enabled modem, your OS X laptop can connect to the Internet anywhere you have cellular service and your phone never has to leave your pocket

☑ Enabling your firewall is important whenever you are on a hostile network

## Battery Management

☑ By applying a little common sense and making sure to drain your battery periodically, your battery should be able to obtain 80% of its original charge after 300 discharge cycles

☑ If your battery or AC adapter seem to be acting strangely, the power manager in your laptop can be reset to factory defaults in an attempt to troubleshoot

# Frequently Asked Questions

The following Frequently Asked Questions, answered by the authors of this book, are designed to both measure your understanding of the concepts presented in this chapter and to assist you with real-life implementation of these concepts. To have your questions about this chapter answered by the author, browse to **www.syngress.com/solutions** and click on the **"Ask the Author"** form.

**Q:** Can I use Mail.app to securely connect to any of the major free mail services?

**A:** Gmail (from Google) supports free secure POP which is supported by Mail.app. The configuration is largely the same as with IMAP, however Gmail only supports POP.

**Q:** What is PGP key signing?

**A:** Key signing is how a web of trust is built in PGP. By having someone sign your key, they attest that the key really belongs to you. The more people that sign your key, the more likely you are to have complete strangers know someone on who has signed your key. And if that stranger trusts the person that signed, they will probably trust that your key really does belong to you. It's a bit confusing at first, but ultimately it allows two people who have never met to have some degree of assurance that each others keys are valid.

**Q:** Do Lithium Ion batteries suffer from the memory effect?

**A:** While Lithium Ion batteries do not have as large a problem with memory as older NiCad and NiMH batteries, they still do suffer from some memory effect. It is important to recognize that even Lithium Ion batteries need to be fully discharged once in a while to get the longest life possible out of them.

**Q:** Why do SSH sessions on my cellular packet connections seem so slow?

**A:** An SSH session is very susceptible to latency in the connection (that is, if there is a large latency in your connection, there is a very noticeable difference in time between when you type a character and when it shows up on your screen). While an EDGE connection (for example) may provide 160kps of bandwidth, the back end network on the cellular provider side may add a second or more of one-way latency. This can add up in an interactive environment like SSH and make SSH sessions almost unbearable at times.

**Q:** Why do the first few minutes of my GPRS connection seem so slow?

**A:** When OS X first connects to the network, many programs may attempt to access network resources at the same time. Mail.app will try and check your mail accounts. Safari will check all its RSS feeds. iChat will log back into AIM. When you are on a slow connection like GPRS, shut down unnecessary programs that are network aware in an effort to try and keep the "bandwidth land grab" to a minimum.

# Appendix A

# Hacking the iPod

## Hacks in this chapter:

- Opening Your iPod

- Replacing the Battery

- Upgrading a 5GB iPod's Hard Drive

- From Mac to Windows and Back Again

- iPod Diagnostic Mode

# Introduction

The iPod (see Figure A.1), was announced in October 2001. It has an impressive array of features not previously bundled together in a portable MP3 player. Highlights of the initial iPod model included:

- A 5GB internal hard drive
- A FireWire port for transferring files to and from the iPod; this port is also used to charge the iPod when connected to a Macintosh computer or the separate charger
- A compact form factor
- An intuitive and easy-to-use interface, which includes a wheel mechanism on the front that allows you to quickly scroll through menu items and lists of songs
- A backlit LCD screen for navigating the user interface
- The ability to be used as an external hard drive for storing files and transferring them between computers

**Figure A.1** The 5GB First-Generation iPod (Left) and the 20GB Third-Generation iPod (Right)

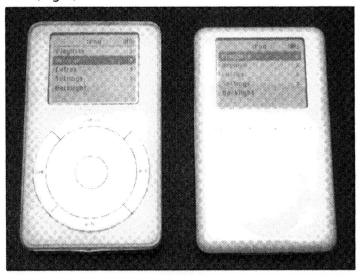

Apple packaged all these features into a very sleek enclosure with a white face and reflective, stainless steel back. At the time the iPod was introduced, Flash ROM-based MP3 players were the norm, and hard drive-based devices were not very common. Because of the large capacity of hard drives compared to solid-state memory, the initial 5GB version of the iPod allowed the user to carry around an impressive amount of music relative to other players. The FireWire interface also addressed the growing problem of the USB interface employed by most MP3 players, since that version of USB (not the newer USB 2) is notoriously slow at copying large amounts of data. With all these features so well integrated into a small form factor, iPod sales immediately took off. Since the iPod's introduction more than four years ago, Apple has sold over 2 million iPods and has captured the majority of the MP3 player market. Along the way, the iPod has seen several updates, which are described later in this chapter.

The iPod is only half of the equation, though. Apple also released a free piece of software called iTunes (see Figure A.2) that works seamlessly with the iPod. iTunes allows you to organize and enjoy your music collection using a slick, powerful interface, and it connects effortlessly to your iPod. In April 2003, Apple introduced the iTunes Music Store (iTMS, as shown in Figure A.3), which integrates a full-fledged online music store into iTunes, allowing quick and painless purchase of music online. As of this writing, Apple has over 400,000 songs available in the iTMS library. Individual songs can be purchased for 99 cents, with most albums going for $9.99. Over 30 million songs were purchased through iTunes as of January 2004.

**Figure A.2** iTunes for OS X

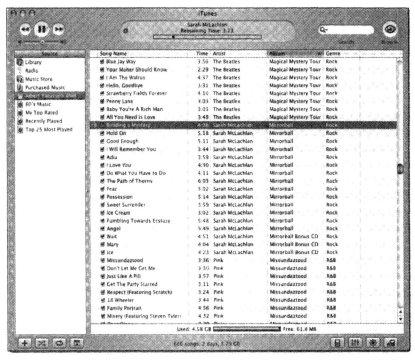

**Figure A.3** The iTunes Music Store

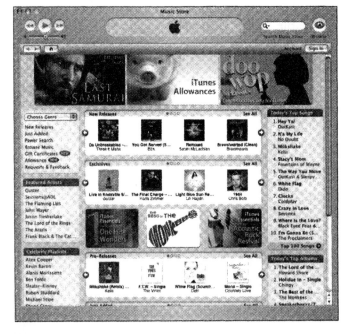

Hoping to capture an even larger share of the MP3 player market and understanding that the Macintosh market is dwarfed by computers installed with Windows, Apple has started selling Windows-compatible versions of the iPod, formatted with the FAT32 file system instead of Mac HFS+ (which is the standard Macintosh file system that Windows computers do not understand). Third-generation iPods, unveiled in April 2003, no longer distinguish between Macs and PCs; the included Windows software will properly initialize the iPod to work with Windows. In early 2004, Apple introduced a smaller, less expensive version of the iPod called the iPod mini, targeting the high-end Flash ROM-based player market. Apple has also released a version of iTunes for Windows, which is virtually identical to the Macintosh offering, giving Windows users access to the same, high-quality software that Mac users have been enjoying with their iPods.

Since the iPod's introduction four years ago, Apple has updated the device several times. Some of these revisions have simply involved adding larger-capacity hard drives, but others have been more significant. Five generations of iPods, known simply as first, second, third, fourth, and fifth-generation iPods, as well as the iPod mini, are now on the market. Differences are minor between the first and second-generation iPods, and those models are very similar in physical appearance. However, in 2003, Apple released the third-generation iPod, which is a new design over previous models and can quickly be distinguished from those earlier models. In this Appendix, we will concentrate on the first, second, and third-generation iPods. Figure A.4 shows the backside of the 20GB third-generation iPod.

**Figure A.4** The Backside of a 20GB Third-Generation iPod

Due to their popularity, iPods have become a target for hardware hackers and other curious people wanting to open them up and poke around inside. However, there are very practical reasons to open an iPod—mainly to replace the internal battery. The Li-Ion battery chemistry the iPod uses is generally better than previous battery technologies (such as nickel cadmium or nickel metal hydride, neither of which were used in any iPods), but people tend to use their iPods quite a bit, and even Li-Ion batteries do not last forever. The most common concern regarding the iPod is the fact that Apple designed it so the battery cannot be replaced by end users Apple has a battery replacement program, which requires you to send your iPod to Apple and pay $99 plus return shipping charges for them to install a new battery in your iPod. And there is no guarantee that you will even receive the same iPod in return! If you're willing to dive into opening your iPod yourself (something that requires a bit of patience), you can replace the internal battery for about half the cost of sending your iPod to Apple, and you won't be without an iPod while you wait. We'll show you how in this chapter.

In addition, we'll describe how to upgrade the hard drive in a 5GB iPod as well as reformatting an iPod so it can be used with either a Macintosh or Windows system. Finally, we'll discuss the iPod's built-in (but undocumented) diagnostic mode. At the end of the chapter, we'll touch briefly on some other hacks you can perform, such as installing Linux on your iPod, and present a list of additional iPod resources so you can further explore the device on your own.

# Opening Your iPod

One thing that iPod owners will quickly notice is there is no obvious way to open the case. There are no visible screws, tabs, or anything of that nature—just a sleek, metal plate somehow affixed to the back of the iPod. The two halves of the iPod are held together by a series of plastic tabs that run along both sides of the case, holding the metal half of the device securely in place. Unfortunately, this ensures that taking apart the iPod, which was never intended for end users, is a tricky proposition.

However, there are compelling reasons to open the iPod, especially if your battery has died (or is nearing depletion) and you want to save some money by replacing it yourself. Be warned, however, that you must be patient when opening the iPod or you can easily damage the case.

# Preparing for the Hack

We will separately describe how to open a first-generation iPod and a second or third-generation iPod. The best tool to open your iPod with is some type of stiff plastic, such as the chapter wedges we'll use below. If you can avoid it, do not use a metal screwdriver to pry your iPod open, as the risk of damaging the case is much greater. The metal case can be permanently bent and the plastic of the case will scratch easily, so care and patience must be applied when opening the iPod. One of the battery kits we purchased came from PDASmart (www.pdasmart.com) included two plastic sticks with tapered, wedge ends (not unlike a flathead screwdriver) which are ideal for opening iPods (see Figure A.5). We also purchased batteries from Laptops For Less (www.laptopsforless.com), and they include a single jeweler's screwdriver for opening the iPod. We do not recommend using such a metal screwdriver if you can avoid it.

## WARNING: HARDWARE HARM

Apple never intended end users to open the iPod and thus made it rather difficult to do so. The iPod is held together by a series of plastic tabs that clip onto the metal part of the case. To open the case, you must exert force between the plastic half of the case and the metal half to flex the case enough so the tabs become detached from the metal. In doing this, you can permanently bend the metal half of the case, as well as cause cosmetic damage to the plastic half along the seam where the two halves come together.

Therefore, extreme patience and care are required when you're attempting to open an iPod. Using a tool to pry into the case can very easily bend the metal, so you must be diligent and work slowly. If you use a small screwdriver you'll want to be especially careful not to slip when exerting force while prying, as you can easily put a nice gouge in the case exterior.

**Figure A.5** Plastic Wedges for Opening an iPod

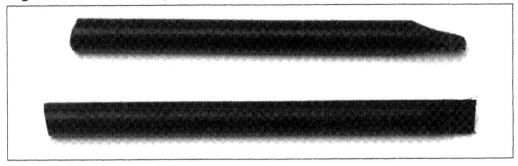

First-generation iPods are easier to open as you can begin prying at the top of the case near the FireWire port. Second and third-generation iPods do not have this advantage, so you must start along one of the sides. We will describe separately how to open first-generation iPods versus second and third-generation iPods.

# First Generation iPods

Let's begin:

1. Using one of the wedges, start by prying between the stainless steel cover and the plastic of the case at the top of the iPod (see Figure A.6). Prying at the top will allow you to open a small gap on the side of the case where you can then use one of the other wedges to start undoing the plastic tabs. To see what you're aiming for, look ahead to Figure A.9, which shows what the tabs look like when the case is open.

**Figure A.6** Start Prying at the Top of the Case

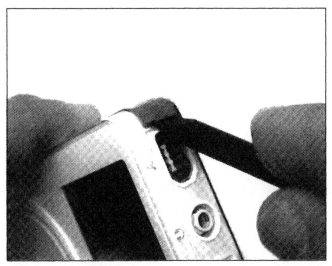

2. With one wedge firmly in place at the top of the iPod, use a second wedge to start working along the side, as shown in Figure A.7.

**Figure A.7** Working Along the Edge

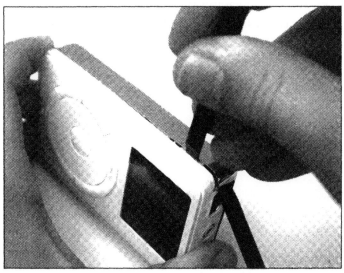

3. Continue working your way along the edge of the iPod until you have all the clips on one side undone (see Figure A.8).

**Figure A.8** Continue Working Down the Edge

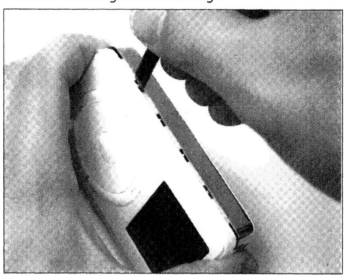

4. Once you reach the corner opposite from where you started and have all the clips undone on one side of the iPod, you are past the most difficult stage and can separate the two halves (see Figure A.9). You may now proceed with other hacks, such as replacing the iPod battery or swapping out the hard drive, which are described later in this chapter.

**Figure A.9** Lifting Apart the Two Halves of the iPod

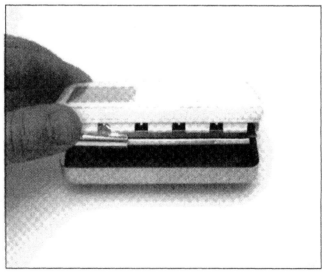

# Second and Third-Generation iPods

Apple changed the design of the second-generation iPods so you can't start prying at the top of the unit near the FireWire port. Third-generation iPods constitute a completely new design over the first two iPod generations and suffer a similar problem. Unfortunately, this makes them a bit trickier to open. While we depict a third-generation iPod in the pictures, the procedure is similar for second-generation iPods.

1. Work one of the plastic wedges along the seam on the side of the iPod until you are able to insert it between the metal back and the case (see Figure A.10).

**Figure A.10** Prying into the Case

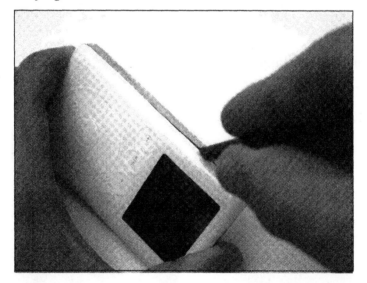

2. With one of the wedges inserted in the case, insert a second wedge into the gap you've created and work it along the edge to pop out the tabs holding the case together. Your goal is to push each of the tabs inward until they release from the metal half of the case.

**Figure A.11** Continue Prying Along One Side

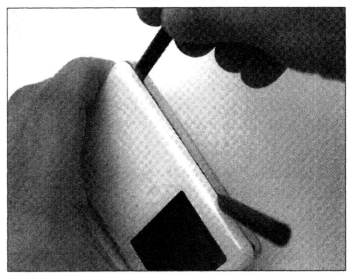

3.  Continue working along the one side until you have all the tabs unclipped (see Figure A.12).

**Figure A.12** Unclip all the Tabs

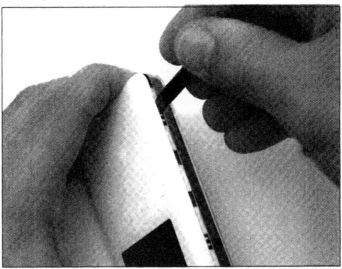

4.  With one side unclipped, you should be able to separate the back of the iPod from the front half (see Figure A.13).

**Figure A.13** Opening the Case

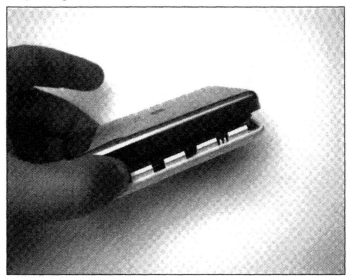

If you're opening a third-generation iPod, the metal half of the case is connected to the bottom half by a thin ribbon cable. Do not try separating the two halves completely without first disconnecting the cable or you may do permanent harm to your iPod. Figure A.14 shows where the cable is connected to the top half of the case. You can choose to either disconnect the cable or leave it connected and flip the metal half of the case over so it is resting next to the top half of the case.

**WARNING: HARDWARE HARM**

Unlike first and second-generation iPods, the third-generation iPods' metal cover is connected to the top half of the unit with a thin ribbon connector. Do not be hasty in separating the two halves, because you can easily damage this cable. You can choose to disconnect the cable (the connector is shown in Figure A.14) or carefully place the two halves of the case close to each other on a flat surface while working on the iPod internals.

**Figure A.14** Connector Holding Two Halves Together

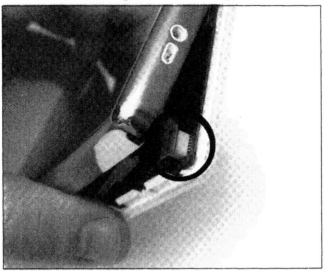

With your iPod open, you may now proceed with the hack of your choice, including replacing the iPod battery or swapping out the hard drive, both of which are described in this chapter.

# Replacing the iPod Battery

Sooner or later, it will come time to replace your iPod's battery. Li-Ion power cells are a big improvement over older battery chemistries, but they are not infallible. Eventually your iPod's battery will no longer hold a charge or it will be sufficiently weak where you're not getting nearly as much time out of your iPod as you did when it was new. When that time comes, you have three choices:

1. **Throw out your iPod and buy a new one**  Apple would love you to choose this option, but most people do not consider the iPod a "disposable" item, given its high price tag. Thus, this is not an option for the majority of people.

2. **Send your iPod to Apple and pay them to replace the battery**  Apple has a program whereby you can send them your iPod and, for $99 (plus shipping and sales tax if applicable), they will replace its battery. Besides being relatively expensive, this choice

deprives you of your iPod while you're waiting for Apple to return it. Also, Apple makes no guarantee that you'll receive your original iPod back.

3. **Open your iPod and replace the battery yourself** Several companies sell iPod batteries for around $50 and often include a tool (a screwdriver or plastic implement) that you can use to open your iPod. Once you have the device open, swapping the old battery for a new one is relatively trivial. Opening the iPod is the hard part.

Since you're reading a book on hardware hacking, we'll assume that you're opting to replace the battery yourself.

# Preparing for the Hack

For this hack, all you need is a tool to open the iPod (a plastic wedge or two, a firm piece of thin plastic, a small screwdriver, or something similar) and a replacement battery.

To demonstrate this hack, we ordered new batteries from Laptops for Less (www.laptopsforless.com) and PDASmart (www.pdasmart.com). At the time of this writing, the batteries cost $50 to $60 each, plus shipping. PDASmart also offers a mail-in service that is less expensive than Apple's battery replacement program. You can also find iPod batteries for sale on eBay, but if you go this route you need to be careful not to end up purchasing a used battery that might be in worse condition than the battery you intend to replace.

When ordering a battery, it is important that you order the correct type of battery for your iPod. First and second-generation iPods use one type of battery, and third-generation iPods use another. The two different battery types are shown in Figure A.15.

## Need to Know...

### Third-generation Changes

Apple made many changes to the iPod when it designed the third-generation models, the battery being one of them. Third-generation iPods have a much smaller battery than earlier models, presumably to reduce the thickness of the iPod. Although Apple certainly succeeded in making the newer iPods thinner, the third-generation iPods have a noticeably shorter battery life as a result. Figure A.15 shows the difference in size between the two batteries.

When ordering a new battery for your iPod, you want to make sure you specify the correct battery type. You'll be pretty disappointed if you open your iPod up only to discover that you ordered the wrong battery.

**Figure A.15** iPod Batteries: First and Second-Generation (Top) and Third-Generation (Bottom)

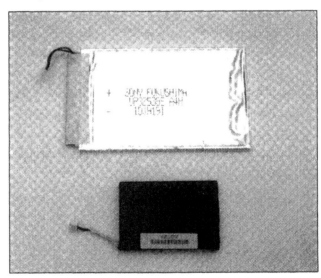

Since the battery and internals are unique between first and second-generation iPods and third-generation iPods, we will describe battery replacement separately.

# Battery Replacement: First and Second-Generation iPods

Follow these steps:

1. The first thing you'll want to do is open your iPod, as described in the first section in this chapter. Once you have the iPod open, put aside the metal half of the case and place your iPod face down on a flat surface, as shown in Figure A.16. The battery is sitting on top.

**Figure A.16** The First-Generation iPod Opened and Ready for the Hack

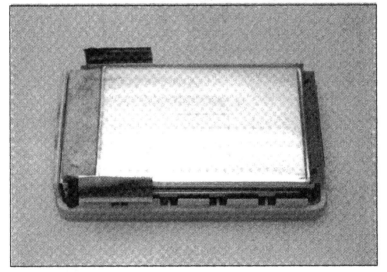

2. The battery is connected to the iPod motherboard by a power connector visible at the lower-left corner of Figure A.16. Holding the battery in place are two thin rubber strips at both ends of the iPod, sandwiched between the battery and the hard drive (which is directly underneath the battery). Figure A.17 shows one of these strips at the top of the iPod. In this picture, you can also more clearly see the battery power cable plugged into the motherboard.

**Figure A.17** Rubber Strips

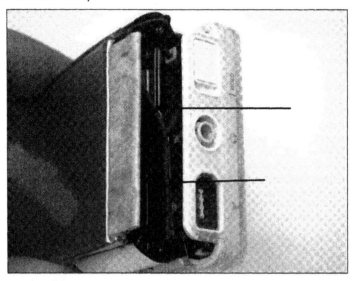

3. Using a screwdriver, carefully pry between the hard drive and the battery, undoing the glue on the rubber pieces, as shown in Figure A.18.

**Figure A.18** Prying the Battery from the Rubber Strips

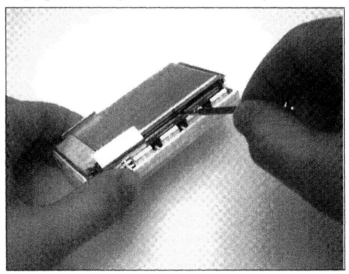

4. Once you have separated the battery from the rubber strips, you can unplug it from the iPod motherboard and properly dispose of it (see Figure A.19).

**Figure A.19** Removing the Old Battery

5. With the old battery removed, you can now swap in the new battery that you purchased (see Figure A.20). Orient the new battery in the same direction as the old battery. Plug the power connector into the iPod motherboard, taking care as you insert the connector. The connector will fit in only one orientation; so do not force it into place. For easier access to the connector on the motherboard, you can temporarily move aside the rubber strip that partially covers it.

**Figure A.20** Connecting the New Battery

6. With the new battery connected, move the rubber strip back into place (if you moved it out of the way) and firmly attach the battery atop the hard drive, as shown in Figure A.21.

**Figure A.21** Affixing the Battery to the Hard Drive

7. Take care that the power cable is tucked away at the top of the iPod (see Figure A.22).

**Figure A.22** Power Cable Safely Tucked Away

8. Once you have the battery securely attached into place, you can reattach the cover (see Figure A.23). The metal cover should snap easily into place. If it does not, make sure there are no obstructions before you attempt to close the cover.

**Figure A.23** Reattaching the Metal Half of the Case

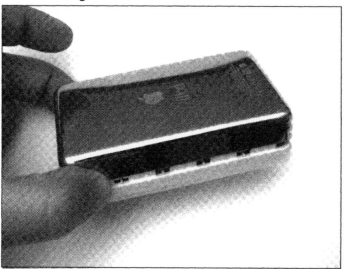

9. Once you have your iPod back together, you'll want to charge the battery for a minimum of three hours before using the device (see Figure A.24).

**Figure A.24** Charging the New Battery

# Battery Replacement: Third-Generation iPods

Follow these steps:

1. Carefully open your third-generation iPod as described in the first section of this chapter. Once you have your iPod opened, it should resemble the image in Figure A.25.

**Figure A.25** The Third-Generation iPod Opened and Ready for the Hack

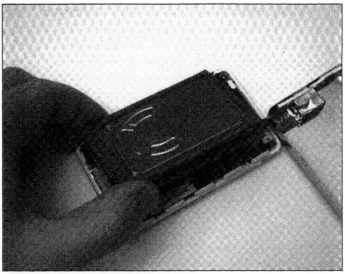

2.  First, you'll need to remove the hard drive (see Figure A.26). The hard drive is sitting on top of the other iPod circuitry, buffered by a piece of blue rubber. The hard drive is connected to the iPod via a small ribbon cable that connects directly to the motherboard. Slowly lift up the hard drive to disconnect this cable, and set the hard drive aside.

**Figure A.26** Removing the Hard Drive

3.  Now that the hard drive has been removed, we have easy access to the battery. The battery is the large black component highlighted in Figure A.27. The battery connector is immediately to the left of the battery (see Figure A.28).

**Figure A.27** The iPod Battery

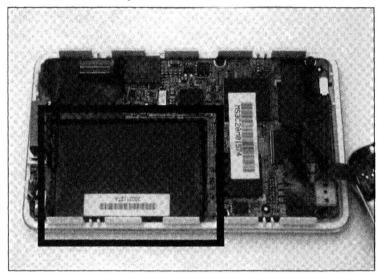

4.  Carefully use a small screwdriver to pry the battery from its compartment. Be careful not to make contact with the circuit board below the battery, because you could damage it. Before the battery can be completely removed, you will need to disconnect the power cord. However, the cord is wrapped around a part of the circuit board, as shown in Figure A.28. You can use a screwdriver to help remove the wires from underneath the board.

**Figure A.28** The iPod Battery Connector

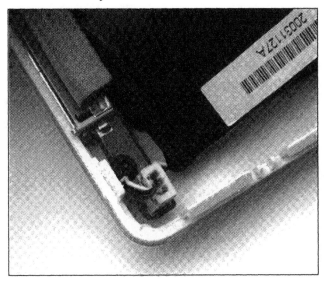

5. With the wires out of the way, you can remove the battery from its compartment in the iPod, as shown in Figure A.29.

**Figure A.29** The iPod Battery Removed

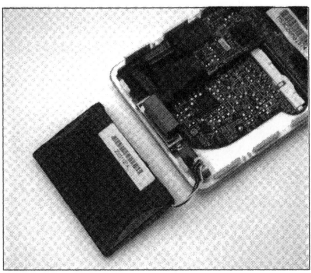

6. Disconnect the battery from the motherboard by gently pulling the power connector straight up. With the old battery removed, you can

now plug the new battery in, taking care as you insert the connector (see Figure A.30). The connector will only fit in one orientation, so do not force it into place.

**Figure A.30** Inserting the New iPod Battery

7. Before you can place the battery back into its compartment, you must first wrap the battery power cord around the tip of the circuit board. You can use a small screwdriver to assist you, as shown in Figure A.31.

**Figure A.31** Tucking In the Power Cable

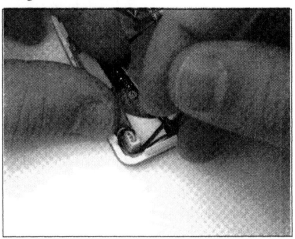

8. Once you have reattached and properly routed the power cable, you can place the new battery inside the case. Your iPod should now resemble the image in Figure A.32.

**Figure A.32** New Battery Installed in Place

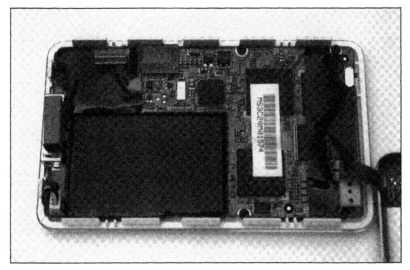

9. Now you can reassemble your iPod. Reattach the connector on the hard drive to the connector on the motherboard. The connectors are highlighted in Figure A.33.

**Figure A.33** Reattaching the Hard Drive

10. After you've plugged the hard drive back in, you can then place it back on top of the board (see Figure A.34).

**Figure A.34** Hard Drive Back in Place

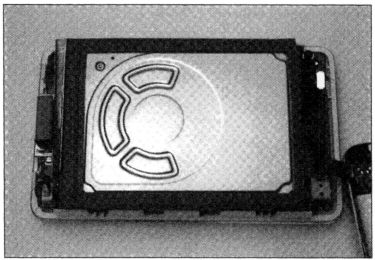

11. Finally, place the metal half of the case back on top of the iPod and snap it into place (see Figure A.35). Take care not to pinch or put too much stress on the thin ribbon connector on the iPod motherboard while you are manipulating the two halves of the case.

**Figure A.35** Snapping the Case Back Together

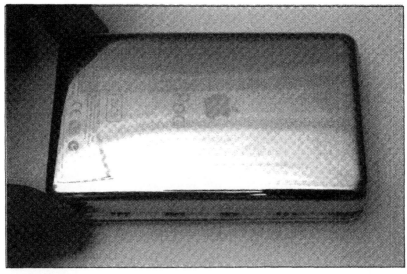

12.  Once you have your iPod back together, you'll want to charge the battery for a minimum of three hours before using the device (see Figure A.36).

**Figure A.36** Charging the new Battery

# Upgrading a 5GB iPod's Hard Drive

The first iPod Apple released contained a 5GB hard drive, which was an impressive amount of storage at the time. However, it has since been eclipsed by iPods with much larger disk space. The largest iPod available as this book goes to press is a 40GB version, allowing for up to eight times the storage of the early 5GB iPods. Unfortunately, the iPod uses a PCMCIA form-factor 1.8-inch hard drive made by Toshiba, and replacement drives are not easy to obtain. However, used iPod drives come up frequently for auction on eBay, giving you an opportunity to either upgrade your 5GB iPod to a higher capacity or replace a nonworking drive with a good one to get your iPod back in working order.

Keep in mind that there is a fairly limited upgrade path for the 5GB iPod. Drives from third-generation iPods will not work in the first-generation iPod, and drives larger in capacity than 10GB (such as the 20GB drive used in the second-generation iPod) will not fit in the first-generation case due to the increase in thickness.

# Preparing for the Hack

For this hack you'll need the following:

- A 5GB iPod that you want to upgrade

- A replacement hard drive (an example is shown in Figure A.37)

- A tool for opening the iPod (such as one or two plastic wedges, a thin, firm piece of plastic, or a flat-head screwdriver)

eBay is a good source for used iPod drives, and they can often be found for much less than you'd pay to buy a new (or used) iPod. If you're unsure of the drive's capacity, you can find it printed in the lower-left corner of the sticker on the top of the drive (highlighted in Figure A.38).

**Figure A.37** A 10GB iPod Hard Drive

**Figure A.38** Drive Capacity printed on the Hard Drive Sticker

# Performing the Hack

The first thing you'll want to do is open your iPod as described in the first section in this chapter. When you have the case off, your iPod should resemble the image in Figure A.39.

**Figure A.39** iPod Opened and Ready for the Hack

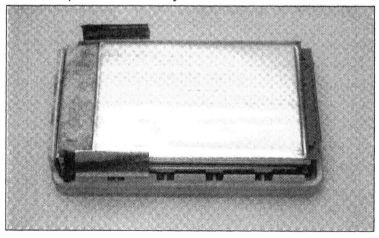

1.  To get to the hard drive, we first have to remove the battery that sits on top of it. The battery is held into place by sticky rubber pads sandwiched between the battery and the hard drive. The battery is

also connected to the motherboard with a power cable. The easiest way to remove the battery is to use a small screwdriver as a lever (see Figure A.40). Take care not to exert force with the tip of the screwdriver on either the battery or the hard drive, because you may puncture them; instead, use the shaft of the screwdriver to pry between the battery and the hard drive.

**Figure A.40** Pulling the Battery and Hard Drive Apart

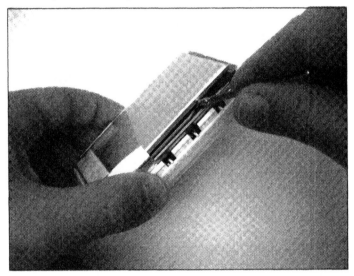

2. Once you have peeled the battery off the top of the hard drive, it will still be connected to the motherboard. Before disconnecting the battery, let's first remove the rubber pads from the top of the hard drive (see Figure A.41), because one of them may be obscuring access to the battery connector and we need to remove the pads anyway to apply them to the new drive. Note that the rubber pads in your iPod may not look exactly the same as those pictured.

**Figure A.41** Rubber Pads on Top of the Hard Drive

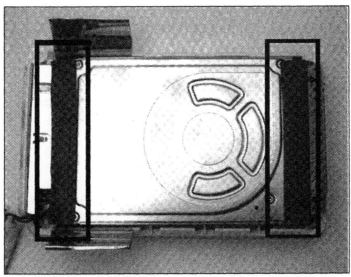

3.  Carefully peel the rubber pads from the top of the drive (see Figure A.42). Put them aside for now; we will be attaching them to the new drive once we've installed it into the iPod.

**Figure A.42** Removing the Rubber Pads

4.  With the rubber pads removed, we can now easily unplug the battery. Although it's not imperative that we disconnect the battery, it

does make removing and installing the new hard drive easier. Carefully unplug the battery connector by pulling it straight up off the motherboard (see Figure A.43). Once the battery has been disconnected, set it aside.

**Figure A.43** Disconnecting the Battery

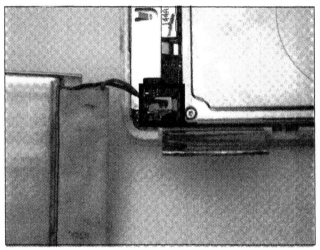

5.  With the battery out of the way, we can now remove the hard drive. The hard drive is resting on four small rubber pads and is plugged into the motherboard with a connector on one edge of the hard drive. Carefully pry the bottom of the hard drive from each rubber pad (see Figure A.44).

### Warning: Hardware Harm

Be extremely careful in performing this procedure. Do not use the motherboard as direct leverage for prying up the hard drive, because you can easily damage the motherboard and render your iPod inoperable. Instead, wedge the screwdriver between the rubber pads and the hard drive, as shown in Figure A.44.

**Figure A.44** Prying the Hard Drive from the Rubber Pads

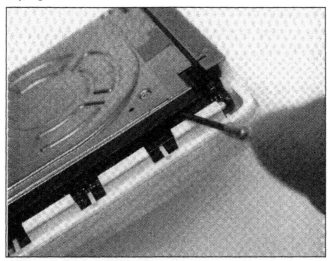

6.  Once you have separated the drive from the rubber pads, you can disconnect the drive from the connector on the motherboard. This connector is very fragile, so take care when unplugging it from the drive. The easiest way to do so is to wedge a flat-head jeweler's screwdriver between the drive and connector to work it loose (see Figure A.45). After you disconnect the drive, you can set it aside.

**Figure A.45** Disconnecting the Hard Drive

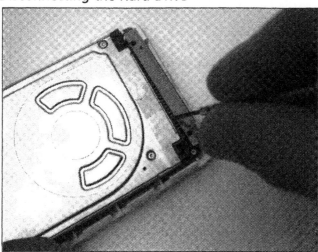

7. If any of the rubber pads are still attached to the hard drive, remove them and place them in the appropriate corner of the motherboard, where they were originally resting. Your iPod should now resemble the image in Figure A.46.

**Figure A.46** Exposed iPod Motherboard

8. Now it's time to attach the new drive. Before you plug the drive in, make sure it is oriented the same way as the old drive. The drive connector is keyed and can be plugged into the motherboard only one way (see Figure A.47).

**Figure A.47** The Hard Drive Connector

9. Taking care that the drive is oriented properly (the label side of the drive should be facing the iPod motherboard), plug the hard drive in as shown in Figure A.48. Do not exert too much force when plugging in the drive—if it doesn't slide in easily, make sure the drive is not upside down.

**Figure A.48** Plugging In the New Hard Drive

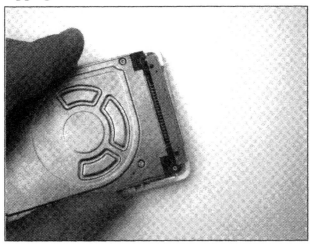

10. After plugging the drive into the connector, place it back on the motherboard's rubber pads, taking care that the drive is properly centered in the case. With the drive placed in the case, it should resemble the image in Figure A.49.

**Figure A.49** The New Hard Drive Resting in the Case

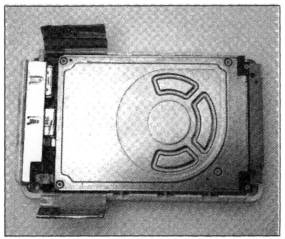

11. Now it's time to plug the battery back into the motherboard. Carefully plug the connector into the board, taking care that the plug is oriented in the right direction. The plug is keyed and will fit into the connector only one way, so do not try to force it (see Figure A.50).

**Figure A.50** Reattaching the Battery

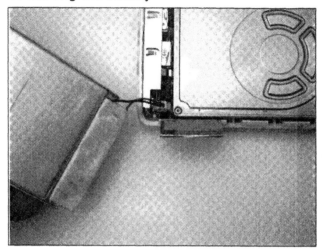

12. Now replace the long rubber pads that you removed earlier by attaching them to the replacement drive in the same locations as they were on the old drive (see Figure A.51). Note that the rubber pads in your iPod might not exactly resemble those in the picture.

**Figure A.51** Replacing the Rubber Pads

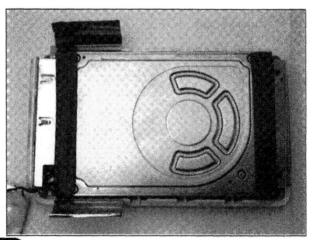

13. After replacing the rubber pads, you can place the battery on top of the hard drive. Take care to properly align the battery on top of the hard drive, or you may have problems getting the case back together. Also, tuck the battery power cable underneath the metal housing at the top of the iPod to move it out of the way (see Figure A.52). Apply enough pressure to the battery to ensure that it is firmly attached to the rubber pads.

**Figure A.52** Battery Back in Place

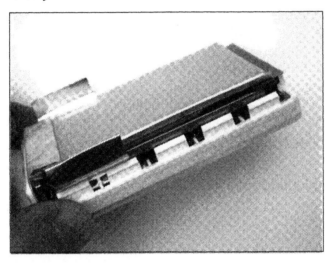

14. Fold the two pieces of metal foil back over the battery. Finally, snap the stainless steel cover back over the case (see Figure A.53). If the cover does not slide easily over the case, make sure there are no obstructions before continuing. The cover should snap into place easily.

**Figure A.53** Replace the Cover

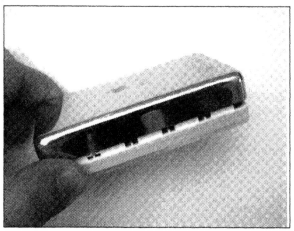

15.  After you've got the iPod back together, turn it on. If the upgrade
was successful, you should be able to use your new iPod immediately
(see Figure A.54).

**Figure A.54** Ahhh, Music!

Of course, you'll probably want to plug your iPod into your computer
and copy your music onto it. If you upgraded your iPod with a larger hard
drive (going from 5GB to 10GB, as we did in this chapter), you now have
twice as much storage space. If the drive was formatted for use with a

Macintosh and you need to use your iPod with a Windows machine, or vice versa, read the next section, which explains how you can perform this magic.

# From Mac to Windows and Back Again

First-generation iPods were intended for use solely with Macintosh computers. As demand for the iPod grew, Apple released the second-generation iPods, which included support for Windows computers. To this end, Apple sold two different versions of the second-generation iPod—models for Windows computers and models for Macs. Third-generation iPods do away with this duplicity in packaging and simply come with an install disk that will properly format the iPod's hard drive for Windows (new iPods come pre-formatted with the Macintosh HFS+ file system). Fortunately, all iPods can be formatted to work with Windows or the Macintosh using software available from Apple.

## Preparing for the Hack

All you need for this hack are the following:

- An iPod you'd like to "switch"
- A Windows or Macintosh computer with a FireWire port (or a USB port if you have a third-generation iPod)
- An Internet connection so you can download the appropriate software from Apple's Web site

**WARNING**

Performing this procedure will cause the iPod Updater software to reformat your iPod's hard drive with a new file system, thus deleting anything stored on the drive. If you have music or other files stored on your iPod and you don't want to lose them, make sure you first back up the files onto your computer!

# Going from Windows to Macintosh

If you're using a first or second-generation iPod, you will need to download the iPod Software Updater 1.3.1. If you're using a third-generation iPod, you will need to download the iPod Software Updater 2.0.1 (or later) instead. The updaters can be found at www.info.apple.com/usen/ipod.

1.  After downloading the correct version of the software for your iPod, run the updater, as shown in Figure A.55. This example demonstrates using the iPod Software Updater 1.3.1, but the procedure is the same for later Updater versions.

**Figure A.55** The Macintosh iPod Software Updater Installer

2.  Go through the install process, which will install the updater on your computer. When installation is complete, plug your iPod into your Macintosh. Locate the iPod Software Updater on your computer, which should be located in your **Applications | Utilities** folder.

3.  With your iPod plugged into your Macintosh, start the iPod Software Updater by double-clicking the **iPod Software Updater** icon (see Figure A.56). Click the **lock** icon in the lower-left corner of the dialog box, type in your password, and click the **Restore** button (see Figure A.57).

**Figure A.56** The iPod Software Updater Icon

**Figure A.57** The iPod Software Updater

4. After you click **Restore**, you will be prompted with a confirmation dialog box. Confirm that you want to restore your iPod to its factory settings. After the updater has completed, unplug the iPod and then plug it back into your computer. That's it! Now you can copy music and other files onto your iPod.

# Going from Macintosh to Windows

If you're using a first or second-generation iPod, you will need to download the Windows 1.3 iPod Updater. If you're using a third-generation iPod, you will need to download the Windows 2.1 (or later) iPod Updater instead. The updaters can be found at www.info.apple.com/usen/ipodwin.

1. After downloading the appropriate software, locate and run the installer, as shown in Figure A.58. Go through the install process, which will install the updater on your computer. This example demonstrates restoring an iPod using the iPod Software Updater 1.3, but the procedure is the same for later Updater versions.

**Figure A.58** The Windows iPod Software Updater Installer

2. If your iPod is connected to your Windows computer, eject it and unplug it from the computer. Locate the iPod Updater that you just installed (see Figure A.59). It should be located under **Start | Programs | iPod | System Software 1.3** (or 2.1 if you're installing that version instead).

**Figure A.59** Locate and Run the iPod Updater

3. After you start the Updater, plug your iPod into the computer. The iPod installer screen should acknowledge that the iPod has been plugged in and resemble the image shown in Figure A.60.

**Figure A.60** The Windows iPod Updater

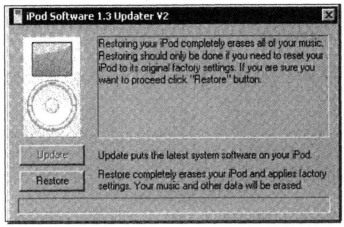

4. Now click the **Restore** button. After the updater has completed, unplug the iPod and then plug it back into your computer. That's it! Now you can copy music and other files onto your iPod.

# iPod Diagnostic Mode

The iPod has several built-in diagnostic features that can help you troubleshoot problems with your iPod. Most diagnostic features are accessed through a hidden, undocumented menu, but there is also a disc scan mode that you can access separately. Each version of the iPod firmware contains a diagnostic mode, though some of the commands differ.

## The Diagnostic Menu

To enter the diagnostic menu:

1. Reset your iPod by pressing and holding the **Menu** and **Play** buttons for 5 to 10 seconds. When the iPod resets and the Apple logo appears, press and hold **Previous**, **Next**, and **Action** (the center button). If you do this properly, you'll briefly see a reversed Apple logo, and a menu will then appear. The menu may differ based on the firmware version installed in your iPod. Figure A.61 shows the diagnostic menus for first-generation and third-generation iPods.

**Figure A.61** The iPod Diagnostic Menu

| First-Generation iPod<br>1.3.1 Firmware Installed | Third-Generation iPod<br>2.1.0 Firmware Installed |
|---|---|

2. The menu is two screen pages long, and you can scroll through the items by pressing the **Previous** and **Next** buttons. Pressing the **Action** button will start the test of the highlighted selection. Press the **Play** button after a test has completed to return to the menu. To exit the diagnostic mode, reset your iPod by holding down the **Menu** and **Play** buttons for 5 or more seconds.

Some of the menu items are fairly obvious, but the function of others can only be guessed at. Table A.1 describes what we know about each test.

**Table A.1** iPod Diagnostic Menu Functions

| Item | Name | Description |
|---|---|---|
| A | 5 IN 1 | Runs tests J through N in succession. |
| B | RESET | Resets the iPod (equivalent to pressing and holding **Menu** and **Play** for more than 5 seconds). |

**Continued**

**Table A.1 continued** iPod Diagnostic Menu Functions

| Item | Name | Description |
|------|------|-------------|
| C | KEY | Gives you several seconds to press all the buttons. If all buttons aren't pressed within the allotted time, you see a "KEY FAIL" message. |
| D | AUDIO | Presumably tests the audio hardware. |
| E | REMOTE | If a remote control is not found, displays "RMT FAIL." |
| F | FIREWIRE (or FW ID) | Displays "FW PASS" if successful. Most likely tests the FireWire bus. |
| G | SLEEP | Puts the iPod to sleep, requiring a reset to wake it up. |
| H | A2D (or CHG STUS) | Appears to test the power subsystem, displays a hex value and the text "CHG OK FW 1 BAT 1." Text displayed differs based on firmware version and whether the iPod is charging. |
| I | OTPO CNT | Tests the scroll wheel. |
| J | LCM | Tests the display. Press the **Action** button to view each of the four test screens (the first being a blank screen). |
| K (1.3.1) | RTC | It's not clear what this test checks, although RTC most likely refers to the on-board Real-Time Clock. |
| K (2.1.0) | CHG STUS | Appears to test the power subsystem, displays a hex value and the text "CHG OK FW 1 BAT 1." Text displayed differs based on firmware version and whether the iPod is charging. |
| L (1.3.1) | SDRAM | Memory test. Displays "SDRAM PASS" upon success. |
| L (2.1.0) | USB DISK | Doesn't do anything noticeable, but presumably it tests the USB subsystem on third-generation iPods. |
| M | FLASH (or CHK SUM) | It's unclear what this test is for, but it's possible it may be related to the firmware version installed or calculating a checksum of the Flash ROM. |

**Continued**

**Table A.1 continued** iPod Diagnostic Menu Functions

| Item | Name | Description |
|------|------|-------------|
| N (1.3.1) | OPTO | This test cannot be activated on first-generation iPods featuring a mechanical scroll wheel. iPods with a touch wheel list the test as "WHEEL A2D." When activated, a screen appears with the text "Wheel A2D" and a bar, requiring a reset to exit. Presumably tests the optoelectronic circuitry of the touch wheel. |
| N (2.1.0) | CONTRAST | Allows you to test the contrast control using the touch wheel to adjust the contrast. |
| O | HDD SCAN | Performs a scan of the hard disk. This test will take several minutes to complete. |
| P | RUN IN | Runs through a repeating series of tests of various aspects of the iPod's hardware. |

# Disk Check

The disk check mode scans your iPod's hard drive for problems while displaying a progress bar.

1. To enter disk scan mode, first reset your iPod by pressing and holding the **Menu** and **Play** buttons for 5 to 10 seconds. When the iPod resets and the Apple logo appears, press and hold the **Previous**, **Next**, **Menu**, and **Action** buttons. If done properly, the disk scan will start and you'll see a graphical display with a scrollbar at the bottom (see Figure A.62).

**Figure A.62** iPod Disk Check Mode

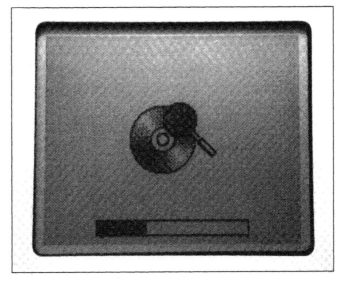

2. The disk check will take several minutes to complete, so be patient. If the disk check completes without problems, your screen will resemble the image in Figure A.63.

**Figure A.63** iPod Disk Check Mode Complete

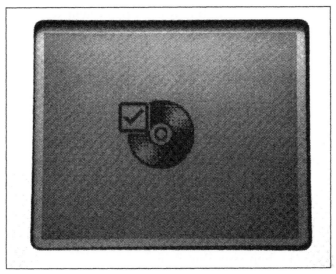

# Additional iPod Hacks

Given the iPod's popularity, users have developed many iPod-related hacks. The following are a few interesting hacks that we don't have space to explore here in detail but that you should be aware of in case you're looking for additional ways to void your warranty. Further information about each hack can be found at the provided links.

## Installing Linux on an iPod

If you're a Linux fan, you've probably heard the phrase, "But can it run Linux?" Most of the time the answer is a resounding, "Yes!" This answer rings true for the iPod as well. A version of uClinux (www.uclinux.org and www.ucdot.org) has been ported to run on the iPod. uClinux is a derivative of Linux intended for constrained embedded systems and devices without Memory Management Units (MMUs). Although the iPod does have an MMU, its features are not sufficient to support the standard Linux kernel.

To install Linux on the iPod, you must overwrite the existing software on the iPod to allow the iPod to boot into Linux. Therefore, you should back up your iPod hard drive before attempting to install Linux. Instructions on how to do this are provided at the *Linux on iPod* site listed at the end of this paragraph. If you're a Linux fan and want to experiment with Linux on the iPod, you can have some fun with this, but you probably will want to continue using the software that came with your iPod to play music—at least until Linux-based iPod software further evolves. You can learn more about installing Linux on the iPod at http://ipodlinux.sourceforge.net.

## Repairing the FireWire Port

On first and second-generation iPods, the act of inserting and removing the FireWire cable on your iPod causes a good amount of stress on the iPod's internal FireWire port (see Figure A.64). Because there is no strain relief on the port, over time the solder joints connecting the FireWire port to the iPod's motherboard can break. Signs of this problem include a loose or wiggling connector, not being able to charge your iPod, or your computer not recognizing the iPod when you plug it in.

**Figure A.64** An iPod FireWire Port

If you suspect your FireWire port might be damaged and you're comfortable with soldering small devices, you can open your iPod and resolder the connections to the FireWire port yourself. You can also apply some hot glue to the FireWire port to help provide some stress relief so this problem (hopefully) does not reoccur. If you'd prefer not to do this repair yourself, PDASmart (http://pdasmart.com/ipodpartscenter.htm) offers a mail-in service whereby they will fix the FireWire port for significantly less than Apple would charge for the same repair.

## Scroll Wheel Fix

First-generation iPods feature a mechanical scroll wheel that spins around a center point, as opposed to later iPod models that use a solid-state touch wheel. The scroll wheel tends to become loose or "sloppy" with time, allowing it to spin more freely. Unfortunately, this can result in frequent and undesirable volume changes when you're using your iPod, especially if you're in motion. However, this problem can be solved with a small amount of effort.

1. This hack involves removing the scroll wheel and center button, preferably by using a piece of masking (or similar) tape to lift up the wheel and button. (Do not use a knife to pry up the wheel!) Under

the scroll wheel is a small metal bearing that the wheel snaps onto, which allows it to spin in place (see Figure A.65).

**Figure A.65** iPod Scroll Wheel Internals

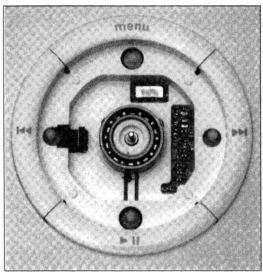

2.  Once you have the device open, you can clean away any grease or debris from the bearing and then apply new grease. Be careful of petroleum-based products, however, since they can degrade plastics.

You can find more information on this hack at www.ipoding.com/modules.php?op=modload&name=News&file=article&sid=486.

# iPod Resources on the Web

A large number of Web sites have sprung up on which you can learn more about the iPod, buy various iPod accessories and products, and discuss the iPod with other fans. The following is a short list of such sites; a quick search on Google will reveal many more:

-   **iPod Home Page: www.apple.com/ipod** This should be your first stop when you're looking for iPod information. From here you can download the latest iPod software and browse through a wealth of information about the iPod and, of course, links to the Apple Store, where you can buy iPods and iPod accessories.

- **iTunes Home Page: www.apple.com/itunes**  No iPod is complete without iTunes, Apple's free digital jukebox that is custom-tailored for the iPod. Versions for Macintosh and Windows computers are available. iTunes also provides you access to Apple's iTunes Music Store, allowing you to browse a large library of music that can be purchased and downloaded to your computer online.

- **iPodLounge: www.ipodlounge.com**  If you'd like to keep up on the latest iPod news, the iPodLounge is a great place to start. Updated frequently with iPod-related news, iPodLounge also features original editorial content, reviews of iPod products, an informative FAQ, active iPod forums, and much more.

- **iPod Hacks: www.ipodhacks.com**  iPod Hacks contains a variety of information about the iPod, including hacks and mods as well as iPod-related software you can download. There's also a forum where you can discuss the iPod with other iPod fans.

- **Everything iPod: www.everythingipod.com**  If you're looking for iPod accessories, this site has quite a bit to offer. Product categories include accessories, cables, cases, headphones, speakers, and more.

- **Laptops for Less: www.ipodbattery.com**  If you need a replacement battery for your iPod and don't want to pay $99 for Apple's iPod Battery Replacement Program, you can order iPod batteries here.

- **PDASmart: www.pdasmart.com**  Another source for replacement iPod batteries, PDASmart also offers a mail-in service that is less expensive than Apple's iPod Battery Replacement Program.

# Index

# X

# Y

# Z

# Syngress: *The Definition of a Serious Security Library*

**Syn·gress** (sin-gres): *noun, sing.* Freedom from risk or danger; safety. See *security*.

Printed and bound by CPI Group (UK) Ltd, Croydon, CR0 4YY

03/10/2024

01040341-0001